Bud Ballew

LEGENDARY OKLAHOMA LAWMAN

Elmer D. McInnes

and

Lauretta Ritchie-McInnes

TWODOT®

GUILFORD, CONNECTICUT
HELENA, MONTANA
AN IMPRINT OF THE GLOBE PEQUOT PRESS

A · **TWODOT**® · **BOOK**

TwoDot is an imprint of The Globe Pequot Press.

Text design: Lisa Reneson

Library of Congress Cataloging-in-Publication Data is available on file.

ISBN 978-0-7627-4477-0

Printed in the United States of America

10 9 8 7 6 5 4 3 2 1

Contents

Acknowledgments

We must extend a gracious thank you to our good friend and editor Garry Radison of Yorkton, Saskatchewan. A writer, historian, poet, and high-school English teacher, Garry's reading and editing of the Bud Ballew manuscript went the longest way to making the finished product presentable to a publisher.

We must also send a special thank-you to Ed Kirby of Sharon, Connecticut, and the members of the National Association for Outlaw and Lawman History, Inc. (NOLA) Research Grant Committee for awarding me a research grant in 2000, helping greatly toward the Oklahoma research trips. Thanks also, to NOLA editor, Chuck Parsons of Luling, Texas, for his kind considerations of the manuscripts over the years.

Another large debt of gratitude must be extended to members of the Ballew family and Ballew relatives, specifically Bud Ballew's great-granddaughter, Ann Ballew Carlton, and granddaughter in-law, Ann Lum Ballew of Natchez, Mississippi. Their magnanimous sharing of information and family photos is most appreciated and impossible to repay.

Many others helped in some way in the making of the Bud Ballew story. They are:

Ardmore, Oklahoma—Allen at Ashley's Bookstore; staff of the Ardmore Public Library; Butch Bridges; staff of the Carter County Court Clerk office; staff of the Chickasaw Regional Library; staff of the Daily Ardmoreite; Norman Flowers; Joyce Franks; Sharon Graham; Sally Gray; staff of the Greater Southwest Historical Museum; Libby Long; and Carter County Deputy Sheriff Steve Maxwell.

ACKNOWLEDGMENTS

Oklahoma City—Richard E. Greene and staff of the Oklahoma Department of Corrections; Richard E. Jones; staff of the Oklahoma State Department of Health, Division of Vital Records office; Scott, Delbert, Mary, and staff of the Oklahoma Historical Society.

Other Oklahoma locations—Allie Gardner, Ringling; Don and Vella Howard, Ringling; Liberty Home Video, Tulsa; staff of the Pontotoc County District Court Clerk's office, Ada; staff of the Tulsa County Court Clerk office, Tulsa; staff of the Washington County Court Clerk office, Bartlesville; Claude Woods and staff of the Healdton Oil Museum, Healdton.

Texas—Malcolm R. Dixon, San Antonio; staff of the Texas Department of Health, Austin; staff of the Texas State Library and Archives, Austin; Diane Walser, Wichita Falls; staff of the Wichita County Clerk office, Wichita Falls.

Other locations—Jeannie Ballew, Natchez, Mississippi; Donna Malinowski, Yorkton, Saskatchewan; Nancy Manning, professional researcher, Fairview, North Carolina; Linda Sexton, somewhere on the World Wide Web; staff of the state of North Carolina, Department of Cultural Resources office, Raleigh, North Carolina; staff of the Yorkton Public Library, Yorkton, Saskatchewan. Finally to Erin Turner and Globe Pequot; your assistance with this project and patience throughout has been greatly appreciated.

To anyone we may have missed, we extend our deepest apologies, but know your help was greatly appreciated.

May it also be known that any errors contained within this volume are strictly those of the authors and have no reflection on the individuals and institutions mentioned above.

Preface

By the second decade of the twentieth century, the Old West gunfighter was an anachronism in America. Technology in every area, including transportation, communications, medicine, and every facet of scientific development, had advanced more in twenty years than it had in the previous hundred years. Societal development, and with it law enforcement techniques and efficiency, had also moved apace. Such men as Billy the Kid, Jesse James, and John Wesley Hardin were disappearing from the landscape. However, another of these modern innovations—the "moving picture show" or movies as they came to be known—had begun the process of turning the Old West gunman into a mythological figure.

In many areas of the southwestern United States between 1910 and 1920, however, certain circumstances would arise that would be responsible for the re-creation of pockets of the Old West. It was a decade of large-scale oil development throughout Kansas, Oklahoma, and Texas, and oil boomtowns sprang into existence throughout the Southwest. The oil boomtowns fostered a fast-paced, rough existence akin to that in the rip-roaring communities of early western expansion. At first glance it was likely hard to tell such early oil towns as Ranger and Burkburnett, Texas, and Tulsa and Bartlesville, Oklahoma, from the earlier fabled frontier towns of Tombstone, Dodge City, or Abilene. A second glance would then reveal the rows of power and telephone poles and the new gasoline-powered automobiles careening down muddy streets rather than high-stepping steeds.

One of the wildest of the twentieth-century oil boomtowns would develop in southern Oklahoma in Carter County. Christened with the name Wirt, the early collection of tent structures quickly gained the appellation Ragtown. Ragtown would have given the previously mentioned towns of Tombstone and Dodge City a run for their money when it came to frontier lawlessness and gunplay. Lawmen with "sand in their craws" were necessary to keep a tight rein on such a place, men who harkened back to the likes of Wild Bill Hickok, Wyatt Earp, and Pat Garrett. Such a man was David "Bud" Ballew.

In many ways Bud Ballew was a man out of his time. He had grown up on the cattle ranges of Texas during the 1880s and '90s when cowboys still rode the backcountry with loaded revolvers on their hips and loaded Winchesters in their scabbards. Throughout his law enforcement career in Carter County, Ballew would favor the Colt .45 rather than the new automatic pistols, which were considered the height of firearms technology.

In the realms of criminology and law enforcement, the decade of 1910–1920 would be a period of evolution. The Old West gunfighters, outlaw or lawman, were in final fade-out. The era of the gangsters and G-men was just beginning. The fact that Bud Ballew stepped onto the stage of southern Oklahoma as one of the last of the frontier-style gunmen and lawmen while his prototypes were being aggrandized in the Hollywood tradition may have had much to do with the localized fame he achieved during his lifetime. Some believed he naturally lived the life of a silent movie idol; others, that he felt compelled to pattern himself after the ideal. Either way, while he lived, he managed to gain national, even international, notice and notoriety.

Conversely, Ballew's emergence in this period rather than in earlier frontier days, may have had a great deal to do with his celebrity during his career as a Carter County lawman, but it may also be the reason that celebrity failed to follow him into the future. If Bud Ballew had lived in the 1870s, he would be remembered today as a gunfighter on par with Hardin or Billy the Kid. If he had lived into the 1930s and continued his law enforcement activities, he would probably be as well known today as the mythical Elliot Ness or the real-life Frank Hamer.

Between 1910 and 1920, Ballew fought in numerous gun battles, killing an opponent in almost every one of them, but students of the Old West rarely study the time period, and students of the later gangster era consider it only a prelude to their major focus. It is a decade in limbo. What happened there is known only to special-interest groups and those with a special agenda. Bud Ballew has been our agenda. The quest for Bud Ballew has been enlightening, engrossing, and surprising. For such a character to be overlooked has been a major injustice.

Ballew's mental attitude was one of "do your damnedest and let the devil take care of the rest," a frontier attitude from a frontier character in a new world.

In researching this biography of Bud Ballew, I became aware that this frontier way of thinking still exists in the minds of many present-day Oklahomans. At one point an interviewee launched into the story of his cowboy grandfather, who had engaged in a shooting scrape on an Oklahoma ranch in the early 1900s. When asked the cause of the shoot-out, the man looked thoughtful for a moment. Then, as if his answer would explain the whole thing, drawled, "Well, they was just cowboys."

Perhaps that's it. After all, Bud Ballew was just a Texas cowboy.

—Elmer D. McInnes
Yorkton, Saskatchewan

CHAPTER 1

Beginnings

The Wichita Falls Round-Up, an annual tradition in Wichita Falls, Texas, for the past eight decades, was only three years old in May 1922. Despite being in its infancy, the event drew the best cowboy and cowgirl talent from the entire Southwest. Among those competing in the various events were world champion fancy roper Chester Byers; future Hollywood movie stunt man Yakima Canutt, one of the best bronc busters in the business; local hometown favorite Slim Caskey, an expert bulldogger; and bull rider John Hartwig, a man with a record in that bone-jarring and dangerous sport.

Another of those specially invited to participate in the rodeo spectacle was a forty-five-year-old former lawman and eminently successful stockman of nearby Carter County, Oklahoma, named Bud Ballew. A peace officer of renown as well as a rancher and stock handler of note, Ballew was to act as a special guest judge at some of the events and also to try his hand as a contestant in the calf-roping competition. Introduced to horses and cattle at an early age, Ballew knew the cowboy trade as well as he knew gun handling.

Wichita Falls was familiar territory to Ballew, as it was to most people from Carter County, being only some eighty-five miles southwest of the Carter County seat at Ardmore. In fact a Ballew kinsman and namesake had been one of the first settlers of The Falls in the early 1880s and had operated one of the first businesses in downtown Wichita Falls on historic Ohio Avenue.

1

As Ballew and his son, Dorris, climbed into their automobile and commenced the trip to Wichita Falls this fine May day in 1922, Bud probably thought little of such history. He had just recovered from a nasty bullet wound to the leg and was still adjusting to life without his deputy sheriff's commission. He most likely only anticipated an enjoyable few days at the roundup.

Still, while he made that long eighty-five-mile drive through the warm Oklahoma sun, Bud Ballew, if he had the inclination, might have had time to reflect on the past episodes of his life. It was a life full to the brim with opportunity, danger, and the type of life-defining events that try men's mettle and shape men's souls.

Bud Ballew's earliest known ancestor was his great-grandfather, George Ballew. George was born in North Carolina in 1768, but little else is known of his immediate family or life except that he tilled the soil in Burke County, North Carolina[1], in order to provide a livelihood for his wife and children.

One of those children, a son named Harvey born in 1802, would follow in his father's footsteps and take up farming as an occupation.

Sometime before late 1831, for reasons unknown, George and Harvey decided to look for better prospects in Kentucky. Records indicate that on December 21, 1831, twenty-nine-year-old Harvey Ballew married seventeen-year-old Pernette Prather in Russell County, Kentucky.[2] Miss Prather was a native Kentuckian born about 1814.[3]

For close to three decades, Harvey Ballew dedicated himself to tending the fertile Kentucky soil. Records reveal that in 1832 he was granted land near the Cumberland River. Again in 1847 he received another land grant along Roaring Lily Creek, Russell County.[4] Gradually the farm prospered.

These years also proved fertile for the Ballew family. Harvey and Pernette would have ten children during this time: James born in 1835; Mary, 1837; Lucinda, 1839; Louisa, ca. 1842; Bryant Y. "Bud," ca. 1843; George, 1845; William, 1847; Orsemus, 1850; Joseph, 1851; and Margaret, 1853.[5] No doubt as the children came of age, they pulled their weight around the farm in the form of chores and fieldwork.

By the 1850s stories of cheap arable farmland and grandiose opportunities began to drift eastward from the burgeoning state of Texas. These rumors reached Harvey Ballew. By 1855 he may already have been planning a move from Kentucky. In that year he sold some of his land in Russell County to a Mason Flanagan. Three years later the decision had been made. Sometime in 1858 Harvey and Pernette Ballew bid farewell to Kentucky, packed up their belongings, and moved their brood westward to Fannin County, Texas.[6]

Fannin County, situated in the northeast portion of Texas and bordered on the north by the still sparsely settled Indian Nations, was prime farming country in the late 1850s and early 1860s. Without delay the Ballews would have set to work making their parcel of land profitable. The county had also been the birthplace of one John Wesley Hardin in 1853, a boy who would grow up to be perhaps the most notorious gunman in the history of the Old West. The activities of gunmen were alien to Harvey and Pernette Ballew, however, as they tended the farm and raised their own children to the best of their ability. They could not know that fifty years later their own grandson would cause a stir reminiscent of the soon-to-be-infamous Hardin.

The 1860 census shows the Harvey Ballew family living near the post office of Garnetts Bluff.[7] Harvey is listed as having a personal estate valued at $300, an average amount for the time and area. His oldest son living at home at this time was Bryant, nicknamed "Bud" by the family. At seventeen years old Bryant probably spent his days sweating under the hot sun along with his father in the dusty fields. Soon Bryant would be looking to make a life of his own.

In early 1869, Bryant, about twenty-five years old, married Miss Mary Thurman, aged twenty.[8] This union produced five offspring: Tishi and Tom, both of whom died in infancy; Susan A., born ca. 1871; Hattie Electra, born 1874; and David Martello, born September 5, 1877.[9] Early on, young David would inherit his father's nickname and be known almost exclusively to family and friends as "Bud."

Sometime in the late 1870s, tragedy struck the Bryant Ballew household with the death of his wife, Mary. Shortly after this Bryant married a Georgian, named Martha A. Seabourne, who was born in 1859.[10]

A short time after this marriage, Bryant and his family left Fannin County. Looking westward, they pulled up stakes and moved some 180 miles southwest to the Texas county of Eastland. In Eastland County, located about sixty miles east of Abilene, Bryant acquired a suitable farming property on which to raise his growing family.

Although the census of 1880 lists young Bud as the junior member of the family at the age of two years,[11] Bryant and Martha would add another five children during their Eastland County sojourn. Bud's half siblings were Tom J., born in 1881; Ethel, 1884; Stella, 1886; Truman Scott, 1889; and Bryant Jr., born in 1890.[12]

Growing up on the Eastland County homestead proved to have a lasting effect on all the Ballew children, especially young Bud. In conjunction with farming activities, Bud was immersed in the cowboy culture of Texas. At an early age he was introduced to the working of horses and cattle. While in his early teens, he became an expert horseman and roper, skills that would remain with him for the rest of his life.

Another characteristic that would affect Bud's later life manifested itself in the handling of firearms. Like most men in the Texas range country, all the Ballew males always went about armed. The carrying and use of guns became as natural as life itself. Quickly Bud became an efficient shot with both long guns and revolvers. Having been brought up with the Colt .45 six-shooter, Bud would favor this weapon for the rest of his life even when the new automatics came into vogue in the early 1900s. Maturing into a handsome, stocky youth of about five-foot eleven-inches and close to two hundred pounds, Bud Ballew, with his distinctive mop of red curly hair, became a familiar sight on the Eastland County range.

Having remained behind in Fannin County, Harvey and Pernette Ballew would live well into the 1870s and 1880s respectively before finally dying at or near the old home place. It is believed by some family members that both are buried in the "Ballew/Cundiff Plot" of the Porter Cemetery located south of Bonham, Texas.[13]

Meanwhile, their son Bryant continued to operate his Eastland County property. On April 26, 1892, Bryant Ballew received the official patent on his homestead in Eastland.[14] After over ten years of sweat and toil, he officially owned his land free and clear.

By this time, however, a new land of opportunity was beckoning. To the north of the Texas border, the area known as Indian Territory was quickly filling up with eager settlers looking for fresh land and fresh prospects. In fact, by the time of Bryant Ballew's receipt of his land patent in 1892, there is evidence to suggest that his oldest son, Bud, had already made the move ahead of the rest of the family.[15]

CHAPTER 2

Carter County Genesis

Most sources agree that sometime in the year 1890, at the age of fourteen, Bud Ballew left his parents' home in Eastland County, Texas, and headed north.[1] Eventually he ended up just over the Texas line in the Chickasaw Nation, Indian Territory, near the fledgling community of Ardmore. Destined in seventeen years to become a part of the new state of Oklahoma, at the time of Ballew's arrival, the area was being subjected to an invasion of Texas cattlemen. Anxious to take advantage of the territory's miles and miles of cheap grazing land, many cowmen, settlers, and entrepreneurs hastened forth to get their share.

With this heavy wave of mostly Texan migrants came young Bud Ballew. Just what Ballew did at such a youthful age to support himself is unknown. It is likely, however, that, due to his already vast experience in working with horses and cattle, he gained employment with one or more of the many cattlemen in the area.

Soon Bud Ballew would acquire the toughness and confidence to become a top cowhand. Likewise, the land he had adopted as his new home, Indian Territory, was going through its own growing pains.

The area, which would eventually come to be called Carter County, Oklahoma, is situated a few miles north of the Texas border in the south-central portion of present-day Oklahoma. Bordered on the north by the picturesque Arbuckle Mountains and drained by the Washita and Red Rivers and their various tributaries, the land produced a variety of tall native grasses coveted by early ranchmen. The rich soil and what lay beneath this lush carpet would be both a blessing and a curse to the territory.

Before the 1820s the only signs of human habitation in the future Indian Territory proved to be the scattered bands of Plains Indian tribes moving nomadically from place to place. This would all begin to change by 1830. The indigenous populations of the southeastern states of Georgia, Alabama, Mississippi, Tennessee, and the Carolinas had been forced off their homelands by the white settlers wishing to farm the rich soil. Looking for a place to relocate them, the federal government ceded to them a tract of land west of the Mississippi River in present-day Oklahoma. People who would come to be called the Five Civilized Tribes were herded into this area by forced march. The relocation effort became known as the "Trail of Tears" because of the many men, women, and children who died in the relocation process.

In 1830 the treaty of Dancing Rabbit Creek conveyed a southern portion of this Indian Territory to the Choctaw Nation.[2] Most of the Choctaws wended their way to the territory from 1830 to 1835. The Chickasaws, a tribe related to the Choctaws, joined them across the Mississippi during the years 1837 to 1840. Eventually the Chickasaws attempted to find some sort of autonomy from their Choctaw brothers. In 1855 they split from the Choctaws and formed their own Chickasaw Nation in the far southern portion of the area.[3] That same year the Chickasaw Nation was divided into four counties, called Panola, Tishomingo, Pontotoc, and Pickens. Officials placed the capital at the town of Tishomingo near the center of the nation.

As early as the 1840s the white man had been making incursions into the Indian nations. By the 1880s the invasion of Texas cattle ranchers into the territory had become a movement of mammoth proportions, spurred by the quest for cheap, if not free, grazing land. Despite the fact that the land belonged to the Indians and this white incursion was actually illegal, the influx of outsiders continued unabated. The federal government ultimately proved unable, or perhaps unwilling, to stem the tide. As Ardmore historian Sally Gray put it, "These were our first wetbacks."[4]

Reminiscing in later years concerning these events, Carter County pioneer and early County Attorney James H. Mathers stated:

When the original removal treaties were made, there was one promise that Indians insisted on. The federal government must agree to keep white settlers out of this territorial home, and Congress did pass laws known as the non-intercourse acts which made it a crime for a white man to invade the Indian boundaries. But the arrangement was doomed from the beginning and if that fact could have been understood then, a lot of bloodshed and grief would have been averted . . . the government tried to move out the white people, but there weren't enough troops and governmental determination was half-hearted.[5]

Soon the native peoples would be relegated to mere witnesses and bit players in the events of their new homeland.

The community destined to become the largest city in Indian Territory, Ardmore, Pickens County, began as a cattle ranch. Established by cattlemen Richard McLish, L. P. Atkins, and A. B. Roff in the southern portion of the Chickasaw Nation in 1880, the 700 Ranch was one of the oldest organized ranches in the nations.[6] When the Gulf, Colorado, and Santa Fe Railroad decided to continue into the Indian Nations from Gainesville, Texas, the well-known landmark of the 700 Ranch seemed a logical location for a station. Thus was born the town of Ardmore, located about ninety-five miles north of Dallas, Texas, and named after the home of a Santa Fe official who hailed from Ardmore, Pennsylvania.[7]

By the time the first locomotive chugged into the new station of Ardmore on July 28, 1887, merchants Samuel Zuckerman and brothers Bob and Frank Frensley had already set up two canvas mercantile stores beside the tracks. With the lumber brought in on this first train, the Frensleys built a more permanent building on the spot. That same month Jim Staples laid out Ardmore's Main Street by plowing a furrow in the prairie for a quarter of a mile west of the Santa Fe tracks.[8]

When the teenage Bud Ballew arrived in the area in 1890 in the hopes of finding adventure and success, he most likely was not disappointed in the Ardmore area. In 1890 the former Indian Nations in the western half of the future state of Oklahoma had been formed into the new Indian Territory and thrown open to white settlement. By 1890 Ardmore could boast a population of some two thousand residents. That same year the federal government decided to establish a U.S. court closer to the Indian Territory to take the pressure off the courts at Paris, Texas, and Fort Smith, Arkansas, which were being over-run with the criminal cases flooding in from the nations. Officials decided to place this court at the budding community of Ardmore, Chickasaw Nation. This proved another boost for the town's economy.[9]

The coming of the railroad to the Chickasaw Nation brought an influx of settlers and small farmers into the region. Although they would never totally supplant the cattle-ranching fraternity, those who followed the agrarian life-style quickly became a major force in and around Ardmore into the 1890s. In agriculture there, cotton was king. By 1892 the area's cotton market ranked as one of the largest in the world. Some fifty thousand bales of cotton were sold in Ardmore that year, and at times wagons piled high with cotton would make the streets almost impassable.[10]

Meanwhile other towns had been taking shape in Pickens County. Heald-ton, founded some four years before Ardmore by early pioneer Charles H. Heald, was located about twenty-one miles north west of Ardmore. Healdton was destined to be the site of a major oil strike of major impact. Graham and Fox, two prominent towns, were founded a bit further north in 1891 and 1894 respectively. Hewitt was located about six miles south east of Healdton.

Closer to Ardmore itself was the community of Berwyn (present-day Gene Autry), ten miles to the northeast. Straight west of Ardmore the towns of Lone Grove and Wilson developed. Quickly the Chickasaw Nation was being occupied by all manner of eager settlers.[11]

The first real calamity to strike the city of Ardmore took place on Friday, April 19, 1895. That evening a fire broke out in Harper's Livery Stable on Caddo Street. By the next morning a majority of the town had been reduced to ashes. The town's courthouse, jail, opera house, Masonic temple, three newspa-per offices, and upward of eighty other buildings were consumed in the blaze. All told, the monetary loss was over half a million dollars. Fortunately, no lives were lost in the conflagration. Although many believed the disaster to have been caused by arson, no one ever faced charges for it.[12]

From the very beginning of white incursion into the Indian Territory, the area had been plagued by lawlessness. Since the white man was an illegal resident to begin with, there were no laws to govern his actions. The nations quickly became a refuge for all manner of criminals and gunmen from the surrounding states and territories. One of the most notorious of these, outlaw Bill Dalton, would be killed only twenty-three miles north of Ardmore in the Arbuckles on June 8, 1894, by Deputy U.S. Marshal Selden Lindsey and a posse of Ardmore lawmen.[13]

All the towns in the Chickasaw Nation, as elsewhere in the territory, had ruffians and cutthroats. But, being the largest city and center of major judicial, political, and economic activity, Ardmore attracted more than her fair share. One portion of the town far exceeded any other when it came to gunfights, knifings, and killings.

The first street to be named in Ardmore's infancy, Caddo Street ran north from Main toward the road leading out to Caddo Creek, about five miles north of the city. Beginning in the 1890s and continuing well into the 1900s, Caddo Street got a bad reputation because of all the deadly violence that unfolded there. The notorious Dew Drop Inn and the other dives lining its sidewalks saw bullets and blades take the lives of many—so many, in fact, that shortly the street came to be known as "Bloody Caddo." Caddo remained violent into the 1950s. It has been recognized as the "street with more killings per block than any in the U.S.A."[14]

Despite the scandalous activities, most of the populace of Ardmore was conscientious and law abiding. These people wished to see the Indian Territory and Ardmore develop in as peaceful and prosperous a manner as possible. Consequently, on April 16, 1898, under the administration of mayor John L. Galt, Ardmore was incorporated as a city of the second class. Other city officials at this time were J. W. M. Harper, street commissioner; W. M. Green, assessor; John S. O'Mealey, fire chief; A. S. Pulliam, city marshal; and W. E. McLemore, assistant marshal charged with controlling the habitués of Caddo Street. A year and a half later, on December 14, 1899, Ardmore became incorporated as a city of the first class.[15] With dispatch the nations were being transformed from barren grasslands into communities for families and soldiers of fortune.

One of the new citizens of Pickens County was young and cocky Bud Ballew. Sometime before 1900 Ballew settled at the hamlet of Lone Grove. Sitting a mere six miles due west of Ardmore, Lone Grove had its own surrounding ranchers and farmers to give it its impetus. Born around the same time as its sister city of Ardmore, The Grove was incorporated in 1898. It soon became a trading center for the agricultural produce of the surrounding area.[16] Ballew took a liking to the lush grasslands ideal for sustaining large herds of cattle and horses. Eventually he would develop his own profitable cattle and horse operations at Lone Grove.

The year 1900 found the twenty-two-year-old Ballew living in more humble than he would eventually acquire but still respectable accommodations at Lone Grove. His abode must have been at least moderately spacious as he was able to accommodate a boarder by the name of William J. Clodus.[17]

Shortly after acquiring title to his property in Eastland County, Texas, Bryant Ballew determined to follow his son to Indian Territory. Liquidating his Texas land, Bryant packed up the family and headed north. By late 1893 the senior Ballew with his wife, Martha, and the children arrived in the Chickasaw Nation. Bryant and Martha would eventually sire two more children in the Nations—a daughter named Ruby, born in November 1893, and a son christened Bernard, born during March 1899. But the year 1900 found Bryant and Martha Ballew along with their seven children living near Bud at Lone Grove.[18]

While Bud Ballew continued to develop his ranch, he also developed a romance with eighteen-year-old Fannie Mariah Harper. Fannie was the youngest of ten children born to Dr. William M. and Ana Eliza Harper. Born October 24, 1882, in Graves County, Kentucky, near the city of Paducah, Fannie moved with her family to the Chickasaw Nation in the early 1880s, settling near Lone Grove.[19]

Quickly the relationship between Bud Ballew and Fannie Harper blossomed. Deciding he had found his life partner, the fledgling rancher asked his sweetheart for her hand in marriage. Consequently, on April 17, 1901, at the age of twenty-three, David "Bud" Ballew and Fannie Harper were wed in a quiet ceremony at Lone Grove, officiated by Rev. J. N. Morris. Mr. and Mrs. Ira Arnold, a local couple known to both bride and groom, acted as witnesses. It was a union that would remain solid for the duration of Bud Ballew's life.[20]

While Ballew and his new bride settled on their ranch at Lone Grove and worked to make it a successful operation, the political machinations continued to work in Indian Territory. For some time parties had been lobbying to gain statehood for the twin territories of Oklahoma and Indian Territory. In 1905 an attempt to make them separate states failed; but finally in 1907, the two territories were able to join and form a single new state called Oklahoma.

With the birth of the state of Oklahoma as the forty-sixth state of the union on November 16, 1907, drastic changes came about in the former Chickasaw Nation. All the old territorial laws were thrown out, and new ones adopted to reflect statehood. Pickens County ceased to exist, being divided into parts of Marshall, Murray, Love, Johnston, Jefferson, Grady, Garvin, Stephens, and Carter Counties. Located in Carter County, Ardmore became Carter County seat with all the added industry and commerce this entailed.

Along with statehood came Prohibition. At the stroke of midnight, November 16, 1907, the possession, consumption, transportation, and sale of intoxicating liquors became illegal under federal laws. Rather than put an end to the trafficking and drinking of liquor, Prohibition only drove the practice underground. It perhaps caused the deaths of more citizen bootleggers and law officers than any other single law in Oklahoma. Scores of deadly gun battles would occur throughout the state during the years the Prohibition Act was in force. Carter County proved no exception.

Evidence suggests that Bud Ballew stayed out of such troubles. He and Fannie concentrated on improving the ranch and marshaling their growing herds of horses and cattle. Gradually their holdings at Lone Grove increased along with their family.

The first addition to the family arrived at the Lone Grove cabin at 9 p.m., February 6, 1904. The couple christened the baby boy Dorris Letcher.[21] Dorris would grow to love ranch life as much as his father. Also like his father, Dorris would eventually excel at choosing and handling the finest horses on the range.

Two years later, a second child was born at 8:45 a.m., October 15, 1906.[22] The parents named their second son Bryant Harper after Bud's father and Fannie's maiden name, but family and friends always called the young boy "Buster." Like his older brother, Buster also took to ranch life. At an early age he could ride as if he were a natural part of the horse and saddle. Bud also taught him to throw a loop with the skill and accuracy of an old hand. Unfortunately, Buster was destined for a short life and a tragic end.

By 1910 Bud Ballew's holdings in land, cattle, and horses had increased and solidified. His younger half brother, Scott, often lived on the ranch with him and helped with various ranch duties.[23]

About this time Bud, with things running smoothly on his spread, was getting restless. Whether from boredom, ambition, or the thrill of the next adventure, Ballew was drawn more and more to the excitement of city life. The dives and gambling dens of Ardmore's Caddo Street attracted his attention. Soon his hearty, booming laugh and shock of red, curly hair would be a familiar sight in towns throughout Carter County from Ardmore to Healdton and Fox to Berwyn. His booming gun was also destined to make a mark. In another five years Bud Ballew would begin his career as one of the last of the old-style western gunmen.

CHAPTER 3

Victim #1—Pete Bynum

O n June 28, 1914, a radical student named Gavrilo Princip put an assassin's bullet into Austrian Archduke Francis Ferdinand, an incident that would eventually drag Carter County and the rest of the United States into what came to be called the "Great War": World War I.

The inhabitants of Carter County, however, were too enthralled in the oil boom to spend much time worrying over the conflict brewing overseas. The discovery of oil under its soil brought not only prosperity to Carter County but a distinctly undesirable element. The resultant crime engendered by the various saloon men, gamblers, con men, and gunmen kept county officials busy twenty-four hours a day in their attempts to enforce the laws against liquor and gambling. The all too common robberies and shootings kept officers struggling to stay one step ahead of would-be lawbreakers. The situation was ideally suited for certain lawmen who wished to make a healthy profit through extortion and protection schemes.

As early as the spring of 1914, Bud Ballew felt confident enough in his ranching operations to be able to devote less time to their day-to-day operation and still have the well-established enterprise turn a profit. He began to look to the city for a suitable circumstance to earn some extra money away from the ranch. This opportunity presented itself when the sheriff of Carter County, Buck Garrett, offered Ballew a job as a deputy sheriff. Garrett apparently recognized in Ballew the type of character he needed to police the roughnecks and assorted ne'er-do-wells of the oil fields.

In late 1913 or early 1914, Ballew went to work with Garrett. Soon the figure of the stocky redheaded deputy became a familiar sight, two .45 Colts strapped around his ample waist, striding down the sidewalks of Ardmore, Healdton, Wirt (or Ragtown as it was called), and the other towns and villages of the county. He was destined to become Buck Garrett's number one trouble-shooter and the most feared and respected lawman in the area.

Ballew's first press notice as deputy sheriff of Carter County came in the May 7, 1914, issue of the local Ardmore newspaper, the *Daily Ardmoreite*:

ANOTHER KILLING AT RAGTOWN
Woman Shoots Husband To Death
After He Had Retired Last Night

Janie Epperson shot and instantly killed her husband, W. A. Epperson, last night at Ragtown in the oil fields. Domestic trouble is said to be the cause of the homicide.

Officers stated that Epperson was shot while in his bed, just below the base of the skull, and death was instantaneous.

The woman was arrested by Deputy Sheriff Bud Ballew, and placed in the county jail, with a charge of murder against her.

The couple have been married about eight years and have one child. The woman had nothing to say about the affair.[1]

Recognizing Ragtown as the wildest of the lively oil towns within his jurisdiction, Sheriff Garrett decided to assign his toughest new deputy to the camp. It would be Ballew's daily activity to patrol the streets of the rowdy community, a task he accepted with relish.

Some of the costs of the magnificent wealth brought by the oil industry proved to be the lives lost in derrick accidents, fires, explosions, and other assorted mishaps. This came into devastating focus on Monday, September 27, 1915, when one of the biggest manmade disasters of the early twentieth-century Southwest and the worst disaster in Ardmore's history struck the county seat.

On that fateful afternoon a 250-barrel tank car of highly volatile casing-head gasoline belonging to the Santa Fe Railroad began a slow leak on a siding at the Ardmore depot. Despite the efforts of Chief of Police Bob Hutchins[2] and various Santa Fe employees, before the car could be moved or the leak sealed, the rail car exploded. The explosion leveled almost every building for five blocks along Main Street and many on Caddo and adjoining streets. Forty-three people lost their lives in the eruption. In the aftermath, Ardmore's business section presented a picture of devastation never seen before or since in the oil fields.[3]

Along with the entire county sheriff's force and city police force, Bud Ballew served long hours in the search for those trapped under the rubble. The deputies also spent the next few days patrolling the ruins in an effort to prevent looting and to bring some sort of order to the chaos. Showing an amazing resiliency typical of early communities, Ardmore had rebuilt its downtown within weeks.

In fewer than two months after the great Ardmore explosion, Bud Ballew would be tested under fire for the first time. He would not be found lacking.

Since its inception, the community of Ragtown had been plagued with various gangs dedicated to the pursuits of petty thievery, mugging, highway robbery, and every other criminal activity imaginable. Two of the worst of this fraternity proved to be a twenty-nine-year-old felon named Pete Bynum, a native of Lawton, Oklahoma, and "Curley" Gray, Bynum's boon companion. The pair had been skulking around Ragtown for a number of weeks hanging out in the various dives and attempting to intimidate all those they came in contact with. By mid November 1915 both Bynum and Gray had acquired a very unsavory reputation in the lively oil camp. On the evening of Thursday, November 18, they decided to pull a major heist.

Joined by another individual who would never be identified, the felonious duo made its way to Ragtown's main street. Though it was almost midnight, the streets were still packed with a milling, reveling throng. Like other oil towns of the time, Ragtown ran wide open twenty-four hours a day.

With bandanas covering the lower portion of their faces, Bynum, Gray, and their companion burst into the 66 Restaurant with pistols in their hands. Covering the proprietor with their weapons, the robbers ordered him to empty the cash register as the customers dashed out the front door.

As chance would have it, Deputy Sheriff Bud Ballew was making his usual rounds in that part of town when he noticed the mass exodus spilling into the streets from the restaurant. Rushing over to the sidewalk in front of the establishment, Ballew enquired of one of the men who had yet to make himself scarce, the nature of the sudden rush in all directions. The man informed the deputy that a robbery was in progress inside the restaurant. Before he himself dashed out of harm's way, he warned Ballew to stay clear or he was liable to get hurt.

As the reporter for the *Ardmore Statesman* put it, this warning "did not bother Bud."[4] Palming his revolver, Ballew alertly strode into the establishment just as the owner was handing over all the money in the till, a mere $6, to the disgruntled outlaws. At that point all hell broke loose.

Turning to face the unexpected intruder, Bynum quickly opened fire. One slug creased the left side of Ballew's stomach (which a newspaper would call "a conspicuous feature of the deputy's make up")[5] just breaking the skin. Ballew swiftly returned the fire with a barrage of pistol shots. Struck in the body with at least one mortal wound, Pete Bynum crashed to the floor. Turning his revolver on the remaining robbers, the fast shooting deputy fired at the now retreating pair. Unscathed, Gray and his mate managed to dash out the back door and make their escape. For Gray it would be only a temporary reprieve.

It was not until the conclusion of the gun battle that the real tragedy of the affair was discovered. Hearing moans from a rooming house adjoining the restaurant investigators discovered Allen Williams, a tank builder in the oil fields recently arrived from Tillman County, lying on his bed desperately wounded. Apparently a stray slug from Ballew's pistol had penetrated the thin board partition separating the 66 Restaurant from Williams's room. By chance the bullet struck the unlucky Williams, dealing him a dire injury.[6]

While Ballew had Williams's stomach wound bandaged, he requested that Sheriff Buck Garrett be notified of the fight. Reached by wire, Garrett quickly made his way to Ragtown from Ardmore. Williams and Bynum were loaded into an ambulance and transported to the Hardy Sanitarium in Ardmore. Despite efforts put forward on their behalf, both men proved too seriously injured to recover. Williams, twenty-two years of age, died at 10 a.m. the following day. Holdup man Pete Bynum succumbed to his wound two hours later.[7]

On the same day as Bynum's death, Deputy Sheriff John Gauntt nabbed "Curley" Gray.[8] Despite Garrett's optimism the third member of the robber trio was never identified or apprehended.

Although the killings had clearly been perpetrated by a law officer in the discharge of his duty, Ballew demanded a quick jury trial. He wished his name to be cleared officially. The entire trial came off between 2 and 4 p.m. on December 10, a mere three weeks after the episode. As could be expected, Ballew walked out of the Ardmore courthouse with a not-guilty verdict.[9]

This shoot-out had repercussions for both Bud Ballew and Carter County in general, some more permanent than others. Perhaps the most long lasting consequences were developed in Ballew himself.

It was most likely soon after this gun battle that Ballew acquired for himself a so-called "steel jacket" or "breast plate," what we today know as a bulletproof vest or flak jacket. The life-saving garment was a new innovation in law enforcement at the time, and both Ballew and Sheriff Buck Garrett, along with some other deputy sheriffs, federal officers, and Ardmore police officers, wisely availed themselves of this extra protection in fast-shooting Carter County. For the rest of his eventful career as a deputy sheriff, Ballew would seldom go on duty without this major article of protection.[10]

Perhaps the most profound effect of the 66 Restaurant shoot-out took place in the psyche of Bud Ballew. There were those in Carter County who claimed that, following this encounter, Ballew seemed to acquire a taste for the thrill of a gun battle. It would seem from his statements and actions that he became that much more of a "gunman." Indeed, Bud Ballew's gun-fighting career had just begun.

The most short-lived effect of the Bynum killing might well have been the perceived peace and quiet the episode was said to have produced in Carter County in general and in Wirt, or Ragtown, in particular. According to the *Ardmore Statesman*:

> It is a noticeable fact that since the killing of these two men (Bynum and Williams) by Deputy Ballew, there has been a cessation of the hold-up business in the oil fields, and less lawlessness in the town of Wirt.[11]

This may have held true for the short term. Soon, however, Ballew's special bailiwick of Ragtown would revert to its former state of wickedness. It was a condition inherent to the community throughout its short and violent existence. And its progenitor was oil.

CHAPTER 4

—— Ragtown and Mighty Oil ———•

The "black gold" waiting to be discovered under the cattleman's paradise of Carter County would bring the greatest prosperity ever seen in southern Oklahoma, but oil would also produce the perfect environment for crime and vice to run rampant. It would transform Carter County from a relatively peaceful farming and ranching area into one of the liveliest booming places on the face of the earth. And Ragtown was the Gomorrah of Carter County.

As early as 1888 oil made its ever-so-quiet debut in the area now known as Carter County. That year the United States Geological Survey, under the auspices of the Department of the Interior, produced a map showing the results of their study of the oil-bearing regions of the United States. Along with Kansas, Arkansas, and Texas, the region that later became Oklahoma showed a huge preponderance of oil-bearing strata. Though this study produced some interest in pioneering oilmen, few acted on the information.[1]

One who did take an interest in the area later that year was a transient petroleum prospector known only as Palmer. Picking a spot in the S1/2 of Section 5-T4S-R3-W, (what in years to come would be the great Healdton Oil Field), Palmer drilled a shallow test well. Employing what was called a "spring-pole" drilling rig, a drill bit attached to a pole made from a supple sapling, the prospector pounded his way into the soil. At four hundred feet he discovered sand bearing a "heavy, black, asphaltic oil," which issued forth from his test hole.

Capping his discovery, Palmer sped to Ardmore with plans of leasing the land around his test and doing more extensive drilling. Unfortunately, he discovered that due to certain federal government restrictions and the lack of a readily available market, his planned venture was a highly unprofitable undertaking. Quietly Palmer drifted from the area never to be seen again, the only evidence of his former presence being his old test well left for future speculators to ponder.[2]

By the early 1900s Oklahoma had become a major oil producer. The fields at Bartlesville and the Red Fork Pool located near Tulsa had developed into successful oil producing operations. Southern Oklahoma had yet to reach its full potential in oil production, however.

In 1903 H. B. Goodrich, a geologist for the Santa Fe Railroad Company, became the first commercial geologist to do exploratory work in the area of present-day Carter County. Though he managed to locate the Wheeler Field about twenty miles northwest of Ardmore, the first paying oil wells in the area, the field failed to produce as expected.[3]

For the next ten years, Carter County would develop into an area much explored by various oilmen and petroleum companies. In 1911 Oil City, located in the Wheeler Field, became an oil boomtown for a number of months. Various test wells throughout the county sustained interest in the region as a possibly viable petroleum-producing area.[4]

The inevitable finally happened in 1913. Roy M. Johnson was a native Wisconsinite and veteran newspaperman who operated the *Ardmore Statesman* in Ardmore. Johnson had dabbled in oil exploration in the past and was of the opinion that a major oil bed lay waiting to be discovered somewhere beneath the soil of Carter County. In November 1911 Johnson—along with Edward Galt, son of John Galt, state legislator and first mayor of Ardmore; A. T. McGhee, a local carpenter; and a "Captain" Cook, an eccentric old-timer who claimed to know the location of some nearby oil seeps—ventured out to do some exploring. The group finally pitched camp near Healdton, where Cook pointed out a spring with crude oil floating at the surface. Palmer's old 1888 test well was also nearby. Johnson felt sure he had found an oil mother lode.

In the intervening two years, Johnson continued to work to bring his dreams of oil wealth to fruition. Eventually, in partnership with Galt, McGhee,

Sam Apple, and Ardmore attorney Wirt Franklin, who owned the land near the proposed test drill area, Johnson began to secure leases in preparation for the initial drilling.

Finally in late July 1913, the group spudded in a test well in the NW/4 of Section 8-4S-3W near the small town of Healdton on land owned by Franklin and Apple. This first well, which would eventually lead to the beginnings of the great Healdton Oil Field and transform Carter County from a largely cotton and cattle economy to one of the largest petroleum-producing areas in the United States, had an initial flow of twenty-five to one hundred barrels of crude per day.[5]

Another enterprise, which ensured the success of the county's oil production, came to pass with the meeting of pioneer oilman Jake Hamon and John Ringling of Ringling Brothers Circus fame. Recognizing the problems of transporting supplies from the nearest railroad at Ardmore to the quickly developing oil regions in the western portion of the county, the pair began construction of the Ringling Railroad through southern Oklahoma in May 1913.[6] The Healdton Oil Field now had all the components to attract interest throughout the Southwest and eventually the entire country.

Quickly the oil companies and oil wells began to multiply at a rapid pace. Towns such as Healdton, Wilson, and Graham, which had previously been nothing more than sleepy farming communities, suddenly came to life as raucous oil towns. Ardmore, the economic supply base to the new oil region, received a mammoth shot in the arm and took on new life.

Situated about two and a half miles west of Healdton was an area especially rich in oil production. Quickly a settlement sprang up to support the thousands of oil-field workers flooding into the area. The instant community acquired the name Ragtown from all the canvas tents initially set up there for residences and business places alike. Eventually the citizens decided to change the name to Wirt in honor of oilman Wirt Franklin. The original appellation of Ragtown, however, was too ingrained to be put aside, and Ragtown it remained to most locals.

Steadily the drilling derricks continued to pop up like mushrooms after a heavy rain. News of oil discovery quickly spread; first, Oklahoma, then neighboring states, and finally the entire country would be aware of the Greater

Healdton Oil Field. Within weeks of the first well, individuals of all stripes inundated Carter County and Ragtown. Almost overnight the region went from barren, uninhabited cattle-grazing and farming land to being literally overcrowded with oil wells, oil workers, and oil towns.

In record time Ragtown evolved into a lively, modern community with clapboard buildings and false-fronted lumber businesses swiftly taking the place of the former canvas enclosures. The town even developed its own bank to handle the copious flow of cash generated by the thriving economy.[7] The one long main street of Ragtown, known as Texas Road, was lined with restaurants, mercantile establishments, oil company offices, clothing stores, bakeries, as well as many drinking and gambling establishments and other businesses. A disproportionately large number dealt strictly in supplying the oil roustabouts with any vice their heart desired.

Like most boomtowns, Ragtown attracted a large number of undesirables. These were individuals drawn to the region by the prospect of an easy buck. They ran the illegal booze and gambling joints, provided prostitution on demand, and supplied the dope fiends with the most popular illicit drugs of the era.

According to John "Slim" Jones, an oil-field roughneck who worked in the fields at Ragtown as early as 1913, "wild women were plentiful, gambling houses were wide open, and whiskey was sold over the bar."[8] The reputation of the town was such that many roustabouts refused to take work there, one exclaiming that "he wasn't interested enough in getting into trouble to go there."[9] Enough did, however, to keep the area a roiling, clambering, tussling mass of frenetic humanity.

Eighty-three-year-old Claude Woods, at this writing the director of the Healdton Oil Museum in Healdton, Oklahoma, proved to be a wealth of information on the history of the Healdton Oil Field in general and Ragtown in particular. As a testament to just how dangerous the community could be, Mr. Woods related an incident concerning his father who, as a young man, worked in the oil fields at Ragtown:

> My father, Ed Woods, a three-quarters Choctaw Indian, came into Ragtown in 1916 to work as an oil field worker. One day he was walking the trail to the drill (oil derrick) where he worked.

My father had just gotten paid and it was dark. Suddenly someone jumped out, hit him on the head and stole all his money. Later the robbers were seen coming out of the bush counting the money.[10]

As in many similar cases emanating from early day Ragtown, the perpetrators of the theft were never apprehended. Just another tale of Ragtown's wickedness, this tableau was played out countless thousands of times in many variations and styles. Eventually Ed Woods, and others like him attempting to make an honest dollar, learned to watch their backs and be ever vigilant. The conditions themselves demanded at least this much.

In addition to its reputation for unrelenting criminality, Ragtown also became known for a propensity to catch fire on a regular basis. On at least one dozen occasions in its history, Ragtown would be hit by major conflagrations. The situation became so dire that in at least one corner, the burg became known as "The Town That Was Always Burning."[11]

Fires took place with so much regularity, in fact, that many took an attitude of nonchalance concerning them. Judge J. B. Orr, later to become justice of the peace at Wilson, worked as a young man in 1916 in a tailor shop at Ragtown. Judge Orr could relate the following story concerning one major blaze that tore through the oil camp's business district:

A fire was raging through the shack businesses. A gambler walked into the street and took a look. He knew the flames would eventually reach his place. "About three hours away," he remarked as he strode leisurely into his busy casino, picked up the phone and ordered enough lumber to build a new building. Then he rounded up a crew and had them set his furnishings in the street at the last minute. Came the fire. The crew then went to working raking the coals of the lot and worked all night throwing up the new building. The gambling hall opened at six the next morning.[12]

Major fires swept through Ragtown at least once every year between 1914 and 1918, some years seeing two or even three disastrous burnings.[13] Always the town quickly rebuilt and resumed its frenzied pace.

Perhaps one of the worst of these fires took place on January 17, 1915, only a few months before Bud Ballew's fight with Pete Bynum and company at the 66 Restaurant. Originating in a "pressing establishment," the blaze swiftly reduced to ashes some forty buildings up and down both sides of Texas Road. Destroyed were "the post office, the telephone exchange, the picture shows, the hotels and rooming houses" along with many other stores and business establishments. Eventually Sheriff Buck Garrett and his force of deputies, including Bud Ballew, had to be called in to restore order and protect property from looters.[14] True to form, Ragtown lost no time in rising from the ashes.

Also making this particular blaze noteworthy was the death of one of Carter County's leading sporting men and gunmen. Having moved his business from Ardmore to Ragtown at the outset of the oil rush, Jonas Fooshee was set up in fine style by the time of the January 1915 fire. During the height of the blaze, Fooshee fell into some sort of disagreement with Bud Roberts, another of the gambling fraternity. Hot words led to hot lead. In the exchange of shots, Jonas Fooshee received a mortal wound. He would die shortly after being shot.[15]

Despite the hardships caused by the destructive flames, Ragtown and Carter County's prime affliction continued to be its chronic criminality. On November 21, 1915, a few days after the Ballew–Bynum gun battle, the *Daily Ardmoreite* blared in front page headlines, "A Disgrace To Oklahoma Says Oil Man." Quoting a veteran oil-field worker the paper reported the man as stating:

> I have been in oil fields for the past twenty-five years but I have never seen a place as rough as the Healdton field is now. Hold-ups are growing very frequent and men are becoming afraid to go on morning tower, which begins at midnight. These men have been accustomed not to take any money with them, but one fellow was badly beaten up because he did not have anything. The highwayman told him next time to carry at least the price of a meal with him.

The newspaper went on to comment:

The person making these statements said that by all means whiskey should be put out of the field, and if the local officers did not do it, that the state officers should be appealed to.

This was a recurring lament, indeed, and one that would be brought forth periodically over the next six years.

Others also found conditions untenable. The Oklahoma State Secretary of the YMCA even got into the act by threatening to have the Carter County oil fields investigated by the governor.[16]

Many reasons were postulated as to why the region had deteriorated in its compliance with the laws. During the height of the oil boom it was estimated some twenty thousand people resided in the oil regions. During this same time period the Carter County Sheriff's Department employed only fifteen officers. At Healdton this left one deputy to cover an average of 17.5 square miles of territory and over 1,300 citizens. The rapid boom caused the population to outstrip the facilities and laws set up for a much smaller populace.[17]

After all was said and done, however, there were those who claimed that law-enforcement corruption was of immense concern. Some felt the reason one illegal joint closed while others flourished had everything to do with protection schemes and extortion on the part of certain officers.

One of the first lawmen in the area to be charged with corruption was Charles King, the chief of police of Ringling, just over the Carter County line in neighboring Jefferson County. King was arrested by federal marshals on December 20, 1915, and charged with being a member of a so-called "whiskey ring" transporting illegal liquor from Wichita Falls, Texas, to the Healdton fields.[18] He would not be the last law enforcement official to face an accusing finger.

Although Carter County Sheriff Buck Garrett would himself face accusations of corruption in office, at the time he seemed the right man for the job. One chronicler has stated:

> The population of the oil field around Ragtown rose almost
> instantaneously from zero to more than twenty thousand men,
> with practically no law enforcement for the oil field. Carter County's

rough and rugged sheriff, Buck Garrett, rounded up 140 gallons of whiskey, ten bootleggers, and a tent full of gambling paraphernalia on his first raid into the area.[19]

Buck Garrett was the kind of man who could engender fierce loyalty in his associates, including Bud Ballew. Ballew became his chief deputy, close personal friend, and a man who would risk his own life to save Garrett's. Garrett was charismatic, a master politician, and a fearless officer. These were traits perfected from years on the frontier. Whatever else he was, Buck Garrett was definitely a man of his time and environment.

CHAPTER 5

Buck Garrett

"Buck Garrett, sheriff of Carter County, is the most feared and respected officer of the law in the southwest. This respect comes not only from the law-abiding citizens, but from the outlaws as well—men with whom Buck has had revolver battles, men he has wounded. Besides possessing necessary requirements of a western officer—exceptional bravery, physical endurance, power of deduction and accurate marksmanship— Buck is endowed with a remarkable personality—a personality which produces an almost hypnotic influence over the person who observes or converses with him."[1]

The man for whom this reverential passage was written was born in Columbia, Murray County, Tennessee, on May 24, 1871.[2] At the age of eight, Buck Garrett moved with his mother and father and at least one sibling, a brother known as J. A., to the vicinity of Paris, Texas.[3] Two years later Buck's mother died of unknown causes. Shortly after the death of his wife, the senior Garrett deserted his children, leaving them to fend for themselves.[4]

The results of this development on Buck's brother J. A. are unknown. It is known, however, that at the tender age of ten or eleven, Buck became an urchin on the streets of Paris, Texas. As a boy he became a well-known figure throughout the town, supporting himself by shining shoes, selling newspapers, or doing various odd jobs.[5] Another young lad about the same age as

Garrett who shifted for himself on the streets of Paris around the same time was Moman Pruiett, later to become one of the most famous criminal lawyers in the state of Oklahoma.[6] It is most likely the pair knew each other at this time and developed a relationship that would come to aid Buck Garrett in the future.

At this time Paris, Texas, some one hundred miles southeast of the future site of Ardmore, Oklahoma, was the lively headquarters of the Eastern Judicial District of Texas with jurisdiction over much of the southern portion of Indian Territory. Buck Garrett often hung around the federal courthouse and Paris police station, making him familiar with the many officers and deputy U.S. marshals who came and went during their duties. He admired these men of strength and authority with the big revolvers on their hips and Winchesters sheathed in scabbards on their horses. He studied them closely. Someday he wished to be just like them.

At the age of fourteen, Garrett took a job as a cowhand on the Leeper spread located near Paris.[7] There he developed into a strapping young man of six foot two inches, weighing around two hundred pounds. After five years on the Leeper Ranch, the seasoned cowpuncher drifted back to the streets of Paris, a tough young brawler who would soon garner a somewhat questionable reputation.

Garrett's employment for the next two years is not known, but he eventually drifted into bad company. On the evening of Monday, November 23, 1891, Garrett, Charles Smith, and Bob Clark attacked a farmer named W. R. Jones on the streets of Boardtown, the saloon district of Paris. While Smith grabbed the unsuspecting man from behind, pinioning his arms at his sides, Clark produced a pair of brass knuckles and struck Jones a number of fierce blows to the head, opening a vicious gash on his skull. At that point Garrett produced a fence post and commenced to wail away on the unfortunate victim's cranium.

Bloodied and bruised, Jones finally managed to break away from his three assailants and stumble to safety, minus his pocket watch. That same day Paris police arrested both Clark and Smith, charging them with robbery and aggravated assault. The following day Garrett was also arrested and jailed by City Marshal James Shanklin on a similar charge of aggravated assault.

After spending a couple of days behind bars, Garrett managed to give bond, and the authorities released him to await further court action.[8] The eventual disposition of his case is unclear. Whatever the results might have been, it would not be the last time Buck Garrett would be at cross-purposes to the law. In the future, however, he would have the might of a lawman's badge behind him.

Garrett found the perfect opportunity to leave his troubles behind him in the spring of 1892 when he and his brother were enlisted, along with other Texas gunmen, by the Wyoming Stock Growers Association to go after "cattle rustlers" in what would become known as the Johnson County War. It turned out to be out of the frying pan and into the fire, however, when the Texans ended up charged with murder languishing in Wyoming until August 10, at which point Garrett and the others were finally released on bail on their own recognizance.[9]

As Wyoming historian Helena Huntington Smith wrote:

> The Texans were paid off and headed for Fort Worth, promising to come back for the trial, set for August 22 . . . They never came back and nobody wanted them, not even the prosecution.[10]

Arriving back in Paris, Buck Garrett was probably more than happy to have left Wyoming and her rustler problems and court proceedings far on his back trail. Enough time had passed for his own legal troubles in the Jones assault to have been largely forgotten. He likely wished to take advantage of that fact and turn over a new leaf.

The young adventurer had not lost his interest in law enforcement. Shortly after his return to Texas, Garrett received an appointment as a deputy U.S. marshal working out of Paris. Domesticity crept into his life in 1893 with his marriage to Miss Ida M. Chancellor, the daughter of fellow Deputy U.S. Marshal James M. Chancellor. Chancellor would be another future chief of the Ardmore, Oklahoma, police force and a man who would always be a close personal ally of his son-in-law. Eventually the couple would have one child, a son named Raymond, born in 1899.[11]

His first serious test and perhaps one of the closest calls he would face in his long career of law enforcement occurred east of Ardmore on November 3, 1894.

While out arresting whiskey peddlers, Deputy Marshals Garrett, Charley Burns, and Ed Roberts stopped in the village of Lebanon. There the trio of lawmen encountered Iveson Keel, the full-blood Indian jailer of the Chickasaw Nation jail at Tishomingo. Keel had been in town most of the day drinking. Following a brief encounter between Keel and Burns, against whom Keel had some sort of grudge, the officers headed toward Ardmore with three prisoners.

About a mile out of Lebanon, Keel galloped up on horseback and over-took the party of lawmen and prisoners. At first expressing friendship, Keel suddenly drew his revolver and opened fire on Burns. The three marshals quickly returned the fire. Bullets narrowly missed Garrett and Roberts while Burns received a grazing slug across the stomach. In return, at least one of the lawmen's shots dealt Keel a serious wound. Turning, the wounded Keel put spurs to his horse and sped down the road.

A mile distant the three officers encountered the badly wounded jailer lying across the road, his horse standing nearby. Upon being commanded to surrender, Keel suddenly raised himself as if to fire the pistol still clenched in his fist. Garrett, Roberts, and the slightly wounded Burns all fired a volley at the prostrate man. Struck by several more slugs Keel finally lay still. Carted into town, Iveson Keel died soon after being shot. Buck Garrett had passed the test of deadly fire.[12]

Garrett continued to be active in the Ardmore area following his transfer to the Ardmore federal court. May 1900 saw him take part in the Lanier mur-der investigation at Centre.[13] He would be involved in other arrests throughout the next year.[14]

If anyone deserved the label of Buck Garrett's major nemesis in his early career, that man would be Marion "Scarface Jim" Watson. A notorious whis-key peddler, Watson received the moniker of Scarface Jim as the result of a long bullet-wound scar running the length of one side of his face. Along with his female consort, Lou Bowers,[15] Watson peddled his illicit booze throughout southern Oklahoma and northern Texas as early as the 1890s. He and Garrett would have many confrontations, at least two of which led to gunplay.

Sometime in early 1901 Garrett encountered Watson near Wynnewood, a little town in Garvin County thirty-two miles north of Ardmore. In the exchange of shots, no one was hit and Watson managed to make his escape.[16]

Again, on the evening of July 4, 1901, while scouting near Sulphur, Oklahoma, Buck Garrett, accompanied by Deputy Marshals Harper, Martin, and Bill McCarty, ran onto Scarface Jim. A fusillade of shots followed in which McCarty had a bullet pass through his hat and Garrett took slugs through his coat and received a powder burn along his face. Garrett managed at the same time to place three Winchester slugs into the slicker rolled up behind Watson's saddle. As before Watson managed to make his getaway.[17]

Over the course of the next two months Buck Garrett and his fellow deputies hotly pursued the whiskey peddler throughout southern Indian Territory.[18] Recognizing Garrett as his main antagonist, Watson formulated a plan to ambush the tenacious lawman.[19] While Watson was on his way back to Ardmore to accomplish his plot, Deputy Marshals Crocket Lee and George Holvey cornered him near Scipio on September 18, 1901, and shot him to death while he was resisting arrest.[20] It was said to have been Lou Bowers, hoping for consideration from the law officers, who led Watson into the trap.[21]

The stature attained by Buck Garrett among his fellow deputy marshals by early 1902 is evident. At the retirement ceremonies for outgoing U.S. Marshal J. S. Hammer, Garrett's fellow deputies picked him to represent them in making a speech to Hammer, wishing him well and presenting him with a gold-headed cane as a token of their esteem. In reporting the incident, the *Daily Ardmoreite* referred to Garrett and Deputy W. E. McLemore, who also spoke and made a presentation to outgoing Chief Deputy R. Herz, with the words "two braver men than (McLemore) and Garrett never served a warrant."[22] The next day the new U.S. marshal, Ben H. Colbert, made his appointments. Buck Garrett received appointment as the deputy marshal stationed at Ardmore.[23]

Garrett continued to make a name for himself while operating out of the Ardmore federal courthouse. Only two days after having his deputy marshal's designation renewed, he and fellow Deputies Dave Booker, Oscar Wilkinson, O. A. Wells, Lute Johnson, and E. S. Adams were instrumental in quelling an uprising of prisoners at the federal jail. Although hit in the back with a "slung shot," Garrett was not seriously injured in the melee.[24]

Within two months Garrett would be involved in perhaps the strangest episode of his career. Probably stemming from an overabundance of alcohol and an exaggerated sense of rough fun, the incident would result in the thirty-one-year-old lawman being charged with an assault to commit murder.

After having consumed a few drinks[25] on the evening of Friday, May 30, 1902, Garrett, Dud Slaughter, Hal Castleberry, and George Hammer found themselves lounging in front of the Ardmore depot. Although the details are somewhat clouded, it would appear that the four men commenced to harass passersby, Slaughter beginning a routine of asking various men if they could lend him a match. With the arrival of a man named W. G. Duley, the encounter became physical, with Duley claiming that the four, specifically Garrett and Slaughter, perpetrated an assault on him. Duley had a badly fractured skull, as well as a number of credible witnesses,[26] to prove his contention.

At the preliminary hearing held June 6–7, the court dropped the charges against Castleberry and Hammer. Despite the fact that Garrett testified to believing he saw a knife in Duley's hand at one point during the fight, both he and Slaughter were bound over for trial under of bond of $1,000 each. The undoubtedly embarrassed Deputy Marshal Garrett paid his bail and gained his release.[27]

As unusual as the case proved to be, it just as quickly faded away. Although records are lacking, it is believed the court eventually dropped the charges against both Garrett and Slaughter.

Despite this serious charge against one of the most respected officers in Ardmore, it would seem to have had little effect on Garrett's career. As early as 1904 the now seasoned lawman resigned his U.S. deputy marshal's commission and joined the Ardmore police force as a regular officer.[28] In February 1905 he declared his candidacy for the office of Ardmore chief of police, which at that time was an elected position.[29]

Winning the Democratic nomination from his old friend and incumbent chief Dave Booker, Garrett found himself on the ballot at the April 4 election. Having run a successful campaign, he defeated his Republican opponent by a plurality of 398 votes to become the new chief of police of Ardmore.[30] Later Garrett would hire his father-in-law, James Chancellor, as a city policeman. In less than a year, trouble once again descended upon him.

During the first week of March 1906, Buck Garrett and his wife, with a number of friends, journeyed to Oklahoma City to take in the Southwestern

Livestock Show and Exposition. By about 3 a.m. on Friday, March 6, Garrett and his cronies, having left their wives behind, found themselves in the combination bordello/dance hall of a notorious lady of pleasure named Eva Ryan. Garrett fell into a brawl with some cavorting cattlemen when the feather duster he was using as a prop while he danced accidentally struck one of the men on the head. Quickly the dispute turned violent. One of the cowmen pulled a knife and slashed at Garrett. At this point Garrett pulled his revolver and jerked a shot at his attacker. Unfortunately the bullet missed its intended victim and slammed into the abdomen of Jim Peters, apparently a long-time friend of Garrett. Peters lived only a couple of hours after being shot. He would expire later that same morning.[31]

After a short delay Oklahoma City Chief of Police John Hubatka sent one of his officers to arrest Garrett.[32] Held in the city until March 27, Garrett was ordered by the court to be bound over pending action of the grand jury, this despite the fact that he managed to produce a dying statement of Peters in which the deceased man appeared to clear the Ardmore chief of all blame in his death. One of the witnesses to this deathbed declaration was Oklahoma County Sheriff George Garrison.[33]

Held under a bail bond of $7,000, Buck Garrett quickly gave the amount and returned to Ardmore to resume his duties as chief of police.[34] In this case the wheels of justice moved slowly. Not until January 1908 would the Oklahoma County grand jury finally bring down an indictment against Garrett for the death of Peters.[35] Eventually he would be cleared of all culpability in the unfortunate affair with the help of his attorney and old friend Moman Pruiett.[36]

Through 1906 and 1907, while the Oklahoma County Court reserved its decision in the Peters case, Buck Garrett continued to function as chief of police.[37] The habitués of Caddo Street would be a continual aggravation. In 1907 his quick and decisive actions in disarming the dangerous Bill Ballew and Jonas Fooshee following the Ike Fooshee killing helped prevent an already deadly situation from becoming even more deadly.[38]

Buck Garrett's stature as a lawman was growing incident by incident.

He was first elected Carter County sheriff in 1911, at age forty, following a successful stretch of over six years as Ardmore police chief. Upon his resignation as chief, Ardmore city commissioners appointed policeman Smith Redmon to replace him in December of that year.[39]

Although his previous years had been peppered with brushes with the law, Garrett's regime as Carter County sheriff would last for the next ten years over which time he would build his political machine into a formidable clique. The word of Buck Garrett would not only be the law in Carter County but could almost be described as dictatorial in scope. Whatever you could say about the man, his charisma and savvy could not be denied.

In order to help run his Carter County bailiwick, Sheriff Garrett hired some of the toughest, hardest working individuals he could find as deputy sheriffs over the years. Men such as A. W. "Gus" Gains, Bill Ward, Frank Bishop,[40] Horace Kendall, Jake Williams, and Fred Williams served under Garrett at various times. They all eventually gained reputations for themselves, which stand to this day in Carter County, as fearless officers of the law.

Garrett's most important hiring during his career as county sheriff occurred shortly before winning his third term of office in 1914. Early that year he would employ Bud Ballew in a deputy sheriff's position. Ballew would become Garrett's closest ally and personal friend and his number one deputy and troubleshooter. The pair would rule Carter County with iron fists for the next eight years. Some would say they became too powerful and this absolute power corrupted absolutely. Be that as it may, eventually Ballew's fame would equal, if not surpass, that of Buck Garrett in Ardmore and Carter County.

CHAPTER 6

Victim #2—Arch Campbell

By early 1916 Ardmore was headquarters to a host of prominent lawmen all attempting to keep the lid on a potentially explosive situation as a result of the vice and corruption wrought by the oil boom. U.S. Deputy Marshal William R. "Dick" Highnight[1] had his office in the Federal Building. At City Hall former Deputy U.S. Marshal Bob Hutchins held the position of Ardmore chief of police; his assistant chief was Will Fraser; desk sergeants were R. Herz[2] and Buck Gardenhise; and the patrolmen were Dave Frazier, Dan Blackburn, Dow Braziel, Mack Pettitt, C. G. Sims, Lee McCoy, Bob Stacy, and Walter Stroud. Both Braziel and Sims were destined to play major roles in the lives of Ballew and Garrett. The constables for Ardmore Township at the county courthouse were Ed Henson and Leslie L. "Les" Segler, the latter also destined to be a future Ardmore police chief and a prominent player in the events to come.[3]

Only a little over two months after the Pete Bynum shooting, Bud Ballew and a number of the aforementioned officers would be involved in another wild shooting scrape.

Arch Campbell was a prominent member of the Ardmore community. He was a former lawman who, in the years 1906 to 1907, had served as a policeman on the Ardmore police force under Chief of Police Buck Garrett.[4] After leaving the police force, Campbell purchased a building and lot in Ardmore, which he operated as a rooming house for a number of years and continued to manage into 1916.[5] He was known as a man who had "many warm friends" and was "always considered a very peaceful citizen," and "a well-known and generally esteemed resident . . . "[6]

For some reason, by early 1916, Campbell had taken to drinking in excess. Shortly after noon on Wednesday, January 26, 1916, the slightly intoxicated man entered the Palace Barber Shop on Ardmore's Main Street. Speaking to the barber working at the first chair closest to the door, Campbell asked him to step into the back room for a moment. Realizing that Campbell had been in the habit of asking those in the barbershop for small loans of cash, the barber told him that he was too busy at the time to talk to him. Walking toward the back of the shop, Campbell requested another of the barbers to go into the back room with him. Following the first barber's lead, the second barber also made an excuse to Campbell and continued cutting his patron's hair. At this point Campbell drew a revolver from his coat pocket and ordered the two men to whom he had just spoken to come to him. As emphasis for this command, he fired a number of shots through the skylight in the shop ceiling.

The sound of the gunshots attracted a number of Ardmore law officers to the scene. As customers and barbers frantically spilled out of the front door, Deputy Sheriffs Bud Ballew and Fred Williams, Constable Ed Henson and Ardmore police officers Dave Frazier, Lee McCoy, and Mack Pettitt almost simultaneously converged on the area.

While Frazier, McCoy, and Pettitt cautiously entered the front door of the Palace, Ballew, accompanied by Williams and Henson, quickly ran through a neighboring meat market and made their way to the back door of the barbershop. Finding the door locked, Ballew smashed his fist through a glass window on the door to access the lock, badly cutting his hand.

When Frazier, McCoy, and Pettitt entered the front door, they encountered Campbell standing at the back of the shop covering them with his pistol. When the lawmen advanced on him and commanded him to lay down his gun, Campbell suddenly opened fire on them. The three policemen quickly returned fire and dove for cover. Likewise, Campbell ducked behind a tall screen separating the main barbershop from a storage area while he continued to trade shots with the lawmen.

At this point Ballew, Frazier, and Henson made their appearance at the rear of the room, behind Campbell. Turning, Campbell began firing at the three men. Quickly Ballew and his companions returned the fire. One of Campbell's bullets struck Ballew in the left shoulder, ranged down through the top of his left lung and exited out his right side. Another slug grazed his side.

As the barrage of bullets continued, a number of shots slammed into Campbell's body. Pierced by at least four bullets, one in each arm and two in the head, he fell to the floor and died within moments. Shortly after the conclusion of the battle, Campbell's body was carted off to T. C. Bridgeman's undertaking parlor.[7]

Immediately following the shooting, Ballew's fellow lawmen, none of whom had been injured in the gun battle, assisted Ballew to the Hardy Sanitarium. Despite his serious wound, Ballew quickly recovered under Dr. Hardy's care and soon was released from the hospital.

Although Arch Campbell had a number of friends in Ardmore and many regretted his death, everyone realized the law officers had no choice in the matter. No blame devolved onto Ballew or any of his fellow officers for Campbell's death. Though it was never definitely determined who fired the fatal shots that killed Arch Campbell, Ballew had been in the forefront of the battle and had at least assisted in claiming his second victim in two months.

Meanwhile, in early January 1916 District Judge W. F. Freeman had called for an investigation of the illegal booze business running rampant in the county.[8] This precipitated a major push by local law enforcement. Almost every day through the early months of 1916 Sheriff Garrett and two or three of his deputies would make a trip out to Ragtown to conduct raids on various businesses. However, as soon as the sheriff's force disappeared over the hill returning to Ardmore, the joints would once again open for business.

During the raid of March 14, Garrett decided to employ a bit of subterfuge. Taking along deputies Will Ward and the now fully recovered Bud Ballew, Garrett made his usual late night attack on the joints of Ragtown. Finding everything legal and above board, the trio of lawmen bid everyone good-night and headed back toward Ardmore. After turning down a side road and allowing time for everything to get into full swing in the sinful camp, the officers surreptitiously returned to town. They caught a number of illegal houses in operation, the surprise raid landing more than one culprit in the county jail with a thirty-day sentence and $50 fine to boot.[9]

In the midst of these events, Judge Freeman's court of inquiry continued to make many people in the county nervous including Bud Ballew. During his investigations Freeman received evidence that parties (whether or not they were connected with Ballew had not been determined) were selling whiskey out of a barn located on Ballew's Lone Grove ranch. While these investigations were ongoing, Ballew entered into an agreement with a friend named Cyrus Pyeatt to sell him a vacant house located on the Ballew spread. With the deal completed, Pyeatt had the house moved about two miles west of Lone Grove where, according to investigators, he commenced the operation of an illegal "roadhouse" dispensing illicit booze. With indictments issued by County Attorney Andy Hardy against him and a number of others, Pyeatt made the rather inappropriate decision to attempt a meeting with Freeman to discuss his case. Enraged, Freeman rebuked Pyeatt and refused absolutely to grant him an interview. Although all involved in the charges would eventually be cleared, Bud Ballew developed an animosity toward Judge Freeman for dragging his name through the muck. In turn Freeman accused Ballew of attempting to protect the parties involved in the case.[10]

About 4:30 p.m. on Saturday, May 20, having only thirty minutes earlier thrown Pyeatt out of his chambers, Judge Freeman and Court Reporter Anderton headed down the stairs from the second floor of the courthouse. Upon reaching the ground floor, they spotted Pyeatt, Ballew, and another individual sitting by the west entrance. In an attempt to avoid trouble, Freeman and Anderton changed course and headed out the north side door, Freeman repairing to his home on D Street four blocks away.

It was Freeman's custom every Saturday at five in the afternoon to walk over to the Palace Barber Shop on Main Street, so recently the scene of the shooting death of Arch Campbell, for his weekly haircut and shave. As he strolled down the sidewalk near the barbershop, he noticed Ballew and Pyeatt engaged in animated conversation as they sat in the doorway of the building next door to the Palace. Ballew looked up and noticed Freeman but let him pass.

Finding the barbershop full, Freeman headed back the way he had come. This time, both Ballew and Pyeatt got to their feet. Ballew walked briskly over and confronted the judge.

"Judge, have I done you any harm lately?" Ballew asked Freeman.

"Not that I recall," Freeman answered. "Why?"

"What in the hell do you keep on punching me for?" the deputy growled.

"What do you mean? How punching?" Freeman came back.

"You know damn well what I mean," Ballew hissed. "Calling these sons of bitches before your damn court of inquiry to swear damn lies on me."

"In calling witnesses before the court I am only doing my duty as an officer, and I am not responsible for what they swear," the judge answered in a calm tone of voice, attempting to divert trouble.

His attempts proved in vain, however, as Ballew's hair trigger temper got the best of him.

Ballew glared fiercely at Freeman. "Yes, and I want to tell you that who-ever swears in your damn court that he bought whiskey out of my barn or in any way connects me with the selling of whiskey is a god damned dirty lying son of a bitch, and you are too!" Ballew roared.

Seeing the confrontation was escalating, Freeman attempted to move around Ballew and continue down the sidewalk. Blocking his way, Ballew suddenly reached out and struck the judge a hard blow to the side of his head, knocking his hat several feet into the street. Staggering, Freeman managed to keep his feet. Ignoring the blow he walked into the street closely followed by the infuriated deputy. Bending over, Freeman retrieved his hat. As he straightened Ballew struck him another blow to the head. Ballew landed three or four more solid blows before someone in the crowd of bystanders who had gathered around the men hollered, "Don't do that, don't do that, that is our district judge!"

"I don't give a damn if it is!" Ballew shouted back, at the same time striking Freeman's face with another hard slap.[11]

At this point Ballew turned and stalked angrily down the street toward the Ardmore police station. At the station Ballew reported his actions, made bond on a charge of disturbing the peace and, still in a fury, headed out to his ranch. Later that same day he telephoned Sheriff Buck Garrett and tendered his resignation as deputy sheriff.[12]

The act of a county law officer assaulting a respected district court judge on the main street of their city greatly outraged many people in Ardmore. The fact that the attack had obviously been premeditated and not carried out in the heat of the moment heightened people's objections to the affair.

Two nights following the assault on Freeman, certain citizens, headed by the Reverend C. C. Weith, organized a so-called "indignation meeting" to be held at a local house of worship called the Tabernacle.

By 8 p.m. close to two thousand people had gathered. Led off by a song service and a speech by Weith, the group then chose W. I. Cruce as chairman and Dr. J. F. Young as secretary. Next, a statement from Judge Freeman concerning the affair was read to the gathering, the reader substituting the word "blank" for all of Ballew's alleged cuss words. Following the reading, Methodist Rev. E.R. Welch and Rev. David Cooper, a Baptist preacher, spoke, Welch condemning Ballew for other acts termed "reprehensible in an officer of the law."[13]

After the two preachers' comments, Cruce opened the floor to anyone who wished to speak. As the crowd sat spellbound Bud Ballew made his appearance and strode up to the platform.

"I have been here all day, and no one has called on me for a statement, or came to see me to get my side of the story," Ballew said in a mild tone. "There are generally two sides to every question, and I am going to give you my side of this one," he said.

As the *Ardmore Statesman* put it, "The crowd began to realize that the lion was being bearded in his den. That the object against which the invective of the meting (*sic*) was being hurled was not only in the crowd, but on the platform."[14]

As most of the crowd squirmed nervously in their seats and whispered apprehensively to one another, Ballew continued.

"Yes, this is Bud Ballew, and I want to give you my side of this matter. I want to tell you that I respect my old mother too much to let anybody speak slightingly about her. And when the Judge called me a son of a bitch I slapped him."

With the crowd partly composed of women and children, many people in the audience took offense to Ballew's choice of language. Calls of "put him out" and "have him arrested" rang through the auditorium. Though his intentions at first had been well meaning, this display of antipathy toward him once again threatened to pique Ballew's temper.

Taking a defiant stance he shouted, "I have a right to be here and speak in my own behalf." He added ominously, "Any effort to put me out by force might not be too healthy!"

At this point, sensing deterioration in the proceedings, Sheriff Buck Garrett got up from his seat in the audience and made his way to the front. As he spoke to Ballew, a voice cried out, "I see a pistol on him, and as he has resigned as an officer, why don't you arrest him for carrying it!"

This comment did not help Garrett in his desired mission. Finally he convinced Ballew to leave the stage and sit down.

Once order had been restored, it was decided that Ballew would be allowed to speak on the proviso that he apologized to the gathering for his unsavory choice of words.

Once again stepping up to the podium Ballew, ever defiant, called out, "I apologize to the ladies for the language I used, but not to the men." He seemed inclined to say more until Garrett again approached and convinced him to return to his seat.

Finally the meeting continued with various speakers declaring their condemnation of the assault on Freeman and their support of law and order. The crowd engaged in a rousing rendition of "America" while a committee composed of Dr. J. F. Young, Thomas Norman, and L. S. Dolman retired to a back room to formulate a resolution for the meeting.[15] The resolution stated:

> *We, your committee appointed to draft resolutions beg to report as follows:*
>
> *Be it resolved, the citizens of Carter county, and Ardmore in particular, that we deplore and heartily condemn the recent assault made upon our district judge because of his efforts to enforce the laws of our country, that said act was a direct assault upon the judiciary, and if continued cannot but result in anarchy.*
>
> *Be it resolved further that our district judge and other officials be assured that the citizens of this city and county are with him and them in his and their efforts to enforce the laws, and we hereby pledge to him and them our united support in this regard.*[16]

With this conclusion the throng, including Bud Ballew, who probably felt no sense of vindication as he had likely hoped he would, filed out and dispersed to their homes. As a display of public support for Judge W. F. Freeman, the meeting could be said to have succeeded to a point. As a lasting monument to the peace and dignity of Carter County, however, the exercise had little, if any, effect.

Thoroughly disgusted Ballew had reportedly told a reporter for the *Daily Ardmoreite* "that he was never accused of dealing in liquor or ever having anything to do with it until he was sworn in as a deputy sheriff. Following his taking the oath of office insinuations and charges [had] been made until he completely lost his patience and let his temper lead him to do what he should not have done."[17]

His distaste for the job, expressed in light of the recent unfortunate developments, would be only temporary.

CHAPTER 7

Ex-Deputy Ballew

In the summer of 1916, following the Freeman incident and the relinquishing of his lawman's commission, Bud Ballew retired to his Lone Grove ranch. Along with his wife, Fannie, and two sons, Dorris, now twelve years old, and Buster, age nine, and assisted by his father, Bryant, stepmother, Martha, and half brother, Scott, and Scott's wife, Nannie, all of whom lived nearby, the ex-deputy sheriff once again put his full concentration into his cattle and horse operations.[1] The ranch responded by developing even more as a prosperous business. He also began to take an interest in the oil fields, speculating in various oil leases and investing monetarily in oil product and equipment companies. At this too he made a success, eventually profiting nicely from his dabbling in the oil wells throughout Carter County.[2]

Always a lover of fine horses, Ballew spent much of his spare time away from the ranch at the racetrack located on the Ardmore Fairgrounds. In partnership with County Commissioner Marion Pierce, Ballew organized and managed many of the horse races that took place there.[3] Racing would be a passion that would continue throughout his entire life.

However, Ballew would be forced to face further court action resulting from his attack on Judge Freeman. On June 13 Freeman had Ballew arraigned before him on a charge of contempt of court, deeming that the assault perpetrated upon him by Ballew came about as a direct result of his court of inquiry. Ballew complained he did not even have time to employ counsel; however, Freeman waived off the complaint. At the conclusion of the proceedings, Ballew came away sentenced to a term of sixty days in the county jail and a fine of $200.[4]

Hiring a bevy of attorneys, including Moman Pruiett, Ballew appealed the case to the Oklahoma Criminal Court of Appeals in Oklahoma City. On June 24 the court of appeals released him on a bail bond of $1,000 pending further investigation.[5]

Carter County continued to be a dangerous locale as summer 1916 eased into fall. In Wirt on July 24, Purris "Slim" Clements, engaged as a cook at the Rogers-Ripey Restaurant, became embroiled in a dispute with John Dennison, a foreman for the Magnolia Pipe Line Co. Clements ended the fracas by hitting Dennison on the head with a board that had a nail in the end of it. The nail penetrated Dennison's skull and killed him instantly. Deputy Sheriff L. O. Bates transported Clements to the county jail at Ardmore later that day.[6]

The very next day Ragtown was to experience another violent death. With the upcoming Carter County elections less than four months away, two separate groups, one supporting incumbent sheriff Democrat Buck Garrett, the other supporters of his Republican opponent, Andy Hutchins, both happened to be in Wirt on campaign tours. Later that afternoon Garrett supporter James A. Smith, a barber at the Roberts Barbershop located in Ardmore's First National Bank building, got into a heated argument with Bob Nabers, a Hutchins supporter from Baum, Oklahoma. Swiftly the exchange of words became violent. Smith brought the altercation to a climax by pulling a revolver out of his pocket and fatally wounding Nabers in the chest. Witnesses at the scene later stated that only the quick action of authorities in hustling the killer to the secure confines of the Ardmore cooler prevented a necktie party being held for Smith.[7]

A little over one month later, violent death again visited Carter County's law enforcement corps. While serving in a posse led by Dow Braziel, now working as a federal government officer combating whiskey peddlers, Special Officer Oscar Alexander was shot and killed by bootleggers on the evening of Friday, September 3.[8] This incident would compound the eventual animosity felt between Ballew and Braziel. Ballew, among others in Carter County, felt that Braziel had been negligent in his duties, allowing the young officer to engage in the actions that caused his death.

In a few months Ragtown would once again be a human shooting gallery. Earlier in 1916 Buck Garrett had hired Frank Jones, a former bootlegger with ties to Carter County's underworld,[9] as a special deputy sheriff and night watchman in charge of keeping the lid on the wild oil town. One night a bandit named Roy McCurtain attempted to rob a Ragtown cafe. Jones caught him as he tried to make his getaway. Leveling his revolver, Jones shot the fleeing outlaw dead.

Later Jones would shoot to death Ragtown badman Curly Gray.[10] Gray had been lucky to escape the bullets of Bud Ballew following the cafe robbery and shooting of November 1915 in which Pete Bynum had been killed. Serving a short sentence and returning to Ragtown, Gray began a simmering conflict of long standing with Jones over matters long since lost to history. Jones put an end to the troublesome Gray by shooting him dead.

Judge Freeman's Court of Inquiry continued to haunt Bud Ballew well into fall 1916. In mid October the grand jury brought down its report for that month's term. In the list of indictments the jury included a charge against Bud Ballew, Scott Ballew, and William Yell, jointly charged with "keeping place for sale of liquor."[11]

It proved to be an all-star list of indicted individuals slated for the October term of court. Besides Bud, his brother Scott, and Yell, the indicted included George and Mose Love charged with the death of Oscar Alexander; brothers Jim and Dock Berryman, well known Carter County bootleggers indicted on four counts of assault to kill; Tom Walker and Carl Pruitt, charged in the sensational shooting of the family of Dr. Paine; Horace Addington and the Key brothers, George and Emmett, well known citizens facing a charge of "maintaining a place, etc.," another way of saying running an illegal booze joint; Jim Smith, held for the July killing of Bob Nabers in Ragtown; Steve Talkington, notorious Carter County gunman, barfly, and future Ballew nemesis, facing a liquor law violation; and Slim Clements, indicted for the death of John Dennison, which had taken place in Ragtown the day before the Nabers killing.[12]

It must have rankled Bud Ballew to be included in this nefarious list of ne'er-do-wells. He probably cursed Judge Freeman again for the trouble his court of inquiry had caused him. As it turned out, however, he need not have worried. Before it came to trial the charges against Bud and Scott Ballew were dropped by the prosecution. The facts of the liquor charges stemming from the Lone Grove ranch incident were never fully brought to light.

Ballew's good friend, County Sheriff Buck Garrett, had his problems to worry about as a result of the October grand jury. On October 14, jury foreman D. H. Dawson submitted the jury's final report. Along with commenting on the duties of the district judge, county attorney, county judge, county commissioners, Ardmore city commissioners, magistrates and constables, the jury found the enforcement of the prohibition laws by county officials "practically a farce, and especially so in the town of Wirt, generally known as Ragtown." The report went on to state, "This last mentioned place is the plague spot of our county, and from the evidence before us we are compelled to believe that all crimes known to civilized man have been committed there."[13]

The grand jury went on to charge that the county jail "was in a filthy condition and recommended that same should be cleaned up and kept clean; that the bedding was dirty and should be renewed." They reported that they had been freely admitted to all parts of the jail except "to a room in the southwest corner of the building on the first floor above the ground, which was locked, and we were told by the jailer that the only person who had a key to that room was the sheriff, and that the captured booze was stored therein."

The most damning part of the report probably came in the following paragraph:

> From the evidence submitted to us, covering a period of the past three years, a great quantity of beer and whiskey has been captured by the sheriff and his force and the constables of the county, and the same was turned over to the sheriff of Carter County, the legal custodian of such contraband goods. Upon examination of the records of the sheriff's office we find no trace of said goods being received or destroyed, or any disposition of same, and further, we can find no record in any court of Carter County, where returns have been made of the seizure or capture of intoxicating liquor by any officer of the county, neither can we find any record of where an application has been made to any magistrate, county or district judge for an order to destroy said contraband goods, nor can we find, of record, where an order has been issued by any of the above said officers, for the destruction of the said contraband

goods, in other words, the provisions of the prohibitory law, relating to the disposition of said contraband goods is wholly ignored and neglected by the officers charged with its enforcement.[14]

Then the jury dropped its bombshell:

Under the laws of our state the sheriff of the county is charged with the enforcement of all the laws applicable to the county in which he resides. We find from the evidence before us, that the sheriff of our county is to be commended for the many valuable services he has rendered in discharging his various duties and in many respects he has made a good officer, but we regret to find, from the abundance of evidence now before us, that he has failed and neglected to do his duty in enforcing the prohibition and gambling laws of our state.

In view of the statements just made, we recommend that the sheriff be requested to resign at once.[15]

The *Ardmore Statesman,* never as friendly to Sheriff Garrett and his regime as its competitor the *Daily Ardmoreite* blared the headline on the front page of its October 19 issue: "Grand Jury Asks for Sheriff's Resignation."

It could not have come at a worst time for Buck Garrett with the county election less than a month away. Ever the consummate politician, however, Garrett prevailed. In a sweeping Democratic victory the voters returned Garrett to the sheriff's office. As the *Statesman* reported:

Buck Garrett was acquitted. The jury of voters of Carter County found him not guilty of the charges made by the recent grand jury. By a majority over both the independent and socialist candidates they said—"We want Buck"—and Buck is our sheriff for the next succeeding term. That should settle the matter, and put to sleep the discussion of the grand jury's suggestion that legal proceedings be instituted to remove him from office.[16]

Thus, it did settle the matter, but only for another five years. Then Buck Garrett would feel the full impact of what, this time, had only been threatened. For now his administration was still on the ascendancy. Shortly he would welcome Bud Ballew back into the fold.

As if in response and self-chastisement to the Carter County Grand Jury calling it "the plague spot of our county," Ragtown again nearly burnt to the ground on November 5. The blaze ignited in the City Cafe on Texas Road as a result of a leak in a gas stove. The town bank, post office, and sixty other buildings were reduced to cinders before the blaze could be brought under control.[17] As in the past, this would only be a minor setback in the exuberant life of the boomtown.

As 1916 gave way to 1917, Ballew continued to enjoy his status as a private citizen. Just after New Year's it became apparent that Bud's love of speed extended not only to racehorses. On Tuesday January 2, 1917, while he was traveling in his automobile at an excessive rate of speed down First Street to the road to Lone Grove, the car blew a tire as he rounded the curve at First and F Street. The auto rolled once, spilling Fannie Ballew and his other passengers into the street, Bud being the only one remaining in the vehicle when it landed upright in a field beside the road. Fannie, knocked unconscious in the ordeal, was taken to the nearby home of Rev. F. W. Howes, where, despite being battered and bruised, she quickly revived and was not to be seriously injured. Taken to the home of Buck Garrett, Bud was discovered to have a dislocated arm and a badly cut and scratched face. After medical attention he too quickly shook off his injuries, gathered up Fannie, and headed home. Both would quickly recover and be up and about in a few days. Luckily none of his other passengers that day was seriously injured.[18] It would not be the last time Ballew would get himself into trouble by speeding his car through the streets of Ardmore.

A near tragedy of another sort struck one of the Carter County sheriff's forces on May 1, 1917, in the Berwyn home of Deputy Sheriff Gus Gaines. While Gaines was receiving visitors at his house that evening, his revolver fell out of his pocket, discharging when it struck the floor. The slug passed through the leg of a Miss Hardy just above the knee, lodging in the knee of Mrs. Henderson who was standing behind her. Fortunately Deputy Gaines's visitors both recovered from the accidental shot.[19] The local wags could perhaps be forgiven for joking that "at least Bud Ballew shot them on purpose."

Sadness struck the Ballew family in July with the death of Bud's father, Bryant, on July 16 at the age of seventy-four years following a short illness.[20] The local press eulogized him as "a respected citizen who had the respect and good will of all of his neighbors."[21]

Later that same evening Ballew, grieving over his father, made his way to the Harvey-Douglas Funeral Home in Ardmore to arrange for his funeral. As he sped his automobile down McLish Avenue at a rate of speed obviously exceeding the speed limit, his car was spotted by the Ardmore Police Department's first, and at the time, only motorcycle patrolman, Officer Earley. Taking up the chase, Earley followed Ballew to the Patterson Motor Company on West Main Street. When Ballew exited his car, Earley confronted him and attempted to place him under arrest on a charge of speeding. Taking umbrage at the actions of the officer and in no mood to meekly surrender, Ballew decided to resist. An all out fistic exchange resulted in which Earley, getting the worst of the encounter, came away badly battered by the husky Ballew. When he learned of Ballew's mission in town, Earley magnanimously decided not to file any charges against Ballew.[22] The following afternoon Bryant Ballew was buried in the tiny Lone Grove cemetery.[23]

Shortly after his father's funeral, Ballew found himself once again a member of the Carter County Sheriff's Department. Buck Garrett, deciding his recent reelection was a mandate from the people to run the office his way, resolved that he needed Bud Ballew's gun beside him. Calculating that enough time had passed for the citizens of Carter County to have largely lost their fervent rancor over the Freeman incident, in late July or early August 1917, Garrett offered Ballew his old job of deputy sheriff. Perhaps desiring a change of scenery from the ranch, now that his father was no longer there to help him, Ballew quickly accepted.

CHAPTER 8

— Victim #3—Steve Talkington —

By the time of Bud Ballew's reentry onto the Carter County sheriff's force, America was well immersed in the brutal trench warfare of World War I. The year 1916 had been the most prosperous year in the history of the country. Unemployment was virtually nonexistent. As prices rose, so too did wages. This trend was felt in Carter County as it was throughout the United States. With the oil industry generating millions of dollars and the average worker making better money than he ever had, the populace of Carter County was able to afford luxuries that had been out of reach only a few short years before.

With Germany's declaration of full submarine warfare in February 1917, President Woodrow Wilson led the United States in breaking off diplomatic relations. Finally, on April 6, President Wilson signed into law the vote of the U.S. Congress declaring the country at war with Germany. With the passing of the Selective Draft Act on May 18, all young American men between the ages of twenty-one and thirty in Carter County and elsewhere in the United States were ordered to register for possible service in the armed forces. In June the first American troops reached the shores of France under Major General John J. "Black Jack" Pershing.[1]

Back on the Carter County homefront, the stocky frame of Bud Ballew, with a badge pinned to his vest, once again became a familiar sight striding down the sidewalks of Ardmore, Healdton, Ragtown, and the other towns of the oil fields. Somehow his appearance seemed even more flamboyant, a wide-brimmed, dust-colored hat perched jauntily upon the mop of red, curly hair, his feet ensconced in the high topped "cow boots." Always fashionably attired, the cocky deputy was almost never caught out without a large diamond tie tack. His image of being an amiable individual with a "cherubic expression" and hearty laugh was always offset by the appearance of two menacing revolvers strapped around his ample waist.

Ballew's unruly temper had not subsided in the least in the months away from the sheriff's office. It has been said that in those times when Ballew would get out of hand and begin to lose control of his emotions, the only other man besides Buck Garrett who could handle him was his fellow deputy and good friend W. A. "Will" Ward. On numerous occasions when Ballew fumed, Ward would take him aside and, somehow, quell the impending volcano. An effective peace officer in his own right, Ward served many years with Ballew and came to know his friend's many moods.[2] Nevertheless, only one month after his return to the deputy sheriff's force, Ballew would once again have occasion to display his gunman's prowess.

Steve Talkington first ventured to Carter County through Ada, Oklahoma, to the north. As early as 1905 he had been a mainstay on the Ada criminal docket. January 26 of that year in the Ada courts, he faced a charge of gaming.[3] Gambling and liquor violations were his mainstays, and answering these charges became routine for the active sporting man.

Talkington also had the reputation of being a dangerous gunman. In September 1905 he attempted to shoot a rival during a disagreement in an Ada nightspot. He was arrested and charged with one count of assault to kill. The eventual disposition of the case is not of record.[4] Although Talkington failed to claim the life of this particular opponent, he added credibility to the rumor that he had killed at least two men in shoot-outs before his arrival in Carter County.[5]

Drawn to the area in the hopes of making big money at his chosen professions of dealing in illegal liquor and gambling, Talkington landed in Ardmore sometime early in the second decade of the twentieth century. A contemporary described him:

Talkington was a man of pleasing personality, always immaculately dressed, and above the average mentally, but he was considered as dangerous when aroused and one that it was not safe to trifle with. Talkington has paid out a small fortune in attorney's fees since he came to this section of the state and has been tried many times in federal, district and county court for violating the liquor laws.[6]

Soon after his arrival in Ardmore, Talkington had the misfortune to witness the shooting death of a man named Clements at the hands of a notorious Carter County bad man named Jake Lewis.[7] Sentenced to a life term at the Oklahoma State Penitentiary at McAlester, Lewis managed to receive pardon in May or early June of 1915. Before leaving the prison, he was heard to mutter dire threats against those who had testified against him at his murder trial.[8]

Early on the evening of June 7 as Steve Talkington strolled down Main Street in Ardmore, a shot rang out. Passing Talkington, the bullet narrowly missed two innocent bystanders on the streets before crashing into the plate-glass window of the T. K. Kearney store. Arrested shortly after the incident by city officer C. G. Sims, the shooter proved to be Jake Lewis attempting to take his revenge on Talkington for contributing to his trip to the state prison.[9] Lewis's imprudent actions would land him back in prison.

By early 1916 Talkington operated an illegal booze and gambling joint in Ragtown.[10] Judge W. F. Freeman's court of inquiry, the bane of Bud Ballew's existence, also came down hard on Talkington. Arrested on a charge of violating the prohibitory laws, Talkington went to trial in February 1916. After deliberating for two and one half hours, the jury returned with a verdict of guilty. On February 29 he received a sentence of two years in the federal penitentiary at Leavenworth, Kansas, and a fine of $1,000. Gus Talkington, apparently a brother of Steve and an alleged partner in the business, came away with a thirty-day jail term and a $100 fine.[11]

Evidently Talkington's lawyers were successful in appealing their client's conviction, as he remained unjailed throughout the spring and summer of that year. Again, in October, he faced another liquor-law violation. On this occasion he came away worse off than he had previously, sentenced to a three-year term in the Leavenworth, Kansas, penitentiary and slapped with a fine of $250.[12] In a seemingly never-ending cycle, Talkington's attorneys filed for another hearing before the circuit court of appeals. Posting a bond of $5,000, he once more gained his release pending court action.[13] For another resident of Carter County, this would turn out to be a most unfortunate turn of events.

Returning to his extra-legal activities in Ragtown while officials deliberated on his case, Steve Talkington mixed business with pleasure. Sometime in late 1916 or early 1917, he married a young Carter County belle. Continuing his operations in Ragtown, he obtained a cottage in Healdton where he resided with the new Mrs. Talkington.[14] Unfortunately for both they were not destined to enjoy married life for long.

While conducting his affairs on May 26, 1917, Talkington became embroiled in a disagreement with Mike Miller, another Ragtown tough. The difficulty reached its zenith as Talkington pulled a revolver from his pocket and shot Miller dead.[15]

Officials placed the gunman under arrest and deposited him in the county jail at Ardmore. Here Steve Talkington would remain for almost two and a half months. Finally, with the able assistance of his ever-vigilant attorney, the famous Moman Pruiett,[16] Talkington managed to make a bail bond in the sum of $20,000 imposed by Judge Freeman. Released on August 8, Talkington returned to the arms of his wife, Virginia, and his bootlegged hooch in Ragtown, pending his appearance at a future term of the Carter County court.[17] As fate would have it, however, he would never have to face justice in the death of Miller. Deputy Sheriff Bud Ballew had yet to have his say in the matter.

According to Sheriff Garrett and Deputy Ballew and the story disseminated out of the sheriff's office upon his release, Steve Talkington "made a promise to Sheriff Garrett that he would not sell liquor or violate the law."[18] If he made such a promise, the lawmen soon discovered that Talkington was not a man who believed in keeping his promises. Shortly after his release from the county jail on August 8, the accused killer commenced the operation of a gambling and liquor emporium in a building he had erected for the purpose behind Rogers & Rippey's Cafe in Ragtown.[19]

On the morning of Sunday, August 26, Bud Ballew motored to Ragtown for the purpose of serving subpoenas on various witnesses ordered to appear at Talkington's trial for the murder of Mike Miller scheduled for hearing on September 14. Early that afternoon Ballew met Talkington on the street and upbraided him for opening his whiskey and gambling parlor. According to Ballew's later testimony, Talkington brushed off the deputy's comments and "asked him to make return on certain subpoenas that he could not find the parties."[20] This Ballew absolutely refused to do.

A short time later, at about one o'clock, the two men again encountered each other on the street. Again Ballew chided Talkington for opening his illegal business.

Talkington came back angrily, "I am going to run it or commit suicide." He told Ballew that he had to do it as it was the only way he had of making any money for his defense in his upcoming trial in the Miller case.

Not backing down, Ballew replied, "You will have to close up. I don't want to arrest you for this, you are in enough trouble now without getting into more. You must close up," Ballew continued firmly. "If you don't, I will be compelled to arrest you."

Talkington glared at Ballew for a few seconds before turning away and heading down the sidewalk, saying over his shoulder, "I'll be damned if I do and you can't raid my place."

Again according to the later testimony of Bud Ballew, while Talkington strode down the street toward his place of business, Ballew followed along behind calling on the man a number of times to stop as Sheriff Garrett had instructed him that if he could convince Talkington to close up his place, Ballew was not to arrest him. Talkington, however, ignored Ballew and continued down the street to Rogers & Rippey's Cafe to which his building was adjoined at the back.

Talkington walked briskly through the restaurant and into his own parlor at the rear with Ballew hot on his heels. Reaching the bar, Talkington allegedly called to his bartender, Gus Harris, to hand him his "other" gun,[21] at the same time turning toward Ballew and reaching his hand into his right pocket.

In an instant, Ballew's old Colt .45 was in his hand. The lawman's revolver bucked four times, all four shots striking Talkington. One bullet entered his right side puncturing a lung. Another bored into the wounded man at the waistline, completely traversing through his body, severing his spinal cord.[22] Talkington sagged to the floor, desperately wounded.[23]

Ballew later testified that when he approached Talkington and turned him over, the wounded man was grasping an automatic pistol in his right hand. Fred Croson later testified that he was the only person to speak to the seriously wounded man following the shooting. In Croson's words, Talkington gasped to him, "Don't prosecute anybody," as Croson leaned his ear over the prostrate man. Croson said that the rest of the conversation dealt with Talkington's business affairs.[24]

As quickly as possible, bystanders carried Talkington to a summoned ambulance. Taken first to his home in Healdton, Talkington talked briefly with his wife before continuing on his journey to the Hardy Sanitarium at Ardmore. Between Healdton and Ardmore the mortally wounded man began to fade quickly. By the time he reached Ardmore, he was dead.[25]

The following day's *Daily Ardmoreite* reported, "Ballew is detained in the sheriff's office and will have his examining trial Wednesday before Judge J. B. Champion (*sic*)."[26]

As reported, Bud Ballew's preliminary hearing did come off three days later on August 29 in the Ardmore courthouse before Judge Thomas W. Champion. Various witnesses including Fred Croson, John Allen, O. O. Calvin, Tom Law, and a number of other men who had been inside the drinking parlor sampling Talkington's illicit whiskey at the time of the gunplay all testified to what they had witnessed on the fatal day. Dr. Hardy gave his testimony as to the dead man's various bullet wounds. Buck Garrett also gave his testimony concerning his instruction to his deputy before sending Ballew on his mission to Ragtown.[27]

As expected, Judge Champion ruled that there was sufficient evidence to bind Ballew over to the September sitting of the District Court to be tried for Steve Talkington's demise. The court set the trial date for September 29. Paying a $10,000 bail bond, Ballew went home to wait his day in court.[28]

While keeping his Lone Grove ranch holdings, Ballew had recently constructed a new home for his family in the neighboring town of Wilson[29] just nine miles farther west. Here he repaired with Fannie and their two boys to await his September trial. Everyone likely knew that the trial would be a simple formality. Bud Ballew himself probably worried the least of anyone.

Crowds packed the courthouse for Ballew's September 29 trial. Represented by his good friend, James H. Mathers, Judge Champion's brother, J. R. Champion, and R. F. Turner, Bud Ballew proved to be the first man put on the witness stand. Facing District Judge W. F. Freeman once again, Ballew calmly told his story of events. All other witnesses tended to corroborate his testimony.[30] As the *Daily Ardmoreite* summarized:

> It was also proven that Talkington had stated he was going to open the joint two or three days before he did so, although he had promised Sheriff Garrett before benig (*sic*) released from jail on bond for killing Mike Miller, that he would not violate the law.
>
> It was also proven that Talkington was a dangerous man, and had repeatedly violated the state and federal laws; was under sentence to serve in both state and federal prisons for these offenses; was under bonds in both courts; had been a law violator for years; and had formerly resisted arrest by officers.
>
> It was proven that persons bought drinks in the joint that morning and two different ones had drunk with Talkington.
>
> It was also proven that a few minutes before the shooting, a witness saw the automatic pistol in Talkington's right pocket while Talkington was in the joint in his shirtsleeves.
>
> It was also proven that a .45 caliber pistol and Winchester were behind the counter and Talkington was going toward these firearms and asking his barkeeper to hand one of them to him.
>
> It was also proven that when Ballew ordered Talkington to stop that Talkington did not do so.[31]

The case also seemed that cut and dried to most others in the courtroom that day. Late that afternoon the jury—B. F. C. Loughridge, Lone Grove farmer; C. L. Ellis, Lone Grove stock raiser; R. E. Vaughn, Ardmore clerk; J. S. B. Apollos, retired, Ardmore; J. A. Steakley, Ardmore contractor; E. J. Chancellor, Ardmore insurance agent; Van Strickland, Ardmore auto dealer; Otis Coffey, a farmer also from Lone Grove; J. F. Button, Hoxbar farmer; S. J. Reed, painter, Ardmore; Joe Telford, another Ardmore auto dealer; and W. W. Trask, a retired Ardmoreite[32]—retired to deliberate on a verdict. In the record time of six minutes, they returned to pronounce Ballew not guilty of the murder of Steve Talkington on the grounds of self-defense.[33] With Fannie by his side,

Ballew shook hands with his attorneys, members of the jury, County Attorney Andy Hardy, and various friends and well-wishers before heading home in a jubilant mood. Once again his name had been cleared.

While no one in Carter County was surprised at the verdict, there were those who felt that there was more to the killing of Talkington than met the eye. In spite of the official version of the shooting emanating from Garrett, Ballew, and the sheriff's office, a rumor began to make the rounds of impropriety in Buck Garrett's county office. Some whispered that the county sheriff and his chief deputy had organized a protection racket. When Steve Talkington had refused to buckle under and pay the demanded amount, this theory continued, he had been continually raided and arrested until it was decided that he would have to be eliminated.[34]

Indeed, the truth or falsehood of the protection scheme story not withstanding, it was quite evident that while some illegal operators were allowed to continue unhindered, others, such as Talkington, were continually harassed by the law. As one newspaper said of Talkington: *"(He) has paid out a small fortune in attorney's fees since he came to this section of the state and has been tried many times in federal, district, and county court for violating the liquor laws."*[35]

One item that may weigh against the story of Talkington's killing being linked to a protection racket run by Garrett and Ballew is an interview conducted by Ardmore author and historian Kenny A. Franks with an elderly Sam Talkington, brother of Steve, in 1983. Naturally Sam Talkington wished to show his brother in the best light possible and, if Franks' book, *Ragtown: A History of the Greater Healdton-Hewitt Oil Field*, is any indication, attempted to portray Ballew's killing of his brother as a wanton, unnecessary act.[36] Yet, not once does he mention a so-called "protection racket." If such had been the case, or even rumored, one would think that this would be a perfect point for Sam Talkington to use to prove that his brother had been murdered because of his refusal to hand out money for "protection."

The only thing known for certain in the case is that Steve Talkington died at the hands of Bud Ballew and his revolver. There were those who mourned Talkington: his mother and sisters at Mill Creek, Oklahoma,[37] his brother Sam who lived in Ardmore where he worked as a chauffeur, and, of course, his wife, Virginia. Shortly after her husband's death, the widow Virginia moved in with her brother-in-law, Sam, at his room on 420 First Ave. S.W. in Ardmore.[38]

CHAPTER 9

—— Victim #4–Rufus P. Highnote ——

Wartime Carter County proved to be a busy place for Bud Ballew, especially from late 1917 to mid 1918. The traffic in contraband liquor was as prevalent as it ever had been; cases of robbery seemed to have increased tenfold; murder was practically an epidemic. If you had a desire for almost any unlawful substance or activity, you could probably find it in Carter County. There was no shortage of work for any of Buck Garrett's deputies, least of all Bud Ballew.

Ballew still enjoyed his social activities despite this workload. For him, socializing with friends and playing cards were of high priority. In late December 1917 another death occurred in Carter County. On this occasion, however, Ballew would find himself more a peripheral participant while others pulled guns and did the shooting.

December 30 found Bud Ballew in Healdton visiting friends. While Ballew, Bert Tucker, and a number of others enjoyed a friendly visit, they were joined by Joe Ford, a casual acquaintance. At first friendly enough, gradually Ford began to give expression to a grudge he held against Ballew. As time passed that evening, Ford became increasingly belligerent. Finally he declared that if Deputy Ballew did not leave the room, he would surely kill him. Before Ballew could take action, Bert Tucker jumped between the two men and swore to Ford that if he made any move toward Ballew he would kill Ford. Enraged, Ford pulled a revolver from his pocket and pointed it at Tucker. When he pulled the trigger, the hammer snapped on a faulty cartridge, and the gun failed to fire. By now Tucker had his pistol in his hand. Unlike Ford's weapon, Tucker's gun fired once, the slug ripping into Ford's chest. Joe Ford died almost instantly.[1] It seemed death was destined to follow Ballew even if he himself wasn't its instrument.

The first four months of 1918 would be some of the busiest in the law-enforcement career of Bud Ballew. On January 22 Ballew traveled to Tishomingo where he arrested W. E. Royer on a warrant brought by Wilson Justice B. F. Coe for disposing of mortgaged property. The deputy brought his man back and placed him behind the bars of the county jail at Ardmore.[2]

The month of February witnessed a rash of holdups on the main road between Ardmore and the oil fields in the Healdton-Ragtown area. Buck Garrett and his deputies spent most of the month attempting to combat the relentless highwaymen. Eventually two brothers named Carothers from Lone Grove and a man named Gardenhire from Wilson were arrested by Ballew and his fellow deputy sheriffs and lodged in the county jail.

The weekly *Ardmore Statesman* felt moved to praise the county lawmen when it commented:

> Holdups, I.W.W., and similar gentry find it to be rather hard sledding in Carter County. Sheriff Buck Garrett and his force of deputies may let a tiger slip through their fingers occasionally, but when it comes to real crime, the underworld doesn't like the grazing in Buck's pasture.[3]

On the evening of Sunday, March 17, Bud Ballew and fellow deputy James Carter raided the Globe rooms on Caddo Street. Upon bursting into the building, the pair caught bootleggers John Garnand and Jim Moon in the act of attempting to hide their stock. After seizing 148 half pints of whiskey, Ballew and Carter placed Garnand and Moon under arrest. Later that same night the two deputies stormed another Caddo Street joint. Arresting Dugan Griffin, the lawmen took possession of six or seven barrels of beer as well and confiscated a Cadillac automobile said to have been used in transporting the beer from Fort Worth, Texas. This outing proved to be one of the largest seizures of liquor in Carter County in several weeks.[4]

Bootlegging was not the only concern of Deputy Ballew. Four days after the successful Caddo Street raids, the active officer ventured to Ragtown in search of the perpetrators of a recent late-night mugging. Tracking down a recently released jailbird, one J. L. Costello, Ballew cuffed the robber and carted him back to his former residence at the county jail.[5]

Amid the various crimes and vices, murderers also could not be ignored. A taxi driver named F. W. Stolicker had been killed and robbed of $500 in Wichita, Kansas, on January 16. C. M. Bickley, one of the suspects in the bloody crime, was reported to have been spotted with his wife in Ragtown in late March. After some snooping around the oil town, Ballew was rewarded by being able to place Bickley and his wife under arrest on March 31. Notified of the collar, Wichita Marshal E. E. Fitzpatrick journeyed to Ardmore in early April in order to return the Bickleys to the Wichita court.[6]

In the midst of everything, Deputy Ballew continued to work on the rash of highway robberies plaguing the oil patch. On April 5 the relentless peace officer nabbed Joe Alread, an alleged partner of the previously arrested J. L. Costello, at a Chickasha, Oklahoma, dive. Ballew had received a tip that Alread was working as a tool dresser at Chickasha. He was compensated for his detective work by being able to bring Alread back to Carter County to face the robbery charges pending against him.[7] The following day the hard-working Ballew would again be faced with a life-or-death situation in which he would be forced to take a human life.

Rufus P. Highnote[8] was an enigma in Carter County. Arriving in the area in 1915 or early 1916, the almost sixty-year-old man[9] volunteered very little solid information about his background or prior residences. The most he would give out were vague stories about having traveled much of the world, mostly acting in some sort of law-enforcement capacity, trailing various criminals for various agencies.[10] He also boasted of having lived at one time or another in most of the oil towns in Oklahoma where he had engaged in many gun battles and killed his share of oil-camp bad men, at one point claiming over twenty kills to his credit.[11]

A man of small physical stature, Highnote was rarely seen without at least two and sometimes three revolvers on his person. Although he was probably not as deadly as he himself claimed, there is reason to believe that the mysterious man could handle a gun when called upon. Buck Garrett himself would later state that Highnote "had killed six or seven to his personal knowledge."[12]

When he appeared in the Ardmore region, Highnote might have already been holding a commission as a deputy U.S. marshal, a position he was known to be in possession of soon after his arrival.[13] A commission would account for Highnote being allowed to walk the streets heavily armed.

Another story about Highnote was that back in 1892 he had been one of the Texas gunmen, along with Buck Garrett, who had trooped north to fight for the cattlemen in the Johnson County, Wyoming, range war.[14] If so, he traveled under an assumed name as no one named Highnote is listed in the records as being a member of this mercenary group. But then, there were those in Carter County who believed that "Rufus Highnote" was not his real name to begin with. At this late date his life before Carter County must remain obscure.

The verifiable records first begin to shine a light on Rufus Highnote in 1916. That year the Ardmore city directory lists "R. E." Highnote as an "oil operator" with an office in the Guaranty State Bank building and a residence at 105 D Street South West.[15] The actual nature of his business in the oil fields at this particular time is not of record.

Perceiving an opportunity for making money on the rampant criminality in the oil fields, by spring 1917 Highnote began operation of the Highnote Detective Agency with headquarters in Healdton. One of the many cases he was called on to solve proved to be the robbery of the Said and Wehba Confectionary at New Healdton, a newer addition to Healdton proper built closer to the oil rigs. In May 1917 the local media made note of Highnote's sleuthing on the case:

> Bob Patton and Fred Eason, identified as having broken into the Said and Wehba Confectionary at New Healdton Saturday night and robbing the place of $205, are in jail here, awaiting examining trial.
>
> Mr. Wehba, proprietor of the confectionary, identified the men, who were arrested at Wirt, by R. P. Highnote, of the Highnote Detective Agency.
>
> Cash to the amount of $125, and $80 in gold on a punchboard, was the booty obtained by the robbers.[16]

Highnote continued to make a name for himself as a man hunter through 1917 and into 1918. He also organized a new oil-field business, which he christened the Highnote Development Co., with offices in the Dobbins building at Ardmore.[17] Bounty hunting continued to be his first love. On numerous occasions he phoned Buck Garrett's office requesting a requisition to other parts of the country where he wished to go to arrest certain wanted criminals. As Garrett would later put it, "he had a mania for finding escaped convicts and bad men, wanted all over the world."[18]

This "mania" seemed to place Highnote in good stead, at least with the business community in Ragtown. When Sheriff Garrett felt compelled to remove Frank Jones as night watchman at the oil town due to Jones's itchy trigger finger, he canvassed the local businessmen for ideas on a replacement. In early 1918 the Ragtown businessmen's committee suggested Rufus Highnote for the job. Although it had been, according to Garrett, "against his better judgment," he gave Highnote the commission as Ragtown night watchman and special deputy sheriff.[19] It would be a decision he would come to regret.

Sometime in March 1918, Highnote married a young Carter County girl many years his junior.[20] Things seemed to be going nicely for him in other respects as well. He proved to be an effective peace officer who seemed able to earn the respect of the town rowdies.

At first performing his duties in an admirable fashion, Highnote gradually began acting more and more unusual. On one occasion he posted a large sign on the Ragtown jail reading "Hotel Ragtown. Rates $10 per day." On being informed of the sign, Sheriff Garrett ordered one of his deputies to tear it down.[21]

The increasingly eccentric man took to visiting the local movie theater and climbing on the stage, making speeches to the patrons before the films began. On one occasion, shortly after assuming his duties, Highnote lectured the moviegoers, "I came to Ragtown . . . the worst town in the state . . . as a deputy sheriff. I came here to clean it up." With that, according to a local oil-field worker named John P. "Slim" Jones interviewed in later years, Highnote reached into his back pockets and pulled out two revolvers. "I brought two fellows with me for help," he said, brandishing the revolvers, "and here they are."[22] On another occasion he told the assembled crowd, "I am a little man, but here is the difference," pulling his two revolvers around in front for all to see and patting the butts.[23]

When it came to firearms, Rufus Highnote was probably the most heavily armed man in Carter County, if not the entire state of Oklahoma. He always carried at least two revolvers on his person. Many times he was known to be armed with three, or even as many as four pistols, filling both coat and pants pockets. On occasion he would holster two big .45 Colts on a belt and display them prominently as he walked down Ragtown's Texas Road.[24]

The first week of April Highnote seemed to reach a peak of unusual behavior that had many in Ragtown doubting their town officer's sanity. Having received many complaints from Ragtown citizens, Buck Garrett decided he would have to act. Early that week while on business at Ragtown, Garrett took Highnote aside and informed him that he would have to take away Highnote's commission as special deputy. Highnote seemed to take the news calmly. He informed the sheriff that the commission was at his house, but he would give it to one of Garrett's deputies to bring to Ardmore later. Garrett then left it at that and returned to his office believing that the situation had been solved. He would soon realize the trouble had only just begun.[25]

Later that week Highnote encountered Dan Blackburn, a special security officer for the Carter Oil Company, in Ragtown. The obviously angry lawman told Blackburn that "they had better not send Bud Ballew after him." According to Blackburn, Highnote also mentioned the names of others he would "get" if things turned ugly.[26]

The following Friday Highnote went to the office of Dr. S. M. Alexander. Alexander, who described Highnote as being "nervous, excitable and very rough" but apparently not under the influence of any stimulants, later reported that the lawman bragged to him that he had killed twenty-two men and had "a mania for killing."[27]

The next day, Saturday, April 6, saw Highnote in an extended state of excitement. Spotting on the sidewalk A. G. Chapman, an enforcement officer of the U.S. Department of the Interior stationed at Ragtown, Highnote called him to one side and asked for assistance in getting papers to arrest some criminals in town. Chapman told him that this was not in his jurisdiction and he should contact Sheriff Garrett for the papers. With that Highnote seemed to become enraged and told Chapman that he would have nothing to do with any man calling himself a deputy sheriff. Furthermore, he stated to Chapman, if they bothered him in any way he would "get them, from the chief on down."

"I am running Ragtown," Highnote growled to Chapman, "and I am going to keep on running it."[28]

That afternoon Highnote cornered a young man named Cecil Sherell in a Ragtown barbershop and accused him of making disparaging statements against him. He told Sherell that if he believed Sherrell had been talking about him he would blow the top of Sherell's head off. The frightened youth managed to convince Highnote that he had never said anything about him at anytime. Before parting from him, Sherell stated that Highnote mentioned the names of two men whom he wished to "get". They were J. M. Chandler, a special officer for the Roxana Oil Company, and Arthur Johnson, a man who had been making overtures to replace Highnote as special deputy and night watchman at Ragtown.[29]

Later that afternoon the obviously unstable officer met the aforementioned Arthur Johnson. Coercing Johnson into a house by telling him that he wished to have a discussion with him concerning the pay of the Ragtown night watchman position, Highnote suddenly pulled a gun on him. He cursed Johnson telling him that he would kill him. Before leaving the astonished man in the house and walking away, he boasted to Johnson of having killed twenty-three men.[30]

Apparently, soon after his encounter with Johnson, Highnote again pulled his revolver on another man in the middle of Texas Road with the command that "if he moved a hand he would blow his head off."[31] Ragtown citizens realized that something would have to be done before serious trouble resulted. Later that day, Chandler placed a telephone call to the office of Sheriff Garrett. Chandler related that if Highnote was not taken care of, he would surely end up killing someone.[32]

Shortly after receiving the telephone call from Chandler, Garrett tracked down Bud Ballew. He asked Ballew to drive out to Ragtown for the purpose of relieving Highnote of his guns and his commission. Reaching Ragtown early that Saturday evening, Ballew had no trouble in finding the peculiar night watchman.

Immediately Ballew informed Highnote that he had orders from the sheriff to relieve him of his commission. Highnote stalled Ballew by first telling him he had some papers that required his attention. A half hour later, the seemingly cooperative Highnote finally got into the car with Ballew and said he would go with him to Ardmore. Almost at once he changed his mind and told Ballew he would not go, at the same time getting out of the car. While the apparently indecisive man appeared to be in a quandary as to what to do, Ballew continually asked him for his commission.

At about 8 p.m. Highnote finally climbed back into Ballew's car. Telling Ballew that the commission was at his house, Highnote asked the deputy to drive him there and he would get it for him. Before reaching his house, Highnote suddenly asked Ballew to take him to the jail as he wanted to check on the gaslights, which had not been operating properly. Switching course, Ballew steered his vehicle to the Ragtown jail.

Leaving the automobile, both men walked into the jail building. For the next few minutes Highnote played with the gaslights, turning them on and off. With the lights burning, Highnote again said he thought he should turn them off. An exasperated Ballew finally told him to leave them on and he could shut them off when he got back. Now he needed that commission.

Appearing to accede, Highnote walked outside with Ballew close behind. Ballew would later state that he "became suspicious when Highnote acted so queerly and was trying to crowd him into a dark place," and that he "kept close to Highnote so that if he attempted to do anything he could grab him."[33] This natural instinct of Ballew may have been instrumental in saving his life.

Upon leaving the jail, Highnote declared that he would walk to his home and get the commission. Abruptly he began to turn around a dark corner of the jail and head toward a dimly lit alley. With Ballew proclaiming his objections and ordering Highnote to go the other way, Highnote suddenly spun around, with his left hand drawing a revolver from one of his two holsters strapped around his waist. Alertly, Ballew crowded close to Highnote, grabbing the man's wrist just as he pulled the trigger. The shot whizzed past Ballew's head. Ballew swiftly drew his own revolver as Highnote came up with another cocked .45 in his right hand. Ballew's gun came into play first as he pumped three bullets into Highnote's body. The doomed man was dead before he hit the ground.[34]

W. A. Richards, one of the first men on the scene following the shooting, reported seeing three revolvers on the dead man. Along with the two Colt .45s clenched in his fists, which he had drawn from the pair of holsters, Highnote was also discovered to have a .45 automatic pistol in his pants pocket.[35]

Three days later, Ballew's preliminary examination for the death of Rufus Highnote came up before Judge Thomas Champion in Ardmore. A number of witnesses gave their testimony, none shining a very favorable light upon Highnote. A note of humor entered the proceedings during the questioning of Arthur Johnson. When asked what he had done when Highnote had stood before him flaunting his revolvers and threatening to kill him, Johnson looked at his questioner queerly for a few seconds before replying, "I was sober and in my right mind, so I exercised good judgment and did nothing."[36]

Again represented by James Mathers and J. B. Champion with assistance from Ardmore attorney H. H. Brown, Ballew took the stand and matter-of-factly stated his case. For all intents and purposes, he petitioned the court for a jury trial before the district court. Perhaps Judge Champion best summarized the case as most people in Carter County saw it and also gave the best explanation for Ballew's and Garrett's continued policy of trial after every death by gunfire when he rendered his decision:

> It is evident from the evidence in this case that no law has been violated, but that society and the law have been protected. It is unfortunate that in order to do this it became necessary to take human life. No man wants to be obliged to kill another. It is the first duty of every citizen to protect himself, and his duty is not taken from him when he becomes an officer. It is his duty not only to do that but it is his further duty to protect society and the lives of other people. I think this defendant has done society and the people of that community a favor. When a person is discharged on a preliminary hearing, any person may at any time, ten years or twenty years later, charge him again with the offense, and in this case it is the defendant's desire, and his right, that he be held to await a trial in the district court, where his case may be tried before twelve men."[37]

With Champion's ruling, Ballew made bond and gained his release to await the action of a future sitting of the district court.[38] Of course, this would simply be another formality. The incident, it was obvious to everyone, was a simple case of self-defense. In fact, there is no record of Bud Ballew ever standing trial for the death of Highnote.

The people of Ragtown quickly put the strange case of Rufus Highnote behind them. Even before Ballew's preliminary hearing of April 9, three days following the gun battle, Garrett had replaced the deceased special deputy and night watchman with Arthur Johnson.[39] As the new law in Ragtown, Johnson had his hands full. For Ballew, it was business as usual.

CHAPTER 10

Whiskey and Murder

By spring 1918 the war in Europe raged to its bloody, bitter climax. The German forces of Kaiser Wilhelm made a desperate push into the Western Front in March capturing many French towns. Despite this bold offensive, pundits speculated that it would only be a matter of time before the waning German military ran out of men, weapons, and energy. Shock waves reverberated across the battlefields and around the world on April 22 when Allied fighters shot down the Fokker triplane of Germany's ace fighter pilot Manfred von Richthofen, the notorious "Red Baron," during the battle of the Somme. The death of the most feared aviator of the war—responsible for the destruction of almost eighty Allied aircraft in two years of fighting—was a harbinger of things to come for the German cause.

Waging his own war against crime in Carter County, Bud Ballew dealt with a variety of interesting cases throughout 1918. On Sunday, June 2, the deputy sheriff traveled to the oil fields near Healdton where he arrested W. G. "Peg" Overstreet on a charge of "malicious mischief." Apparently Overstreet had previously been arrested for stealing chickens. At Overstreet's hearing a neighbor named Avant appeared as a witness against him. Upon being released, the vengeful Overstreet stole a horse belonging to Avant, led the animal into the brush, and killed it by beating its head in. He then capped this act of cruel retribution by dousing the body of the horse in coal oil and setting it alight. Bringing the animal abuser to Ardmore, Deputy Ballew slapped him behind the bars of the county lock-up.[1] Being the horse lover that he was, Ballew probably wished he could deal with Overstreet in a less peaceful manner.

During the last week of August, a strange rumor developed in Carter County. That Sunday, the 25th, Sheriff Buck Garrett, accompanied by his wife, his son,[2] and his son's wife, took an excursion to the resort town of Sulphur, Oklahoma, to take in the sulphur baths. By the following day Garrett was laid up in bed at the family home in Ardmore with a mysterious ailment.

According to the *Ardmore Statesman*, "Many reports got in circulation over the city as to the nature of his illness, one report, widely circulated, being to the effect that he had been 'shot by a woman.'"[3]

Garrett's physician, Dr. Walter Hardy, quickly came to the defense of the sheriff, when he told the *Statesman*:

> During the night Mr. Garrett had a severe attack of illness, and suffered considerably. On Monday the family started to return home but when between Berwyn and Ardmore Mr. Garrett was again taken sick with a stroke resembling apoplexy, and became unconscious. Mrs. Garrett stopped a passing car and sent for Dr. Hardy who came as quickly as he could and found Mr. Garrett in a very serious condition.[4]

Again according to Dr. Hardy, he at first thought that Garrett's condition was serious enough to prove fatal. Quickly, however, the sheriff rallied and by Tuesday was considered out of danger.[5]

The exact nature of Buck Garrett's malady was never made public. Whether a precursor of the disease that would eventually claim his life in a few more years or something else entirely was never made clear. The element of an outraged woman possibly putting a bullet into Garrett becomes all the more interesting when one considers his known womanizing proclivities.

With his boss still recovering from his mysterious illness, Bud Ballew continued to enforce the liquor laws of Carter County. On August 28 he arrested J. C. Lindsey, a member of the well-known Lindsey clan, near Wilson on a charge of being in possession of illegal "choc" beer.[6] Two days later Ballew again engaged in a matter of gunplay, this time in the middle of downtown Ardmore.

The underworld of Ardmore was highly evolved by summer 1918. Illegal operations specializing in booze, gambling, and prostitution carried on clandestinely with an intricate web of spies, informants, cover men, and paid fixers. A series of tunnels running under the streets of Ardmore connected the various hotels on Main Street with the numerous bordellos and bootleg joints of seedy Caddo Street.[7]

By 1918 unlawful narcotics was also a major problem in the county and shared this underworld scene in Ardmore and elsewhere. Charles Wren, one of the so-called "dope fiends," first appeared in the Carter County seat on Friday, August 30. That afternoon he walked into the office of Ardmore physician Dr. R. S. Willard and presented him with a letter from the war department declaring he had been discharged from the army at Pittsburg, Kansas, as a result of his being "an incurable dope fiend." Dr. Willard advised Wren to leave town as soon as possible. Unfortunately for him, Wren failed to heed the doctor's advice.

Late that evening near 11 p.m., Police Officer Walter Stroud placed Wren under arrest on a charge of vagrancy and illegal narcotics. As Stroud led his prisoner toward the city jail, Wren suddenly wrenched himself free of the officer's grasp near the California Cafe on Main Street and dashed off. Bud Ballew and Policeman Dave Frazier happened to be talking nearby when they heard Stroud yell to his prisoner to halt. Seeing Wren running down the street, both Ballew and Frazier unlimbered pistols and fired at least three shots at the fleeing man. One bullet struck the pavement and ricocheted upward, making a hole the size of a silver dollar through Wren's left foot.

Undaunted for the moment, Wren continued to run. Turning down an alley and running across Caddo Street, the wounded man ran through a house before being captured by the lawmen near an ice-cream factory in the southeast corner of town. The now hobbling prisoner finally made his way to the city jail never realizing how lucky he had been that Ballew's aim had been slightly off that evening.[8]

That same week further excitement of the criminal variety visited Carter County with the arrest of the notorious southwest outlaw Tom Slaughter by Wilson constable Charlie Jones and Carter County Deputy Sheriff Will Ward. Slaughter had been captured in Carter County the previous spring following his escape from officers transporting him back to the Texas state penitentiary from which he had previously made his escape. Slaughter, a well-known bank robber, gunman, and killer, had only a few days before executed another daring escape from the Texas prison only to be corralled again by Jones and Ward. No doubt Bud Ballew wished he had been in on the capture of Slaughter and had some interesting conversations with the bad man before Texas authorities retrieved their escapee and returned him to the Texas pen.[9]

Ballew once again teamed up with his good friend Will Ward on September 7 when they, along with Deputies Horace Kendall and Jim Carter, apprehended bootleggers Otis Rector and J. W. Hines while patrolling west of Ragtown. The lawmen managed to confiscate twelve quarts of whiskey and a 1917 Ford Roadster in the raid while making a slight dent in the traffic of illicit booze.[10]

By October of 1918 Carter County and the entire world were threatened by another menace perhaps even more deadly than the Great War being waged in Europe. Originating in Spain, a new strain of virulent influenza spread rapidly across the globe. Christened the "Spanish flu," the malignant germ disseminated swiftly through the European and American armies causing more death than the actual fighting. Civilian populations were likewise hit hard and health officials estimated that the disease would cause at least twenty million deaths worldwide.

In the United States the death toll eventually far exceeded the number of troops killed in battle overseas. Through September and into October, the flu was well on its way to claiming nearly eighty thousand lives. At the height of the epidemic, the two weeks ending October 26, some forty thousand American lives would succumb to the germ.

Carter County, Oklahoma, like the rest of the country and the world, was hit hard by the raging malady. First recognized in the county about October 7, the Spanish flu quickly claimed a number of lives throughout the area. As happened almost everywhere, genuine fear gripped the communities of Carter County. In the ten days from October 7 to the 17 health officials in Ardmore counted nineteen deaths attributable to the epidemic.[11]

In a perhaps misguided attempt to calm the fears of the local populace, the weekly *Ardmore Statesman* even initiated a writing contest dealing with essays on the dreaded flu. In its October 10 issue the newspaper declared:

$5 IN CASH PRIZES

The Statesman *will pay $3 for first prize, $2 for second prize and $1 for third prize for first, second and third best "quip" on the Spanish Flu . . . Said "quip" not to exceed thirty-five words . . . Merit to be judged by one [newspaper] representative, one teacher and one lawyer, all to be chosen by the* States-man. *Let us see how much fun you can get out of the Flu.*[12]

The influenza was indiscriminate in its victims: Prominent Ardmore businessmen such as J. L. Adair and Cecil B. Williams and lowly Caddo Street vagrants all fell victim to its wrath. Likewise the Ballew family was not immune.

Tragedy struck Bud and Fannie's household on October 8 with the death of their youngest son, eleven-year-old Bryant "Buster," just seven days short of his twelfth birthday. In his death notice it is revealed that the young Ballew boy finally succumbed to pneumonia, a common final blow to those suffering from influenza. Buster was another of the many victims of the global epidemic of 1918. The following day Bud and Fannie buried their youngest child near his grandfather in the Lone Grove cemetery. Many family and friends attended the funeral to pay their respects.[13]

Almost one month to the day later, on November 11, an armistice was signed between Germany and the Allied Nations. The first Great World War was over. With a death toll of more than ten million, the world was once again at peace.

As the American troops began to stream home after their long ordeal Bud Ballew began to get back into the routine of life following the death of his son Buster. One of the more interesting cases the deputy worked on in 1918 was the S. M. Nations murder case of November that year.

S. M. Nations, an oil-field worker, was found dead in the road near Rag-town on the morning of November 13. The cause of death was shown to be a large-caliber bullet wound. Teaming up with Chief Special Officer Dan Black-burn of the Carter Oil Co., Deputy Sheriffs Bud Ballew and Will Ward began to investigate the murder. Blackburn took his bloodhounds to the scene of the crime; however, the dogs were unable to sniff out a trail.

After much detective work by the trio of officers, Ballew finally received information that led to the arrest of a young oil field worker named Bard Caldwell. This arrest led to the apprehension of three more young oil-field roughnecks, Ted Hogue, Hume Tabor, and Ralph Faulkner.

The men, none of whom were over twenty-one years of age, steadfastly denied any involvement in the killing. At one point, the now fully recovered Sheriff Buck Garrett conducted a tedious session of questioning one of the suspects. Following a number of trivial questions, Garrett suddenly asked the man, "When you held him up you didn't intend to kill him, did you?"

Without thinking the suspect quickly answered, "No, I did not." Catching himself he then continued to deny his connection to the murder. The damage had been done. After this the case for the arrested suspects quickly began to unravel, and the story became clear.

The evening before the discovery of his body, Nations had been observed in a restaurant in Ragtown flashing a large roll of bills. That night as he made his way home, the four robbers halted him on the road and ordered him to throw up his hands. Nations began begging them not to shoot him. Ignoring his pleas, one of the young felons fired, the slug dealing Nations a fatal wound. Taking Nations's money, the four men fled the scene.[14]

The *Daily Ardmoreite* felt moved to praise the work of the lawmen when it commented:

> The case appeared at first to be a baffling one, but the sheriff and his deputies, Ballew, Ward, and Dan Blackburn, worked closely on the case until they appear to have woven a chain about the men, even exclusive of the confession, that makes a strong case against them.[15]

It was back to the bootleggers again for Ballew on the afternoon of November 23 when he and fellow deputy sheriff, John Ginn, noticed four automobiles suspiciously parked in front of a house at 111 Q Street in Ardmore. Upon investigation the two officers found a number of men inside the residence indulging in the consumption of whiskey. Eventually it became clear that the owners of the house, James and Myrtle Brockett, had for some time been using their home as a dispensary of illegal liquor. Following the issuance of injunctions and court action, the Brocketts found their operation shut down for good.[16]

On the evening of December 11, Garrett and Ballew engaged in a high-speed automobile chase of some Louisiana bootleggers traveling through Carter County. Receiving a tip that the car would be passing through that night, Garrett and Ballew jumped into Ballew's Franklin roadster and, with Ardmore policeman John Dyer in another car, drove out to the forks of the road south of the town cemetery. As they waited, a car ripped past Garrett and Ballew's vehicle at a speed that Garrett later recalled "seemed to him ninety miles an hour." Giving chase, Ballew had his roadster almost beside the bootleggers' car when the occupants began throwing whiskey bottles in front of the lawmen's vehicle in an attempt to puncture Ballew's tires with the broken glass. As a result, Ballew was forced to slow down, and the liquor traffickers from Louisiana managed to make their escape.[17]

That same night Buck Garrett's family would also be touched by the deadly Spanish influenza. Marion Chancellor, the young son of Garrett's in-laws, Mr. and Mrs. James Chancellor, fell victim to the virus that evening following a short illness. To add misfortune upon misfortune, Marion Chancellor's mother, Mary, had that same day undergone the amputation of one of her arms in an attempt to prevent the spread of a serious infection. The news of her son's death was kept from her for a number of days in order to allow the woman to recover sufficiently from her own ordeal.[18]

Despite the human tragedies being enacted as a result of the rampaging flu epidemic, Garrett and Ballew continued to perform their law-enforcement duties. The violation of the prohibition laws continued apace. In early January 1919 Garrett received information that a major whiskey-peddling enterprise existed somewhere in the northwestern part of the county. Taking Bud Ballew and Will Ward with him, Garrett decided to do some investigating in the area of the village of Tatums, about thirty miles northwest of Ardmore. The lawmen were rewarded by finding a homemade still in operation. In relating the venture, the *Daily Ardmoreite* gave its readers an inside look at the intricacies of the "moonshine still":

The still was found at the home of Joe Carter, a Negro. Carter has built a new house and his old house, left standing, in the center of an enclosure which he is using as a horse lot, is where the still was found.

A hole had been cut in the floor of the old house an (*sic*) under this a slow fire was kept burning beneath a barrel, with an iron bottom, in which was the mash. From this a copper pipe ran into a big trough filled with water. The copper pipe did not form a worm, but was a series of turns and elbows made an imitation of one sufficient to catch the vapor from the cooking mash and transform it into "mountain dew." The sheriff brought the copper pipe with him.

Under a lot of baled Johnson grass, in a barn, was found the whiskey. There was also about fifty gallons of mash in the process of whisky making and this was destroyed.

The officers found part of a barrel of syrup said to have been used in making the whisky. The Negro's place is on Wild Horse creek, in a wild country, but still so well populated as to make the manufacture of whisky, as he is said to have been carrying it on, very daring. It was a white man the sheriff was hunting when he received a tip as to the Negro's plant. It is reported that a white man has been peddling whisky in that part of the county, probably, as the officers think, securing his stock from the Negro's illicit still.

The Negro was brought to jail, and will probably be prosecuted by both the state and federal authorities.[19]

The amount of publicity he had been receiving for not only his gunfighting prowess but also his service as a deputy sheriff had firmly established Bud Ballew's reputation in Carter County. One incident, which probably best illustrates this reputation, is related by Norman Flowers, whose grandmother, Bessie McCullough,[20] was a cousin of Ballew. Although the exact date of the incident is hard to pinpoint, it could have happened at about this time.

According to the story there had been a bank failure in Ardmore. At that time banks were not covered by insurance and, when a bank was forced to close due to financial collapse, all the depositors simply lost their money. As it happened, both Bud Ballew and his cousin Bessie's husband, Henry McCullough, had money in this particular bank.

On the day that the bank closure was announced, great crowds gathered in front of the institution in an attempt to recoup their losses. Ballew pushed his way through the crowd of some two to three hundred people and made his way to the front door of the bank. When banging on the door with his fist failed to get desired results, Ballew pulled his revolver from its holster and commenced to pound on the door with the barrel.

Finally a bank official appeared at the window. Opening the window he enquired of Ballew his business.

"Open the door!" Ballew shouted.

"I'm afraid I can't let anyone in," the bank official answered.

As he was about to shut the window, Ballew strode over and poked his revolver in at the man's head. "I came here to get my money out of this bank," he growled menacingly, "and I will either get my money or you will be carried out in a pine box. I'll give you a few minutes to think about it," Ballew said as he stepped aside.

A few minutes later the bank door opened a crack and the official motioned Ballew over. When the deputy stepped up to the door, the banker quickly slipped him a roll of bills totaling the amount that the bank records showed Ballew had in the institution; then, just as quickly he slammed the door.

According to family tradition, when Henry McCullough, who had been standing at the back of the crowd, saw what was transpiring at the front of the bank he began to shout as loud as he could, "Bud, get my money too! Bud, get my money too!" However due to the noise of the milling, angry crowd, Ballew had failed to hear him. Thus, Henry McCullough was forced to take the loss along with the others.[21]

Although many people feared Bud Ballew and his revolvers, there were others who looked on him as a friend. These individuals were glad to have this powerful, charismatic man on their side. A small number of others, rare men indeed, failed to fear Ballew for other reasons. There were men in Carter County, just as fearless and just as deadly as Bud Ballew when it came to gunplay.

CHAPTER 11

—— Victim #5–Dow Braziel ——

Dow Braziel, who was destined to become a force to be reckoned with in the Bud Ballew-era of Carter County, was born sometime in the early to middle 1880s in Texas. The son of native Tennesseeans—Robert H. Braziel, a teamster and laborer and his wife N. J.—Dow moved to Indian Territory in the early 1890s along with his parents, two brothers, John and Robert Jr., and five sisters.[1] In 1896 the family became one of the early pioneer clans of Ardmore when they moved to that fledgling community.

By 1904 the Braziel family resided at 1133 McLish Ave. S.W. in Ardmore where all four of the Braziel males are listed as laborers in the city directory.[2] In his early adulthood Dow Braziel found time to woo a young lady named Virginia, always called "Virgie," who eventually became Mrs. Dow Braziel.[3] It could not have been an easy marriage as the Braziels were a clannish, feisty tribe.

The three Braziel brothers were constantly in trouble of one sort or another; John and Bob ended up in court over a saloon brawl; Bob was fined for "shooting a gun in a public place"; and all three brothers were suspected of being involved in the handling and distribution of alcohol.[4]

Their criminal career, however, escalated into gunplay in the early morning hours of Tuesday, November 3, 1908. The incident would land John Braziel in the Oklahoma State Penitentiary and two Carter county residents in the Brown and Bridgman Undertaking Parlor.

At about 2:30 a.m. on November 3, John Braziel stood in front of the McCoy Drug Store on East Main Street in Ardmore talking with two friends. At this juncture D. B. Cook, constable at Provence, along with J. A. Sims and Jim Billings, came down the sidewalk. In going around Braziel, Cook bumped into him. Angry words quickly passed between the two men.

"I am an officer," Cook warned Braziel. "I'll arrest you if you get too smart."

"There aren't enough constables to arrest me," Braziel answered defiantly.

Both men simultaneously reached for their revolvers. Braziel was the quicker of the two. Before Cook could bring his gun into action, Braziel fired. The bullet smacked into Cook's chin and passed through his neck. He fell mortally wounded.

Braziel next stepped to one side and turned his gun on Sims. The slug hit the surprised man in the chest dealing him an instant death wound. As Sims crashed to the sidewalk, Billings turned and ran down the street. Jumping to one side, Braziel fired after the retreating man. Hit in the left arm and left hip, Billings literally ran into Patrolman Smith Redmond with the plea, "Help me; I'm shot all to pieces."

In a few seconds Braziel approached Redmond and the wounded Billings. He handed his pistol to the policeman with the comment, "I have killed some fellows. I'm sorry I had to do it."[5]

While John Braziel was taken to the county jail and Sims was carted to the undertakers, Cook and Billings were gathered up and rushed to the Hardy Sanitarium. Billings eventually managed to recover. Constable Cook, however, proved too seriously injured and died three and one-half hours after being shot.[6]

It was, according to one source, "probably the most uncalled for and unfortunate shooting affair [that] ever occurred in this city."[7] Despite the seeming hopelessness of the situation, Braziel's brothers, Dow and Bob, did all they could for their incarcerated sibling. Hiring eminent Ardmore attorney J. B. Champion to represent John, the Braziels did their best in his defense.[8] It all proved in vain.

On a change of venue to Love County, John Braziel received trial at the January 1909 term of court. Found guilty on a charge of murder, he was sen-

tenced to a term of life in prison. The Oklahoma State Penitentiary at McAlester received their newest convict on February 20.[9]

In the months following his brother John's incarceration, Dow Braziel
decided to turn over a new leaf. Whether as a result of John's predicament or
some other catalyst, the former bootlegger took up a career in law enforcement.
By May 1911 he was working as a patrolman on the Ardmore police force
under Chief of Police Joe Atkinson.[10]

In December 1911 Atkinson tendered his resignation, and city commissioners hired Braziel as temporary police chief pending the appointment
of Atkinson's successor. Braziel promoted himself as one of the leading candidates for the chief's position. His competition included Bill McLamore, a
former U.S. deputy marshal and assistant police chief; and Dave Booker, a
former deputy marshal and police chief under a previous city regime. Although
Booker was the early favorite, the city fathers handed Dow Braziel the position
of Ardmore Chief of Police on January 10, 1912.[11]

Braziel's adventures as head of the Ardmore police force were many and
varied and he made an effective chief. The day of his appointment he participated in the arrest of Bud Parks wanted for an attempted murder in Denison,
Texas.[12]

On March 10, he teamed up with Buck Garrett in the arrest of a number
of boys suspected of burglarizing a store at Marietta. Braziel was surprised to
learn that one of those arrested, Freddie Holman, was a brother-in-law of one
of his policemen, Officer J. C. Thompson of the mounted squad. Another of the
prisoners turned out to be the son of Sheriff Cochran of Love County. Despite
these facts, both Thompson and Cochran participated in the arrests no doubt
performing some chastising of their wayward kin.[13]

Chief of Police Braziel faced his first real dangerous test of gunplay as
a lawman on the afternoon of Tuesday, May 12. Shortly after 2 p.m., as Braziel sat in the Canton Restaurant having lunch, a number of shots suddenly
rang out from Ardmore's Whittington Hotel just across the street. At the hotel
Braziel quickly managed to locate the room where the shots had resounded.
Bursting in, the chief encountered two men of prominent ranching families,
J. C. Washington and Cal Stewart, in a desperate struggle to gain possession of
a pistol. As Braziel entered the room, Washington managed to raise the weapon

and fire two more shots narrowly missing both Stewart and the chief of police. Entering the fray, Braziel managed to corral both combatants, the only injury being a slight bullet wound to one of Stewart's legs. Apparently the two ranchmen were attempting to settle an old grudge. Braziel arrested both parties and turned them over to Sheriff Buck Garrett to face trial in county court.[14] Dow Braziel had this time managed to dodge the lethal bullets. He would have less luck against sharp tongues and politics, which would lead to his resignation as chief of police on September 28.

Likely sometime in 1913 Dow Braziel was hired by the Interior Department as a federal enforcement officer in charge of enforcement and investigation of violations to the various Prohibition laws.[15] He may also have been working concurrently as a deputy U.S. marshal.[16] It would be while working in his federal law enforcement capacity that Braziel would see the bulk of his gunplay as an officer. It would also be during this time that he would form a close personal and working relationship with another federal officer stationed at Ardmore, Deputy U.S. Marshal William R. "Dick" Hignight.

By 1914 attempting to enforce the Prohibition laws in Oklahoma had become a dangerous undertaking. In discussing the situation the *Ardmore Statesman* commented:

> The attempts being made throughout the state to enforce prohibition are resulting in most of the killings that are occurring in Oklahoma at the present time. This is particularly true of the old Indian Territory portion of the state, because of the strenuous and continued efforts of deputy U.S. marshals and enforcement officers to do their duty by prohibiting the sale of intoxicants within the old Indian country.
>
> Two such killings have occurred in this locality within the past sixty days, in both of which enforcement officers did the effective shooting, and in addition there are three men under arrest, being held to the federal grand jury at Chickasha, on charges of conspiring to injure or do away with another enforcement officer, Deputy Marshal Dick Hignight, of Ardmore.[17] Whether or not the enforcement officers in this section are better and quicker shots

than those in the more northern portion of Indian Territory can be answered at this time only in the affirmative, for at least a dozen officers have fallen victim to bootlegger bullets in the Tulsa, Bartlesville and adjoining communities, whereas no officer has as yet "bit the dust" in this section.[18]

The first of the shootings mentioned by the newspaper took place on July 25 at Ringling, just over the county line in Jefferson County about six miles southwest of Ragtown. In that incident former U.S. deputy marshal and current federal enforcement officer stationed at Healdton, A. G. Chapman, and three other lawmen were patrolling the annual Ringling picnic watching for liquor violators. While attempting to arrest bootlegger Roy Dorris, Chapman was forced to fire on the lawbreaker as he dashed for the safety of the nearby brush. Dorris died from his wounds a few hours later.[19]

The second killing took place September 14 on Main Street in the middle of a busy Ardmore Monday afternoon. Tom Greenwood was a bootlegger with a reputation in both Ardmore and Oklahoma City. For a number of months Dow Braziel had been investigating Greenwood's activities. By September 1914 Braziel had accumulated enough evidence to place Greenwood behind bars for a long stretch. Because of Braziel's investigation and possibly other matters that would come to light at a later date, the two men had developed a seething animosity toward each other.

That particular afternoon Greenwood strolled down the sidewalk near the California Cafe talking to his friend and fellow whiskey runner, Bob Key. Soon Braziel walked past the pair making some comment to Greenwood, which stirred the bootlegger's ire.[20] An argument broke out between the two men whereupon Greenwood struck out at Braziel. Both men quickly reached down for their revolvers. Coming up with his a split second faster than Greenwood, Braziel fired two quick shots. Both slugs hit Greenwood's torso, one piercing his heart. Greenwood managed to fire once, the bullet grazing the officer's arm. As the fatally wounded bootlegger fell to the sidewalk, his finger spasmodically squeezed the trigger again. The shot shattered the plate-glass window of the J. B. Spragins Hardware Store. Turning and walking into the hardware store, Braziel left his already dead opponent on the sidewalk in a widening pool of blood.[21]

Braziel surrendered himself to Sheriff Buck Garrett immediately following the gun battle. Posting a $10,000 bond to wait a preliminary hearing, the federal officer was just as quickly released. The family of Greenwood hoped to put the killer of their relative away for much longer. A few days after the fight, they hired the renowned barrister of Oklahoma, Moman Pruiett, to assist the prosecution of Braziel.[22]

Represented by attorneys James Mathers and Thomas Norman, Dow Braziel appeared in district court in late September for his hearing in the killing of Greenwood. Held under a bond of $7,500 for his appearance at the next sitting of the court in January 1915, Braziel immediately paid the amount and gained his release.[23] Within a matter of days, the active officer would be back in the field and involved in another shooting scrape.

While investigating reported bootlegger activity west of Ragtown in Jefferson County, Braziel and Dick Hignight discovered the whiskey plant of Joe Colson on the afternoon of November 1. Placing Colson in custody, the officers allowed the whiskey peddler to enter his cabin in order to retrieve his coat preparatory to leaving with the lawmen. Instead, he emerged with a shotgun. Aiming the weapon at Hignight, whose back was turned to him, Colson pulled the trigger. Peppered in the back and shoulders with shot, Hignight fell to the ground. As Colson frantically attempted to reload his shotgun, the surprised Braziel jerked out his automatic pistol and opened fire on Colson.

Wounded in the shoulder, Colson managed to run to his horse, pull himself into the saddle and head out toward Waurika as both Braziel and Hignight emptied their revolvers in his direction. Later that day, while attempting to find medical attention for his injured shoulder, the gunman was corralled by officers and placed in the Jefferson County jail.

Meanwhile Braziel managed to transport his wounded partner to the Hardy Sanitarium at Ardmore. Luckily, Hignight eventually made a full recovery from his gunshot injuries.[24]

As 1914 turned to 1915, Braziel's day in court for the shooting death of Tom Greenwood drew near. The trial commenced January 27, 1915, with the formidable legal trio of James H. Mathers, Thomas Norman, and T. N. Robnett presenting officer Braziel's case. The prosecution proved just as formidable with County Attorney Andy Hardy, Assistant County Attorney Bowman and legal genius Moman Pruiett attempting to prove Braziel's guilt. The case would develop into what one contemporary source would label "the hardest fought of any that has been in the district court since state hood."[25]

After arguments concerning the admissibility of certain evidence were won by the prosecution, they dropped a bombshell early in the trial by entering into the record a document which had been signed by Greenwood before his fateful encounter with Braziel on September 14, 1914. The document was in the form of a petition accusing Officer Braziel of accepting money from certain gamblers and bootleggers in return for immunity from prosecution.[26] Although this would be a continuing theme in the life of Dow Braziel and must have caused him and his attorneys a few anxious moments, it failed to have an overly adverse affect on the jury. Following the closing argument by Moman Pruiett on January 29, the jury returned on the morning of January 30 to find Braziel not guilty.[27]

Without delay Officer Dow Braziel resumed his law enforcement duties in Carter County. The charges of impropriety that had been leveled against him seemed to do him little, if any, harm in his role as a federal officer. On November 12, 1915, he received praise for making a large liquor seizure near Ardmore.[28] The following day he assisted Deputy Sheriff Horace Kendall in arresting Green Canady, an alleged highway robber.[29]

Dow Braziel's reputation as a gunman was firmly established by the Tom Greenwood killing. Outlaws soon developed a healthy respect for the lawman's proficiency as both a gunfighter and investigator and endeavored to keep their distance. Rumors of a Braziel/Hignight protection racket continued to make the rounds; however, Braziel did not allow this talk to interfere with his effectiveness as an officer. On occasion, though, he would apparently allow himself to get carried away with his own mystique as a gun handler.

One such instance almost had disastrous effects for his wife, Virginia. Years later, one resident of Ardmore, who was a schoolboy at the time, remembered the incident:

> I was going from school and had to pass the Braziel house
> to get where I lived. As I started to walk by, Dow Braziel drove up
> to his house [located at 411 3rd Ave. N.W.][30], jumped out of the

car and in one quick motion pulled out his gun and shot into the ground—just to tease his wife who was out in the yard at the time. He scared her all right. The bullet either hit the sidewalk or a rock, ricocheted, and hit her in the leg, knocking her down.

She failed to see the humor of it and didn't think the idea was a bit funny. In fact, she was crying mad. As for Braziel, it almost scared him to death. It had been a rough joke but he had not meant to hit her. But that was the way he was. He could, and often did, draw a gun like greased lightening—sometimes just to show off but often for real.[31]

Braziel eventually had reason to use his gun "for real" in early September 1916. The episode would have dire consequences for one of Carter County's lawmen elite, a thirty-four-year-old federal enforcement officer named Oscar W. Alexander.

Born in Rutherford, North Carolina, on April 15, 1883, Oscar William Alexander moved to Carter County, Oklahoma, with his family sometime in the early 1900s[32]. The likeable young man prospered, married, and sired a son. His first job in law enforcement was as a patrolman on the Ardmore Police Force under Chief Dow Braziel. In September 1912 the young officer would be caught up in the events leading to the dismissal of Chief Braziel and, along with the chief and almost the entire police force, be forced to resign.[33] By September 1916 Alexander was working as a special federal enforcement officer in Carter County. On the job for only a matter of a few short weeks by this time, the lawman had made a good reputation in his new position.

Alerted to the existence of a whiskey trail used on a regular basis by the Love brothers,[34] George and Mose, near Hoxbar, located a few miles south east of Ardmore, Dow Braziel decided to set an ambush for the evening of Friday, September 1. Recruiting Alexander and two other U.S. officers, Tom Adams and George McLaughlin, Braziel arrived with his party near the Hoxbar trail at around 10 p.m. Placing his men at strategic points of concealment beside the wagon road, Braziel sat back to await the appearance of the Loves. Soon the Love brothers made their appearance, their whiskey wagon being pulled by two sturdy mules.

When the wagon reached a position on the trail opposite to him, Braziel yelled out a command for the brothers to halt. Rather than comply, Mose Love raised a shotgun and let loose with a barrel in Braziel's direction. Almost at once Officer Braziel and his three companions opened a barrage of pistol fire at the occupants of the wagon. Impulsively, Alexander rose up from his place of concealment along the trail and ran toward the bootleggers. Catching the movement, Mose Love pointed his shotgun at the running figure and fired the remaining barrel. Struck in the right side, Alexander fell dead in the road.

In the hail of lawmen's lead, the shotgun-wielding Mose Love received wounds in the shoulder and hip. Severely injured, he fell out of the wagon to the ground. Meanwhile George Love, also slightly wounded in the hip, finally lost control of the frightened mule team, which dashed off down the road with him. In an attempt to halt the wagon, Braziel fired at the mules as they dashed by. He managed to hit one of the animals but it remained mobile for the moment and the mules, wagon, and George Love disappeared down the road.

Gathering up the dead body of Alexander and the badly hurt Mose Love, the lawmen returned to Ardmore and deposited Love in the Hardy Sanitarium. He was found to be seriously, though not fatally, injured.

The next day a large posse discovered the Love's wagon in the vicinity of the shooting. One mule was dead, the victim of Braziel's pistol fire. Nineteen cases of moonshine whiskey were found inside the wagon box. Apprehended later in the day, the slightly wounded George Love was incarcerated in the Carter County jail at Ardmore.[35] Officer Oscar Alexander's funeral took place on the afternoon of Sunday, September 3, from his home at 116 C Street N.W. The first lawman killed by bootleggers in Carter County, Alexander was buried in Ardmore's Rose Hill cemetery.[36]

Alexander's death caused a wave of indignation to wash over the city of Ardmore. There was talk of lynching the two Loves, but cooler heads prevailed. Others blamed the leader of the lawmen's party, Dow Braziel, for the death of the young, well-liked officer. These concluded that Braziel had carelessly led his men into an unnecessarily dangerous situation without proper caution and instruction. One of the individuals in this camp was none other than Bud Ballew.

It cannot be stretching the point to state that Bud Ballew and Dow Braziel absolutely hated each other. Although it was obviously a part of the pair's dynamics, the cause of the mutual enmity remains mystifying.[37] Both personal and professional[38] rivalries have been suggested. Others would claim more prosaic motives, which gradually grew to major proportions. Through it all, one thing is clear: Ballew's placing of fault on Braziel for the demise of Oscar Alexander, a fellow officer whom Ballew had come to like and respect, simply added another degree of hatred into the mix between the two peace officers.

The Love brothers came to trial in the shooting death of Oscar Alexander on November 2, represented by J. B. Champion and H. H. Brown. The family of the dead officer responded by hiring James Mathers and Moman Pruiett to assist County Attorney Hardy and Assistant Attorney Bass in the prosecution.[39] On November 5, George and Mose Love were pronounced guilty of murder.[40] Both would receive long terms in the penitentiary.

Despite the events of September 1, it is apparent that some fellow lawmen had not lost their confidence in Braziel's abilities. In late November a gang of alleged train robbers was detected in Purcell, Oklahoma, sixty miles almost due north of Ardmore in McClain County. The gang was said to have robbed an El Paso and Southwestern locomotive near Apache, Arizona, earlier that year on August 6, as well as a Sante Fe train near Bliss, Oklahoma, on October 18. When the group of federal and local officers organized to make the arrest, they chose Dow Braziel to lead the raid. The five train robbers were apprehended in Purcell on November 27 without a hitch.[41]

Braziel continued to operate as an officer into 1917. In May he traveled to Fort Worth with Sheriff Buck Garrett and Deputy Fred Williams in order to question one Joe Lane, a murder suspect linked to a killing at Healdton.[42] Dow Braziel would only serve another year at most as a lawman.

On August 11, 1918, Braziel appeared as one of the first men on the scene following the notorious shooting of Joe Duane by O. S. Bailey on Broadway in Ardmore.[43] Whether he was there as a lawman or as a regular citizen who happened to be a witness to the incident is not known. However, sometime in 1918 the veteran officer resigned his federal commissions and entered the Ardmore business community. Interestingly enough, his biggest gun battle would come upon him as a private citizen and not as a lawman.

By 1918 Dow Braziel had formed a close personal friendship with his fellow federal officer U.S. Deputy Marshal Dick Hignight. A native Texan, the forty-five-year-old career law enforcement officer lived with his forty-year-old wife, Ruth, and their children—Ella, seventeen; Walter, fifteen; Julia, twelve; and Carter, seven—at 21 7th Ave. N.W. in Ardmore.[44] Hignight's brother, Earl Hignight, owned and operated the well-known California Cafe at 15 East Main Street until sometime in 1918.[45] At this time Dow Braziel and Dick Hignight formed a business corporation, which they named Hignight and Braziel. Sometime after this the two business partners purchased the California Cafe from Earl Hignight.[46] Braziel managed the lucrative restaurant while Dick Hignight continued to perform his duties as a deputy U.S. marshal.

The California Cafe of 1918 was anything but a quiet dining experience. While a topnotch meal could be obtained in the main restaurant area, those wishing to partake of a little gambling activity could adjourn to the back of the establishment. Here a "sort of lean-to" had been built on the rear of the premises where games of poker and the imbibing of moonshine whiskey were conducted in semi-privacy. Braziel and Hignight also owned a fleet of service cars employed in transporting men, and any other commodities needed, between Ardmore and the oil fields. The taxi drivers or "chauffeurs" as they were called then, one of who was Dow's ex-con younger brother John,[47] used the cafe as headquarters while waiting for fares. As one early resident observed:

One of the reasons the cafe was so noisy was that it was a hangout for a really tough bunch of men—the taxi drivers who drove the service cars to the oil fields east to the Madill field and west to Ragtown. Dow Braziel owned most of these cars and employed the drivers so naturally they parked them out in front of the cafe while they were waiting for fares. And while they waited, they passed the time drinking and playing cards out back in the "tin" building. With a bunch like this arguments and fights were just bound to come up.[48]

This taxi service may have caused Braziel more grief than he could ever realize. If rumors are correct, the rivalry between the transport of illegal contraband and protection rackets may have been what led to the resultant fatal consequences.

Besides Bud Ballew, another Ardmore lawman who did not see eye to eye with Dow Braziel on any issue was Chief of Police Lesley L. Segler.[49] Born about 1880 in Guntersville, Alabama, Segler moved with his parents and ten brothers and sisters to the old Indian Territory in the 1900–1901 time period.[50]

By 1910 the thirty-year-old Segler lived with his wife, Beulah, and the couple's two children, daughter Stella and son Cecil, on a farm in Morgan Township near Ardmore.[51]

Segler farmed near Ardmore until deciding to change occupations. A colossus of a man at six foot, six inches, and weighing in at around three hundred pounds, he concluded that his imposing presence might be put to best use in law enforcement. Sometime before 1916 he ran for, and was elected to, the position of constable of Morgan Township, at this time moving his family into the city of Ardmore.[52]

The gargantuan lawman proved most effective as a protector of the peace. In 1917 the citizens of Ardmore elected him chief of police in that year's city election to replace outgoing Chief Bob Hutchins. During the latter stages of the First World War, he supplemented his income as police chief by also acting as registrar of all German aliens living in Carter County.[53]

Les Segler did his best to keep the lid on Ardmore. In May 1918 the local press made mention of his attempts to control the vice elements:

CHIEF OF POLICE ORDERS
CLOSING OF RESERVATION[54]

Chief of Police Segler has closed the reservation. Before the announcement of the government's drive on vice, he went to the reservation Sunday evening [May 12th] and told the proprietors that they would have to close up and that all inmates must find some other places of abode, as they can no longer remain in Ardmore. Yesterday afternoon he returned to see what progress they were making toward moving and found that many of the women had departed and the others were packing up and arranging to leave.[55]

As if the job of Ardmore police chief were not tough enough, Segler was also forced to attempt to deal with the strong personalities within Ardmore's law enforcement community. Segler was a good friend of Deputy Bud Ballew, and it may seem at first glance that he fell into the Ballew corner in the Ballew/ Braziel feud simply by association; however, Segler also had his run-ins with the combative ex-federal officer and police chief.

In early January 1919 Segler and some of his officers arrested a friend of Braziel on a charge of carrying a pistol. Braziel, enraged, stormed to the police station where he "made threats of violence against the police chief and some of his officers, and used language of [a] violent character . . . "[56] Braziel vigorously claimed that previously, during his tenure as a U.S. officer, he had given the man a permit to carry the weapon for just cause.[57] Sometime later, still in a huff, Braziel, for some reason, dredged up his old feud with Bud Ballew, reportedly communicating a number of threats against the deputy sheriff to various acquaintances.[58] Perhaps to Dow Braziel's ultimate grief, these angry mutterings were eventually relayed to Ballew. Almost everyone expected fireworks to follow sooner or later. Those betting on sooner won the pot.

Early on the morning of Thursday, January 30, 1919, at about six o'clock, chief of Police Les Segler, followed by Deputy Sheriff Bud Ballew, entered the California Cafe on Main Street. The restaurant contained about a dozen patrons at various tables. Dow Braziel stood behind the counter near the window in the front southwest corner of the building reading a newspaper, as was his custom on most mornings. Harry Brown, Braziel's restaurant manager, sat at his desk behind the counter near his boss. Almost immediately Ballew and Braziel drew their revolvers and started shooting. As the *Ardmore Statesman* put it, Brown, "Being a native of Kentucky, where the rule is, 'if it is not your fight, get behind something,' . . . dropped behind the safe and remained there until the shooting was over."[59]

Braziel managed to get off two shots. One went wild. The other grazed Segler's left side, leaving a large black-and-blue welt but otherwise doing no further damage. Ballew succeeded in emptying his revolver at Braziel. All six rounds thwacked into the former lawman's body. Shot once with a slight wound to the top of the head, three times in the left arm, just below the shoulder and above and below the elbow, once in the heel and once in the right side, where the bullet perforated the liver and kidneys, Dow Braziel fell to the floor a corpse.[60]

The foregoing are facts of the gunfight, which cannot be denied. Everything else has been argued and debated over for the last eighty years.

According to the story put forth by both Bud Ballew and Les Segler, the pair had both been attracted to the Ardmore Depot that morning by the reports of pistol shots in the neighborhood. Both converging on the area simultaneously and finding all quiet and nothing amiss, the two lawmen walked slowly up Main Street together. As they approached the California Cafe, Ballew suggested that they stop and get a cup of coffee (or breakfast, depending on the story). Segler claimed he declined Ballew's offer at first; however, Ballew continued to insist. Therefore, according to Segler, he finally acquiesced.

Moving to the door, Segler entered the cafe first, followed by Ballew. Before the police chief even saw Braziel, he was, he claimed, grazed by Braziel's first shot. Then Ballew returned fire and Braziel pitched over dead. At the conclusion of the battle, Segler arranged for an ambulance to take away the body of Braziel. He then escorted Ballew to the police station from which he was transferred to the county jail.[61] At the county lock-up according to local newspaper reports Ballew claimed, "He was satisfied that Braziel did not intend to shoot the chief, but was shooting at him when the latter was hit by a bullet."[62]

A second story circulating around town put a much more sinister aspect to the actions of Ballew and Segler that morning. At least one witness apparently spotted the pair of lawmen acting "peculiar" as they neared the cafe. It seemed to him that Ballew deliberately concealed himself behind the police chief's bulky frame as they entered the building, then quickly jumped to one side and started shooting.[63]

A careful study of the available evidence seems to point to the very real likelihood of Bud Ballew, perhaps with the aid of Les Segler, carrying out a planned, deliberate assassination of their enemy Dow Braziel. Perhaps the biggest question should be why would Ballew and Segler, known adversaries of Braziel, casually decide to stop for a cup of coffee at the restaurant owned and operated by their bitterest enemy? As historian Richard Jones most succinctly puts it, "Ballew and Braziel *hated* each other. The 'personal' animosity that they felt for one another should have kept them far apart under any other circumstance."[64]

Now the question becomes, if Ballew, alone or with Segler's help, conducted a plot to bring about Braziel's demise, why? The most obvious answer would have to be the known animosity between the men. Ballew and Braziel had a feud of long standing. As the *Daily Ardmoreite* commented the day of the shooting:

> It is a fact very well known and widely discussed that there has been an old feud between the parties to the shooting and a result something like that occurring this morning was not unexpected by the friends of both.[65]

Only recently Braziel had expressed threats against both Ballew and Segler. Knowing the ex-deputy marshal's dangerous reputation, perhaps Ballew, at least, decided to strike first and hardest.

Some have detailed a more involved scenario of a Buck Garrett/Bud Ballew protection racket. When Dow Braziel continued to operate his "unauthorized" taxi service between his cafe and the oil fields while at the same time refusing to pay the required protection money, this particular story says, Garrett and Ballew decided he would have to be eliminated.[66]

The real reason for the shooting may be none of the above. Perhaps at this late date we shall never know the truth of the matter with absolute certainty. One thing is sure: Bud Ballew proved the deadliest on that cool January morning, and Dow Braziel was dead.

Back row, left to right: David M. (Bud) Ballew, Tom J. Ballew, Callie Ethel Ballew, Stella Ballew; *Front row, left to right:* Truman Scott Ballew (face scratched out), Bryant Young Ballew holding Bernard T. Ballew, Bryant Ballew, Martha S. Ballew with Ruby Ballew in front of her

Amy Bear, Carrie Fox, and Bud Ballew, circa mid to late 1890s

Wedding photo of Bud and Fannie Ballew

Buck Garrett *(seated)* and Bud Ballew *(standing)*

A. W. "Gus" Gaines Champion "Hooch" Hound with one of the many whiskey stills he confiscated, circa 1925

Portrait of Clara Smith Hamon

Portrait of Jake Hamon

The town of Wirt, later called Ragtown, was always a busy place.

Ardmore Police Force circa 1910—*Front row* (left to right): Fred Emmerson, M. Butcher, Buck Garrett with son Raymond in front, Smith Redmon, L. A. Throp. *Back row* (left to right): (?) Roberts, Thomas Staples, Jake Williams, Walter Stroud, Tom Tippett, Tom Carter, unidentified, Gene Cook, Old Nuisance (dog)

Myrtle McGuire and Fannie Ballew, post 1923

Bryant Harper "Buster" Ballew

Bud Ballew's revolver—currently in possession of Ballew's descendants

Ballew's badge

Former location of Hardy Sanitarium, Ardmore, Oklahoma

Bud Ballew (left) and Buck Garrett (right) shaking hands

Dorris Ballew

Mildred Ballew

James Mathers, circa 1920

Wirt Franklin, circa 1950

CHAPTER 12

—— Victim #6—Rusty Mills ——

Two days following the shooting, February 1, Bud Ballew appeared in court before Judge Thomas Champion to answer for the killing of Dow Braziel. Ballew waived a preliminary hearing and entered a plea of not guilty. Judge Champion granted bail in the sum of $10,000. Producing the required bond, Ballew gained his release to await a future sitting of the district court.[1]

The day following Ballew's bonding out, Dow Braziel's funeral services were conducted at his home on Third Avenue by the Rev. C. C. Weith of the First Presbyterian Church. Burial followed in the Rose Hill Cemetery. A large gathering of family and friends attended the solemn proceedings.[2]

Bud Ballew must have lived a rather precarious and watchful existence over the next few weeks. Braziel had many kinsmen and friends in and around Ardmore who looked on his death as a case of plain and simple murder at the hands of Ballew and Les Segler. In fact it has been reported that for a time after his brother's death John Braziel would sit on a stool in front of the California Cafe menacingly displaying two shoulder scabbards containing pistols. Despite this obvious parole violation, no lawman, least of all Ballew or Segler, ever molested him. When the deputy sheriff and the police chief failed to confront him, Braziel grew tired of his vigil and left Ardmore for good.[3] He would eventually receive a full governor's pardon on September 11, 1922.[4]

By March Ballew was back performing his regular duties as Sheriff Buck Garrett's chief deputy. A week and a half after having his year old case in the killing of Rufus Highnote dismissed in the county court,[5] Ballew made what was perhaps one of his most embarrassing arrests.

Due to the constant complaints reaching the office of Buck Garrett concerning the transport of bootleg whiskey from Louisiana through to the Healdton Oil Fields, the sheriff encouraged extra vigilance on the part of his deputies. On the early morning hours of Wednesday, March 12, Deputies Bud Ballew and Will Ward stopped a suspicious Dodge roadster near the pair's hometown of Wilson. The lawmen were rewarded when they discovered ninety-six quarts of whisky stashed inside the vehicle.

The two men in the vehicle proved to be local residents of Wilson. One, George Van Dorn, was the operator of an auto repair business in the town. The second man must have given Ballew an uncomfortable moment when he recognized Jim Gauntt, a relative of his brother-in-law, John Gauntt, his sister Hattie's husband.[6] To make matters worse, Jim Gauntt was a fellow lawman in his own right, being the first elected constable of Wilson Township. Both men were arrested and held under a bond of $500 to face charges of transporting illegal liquor.[7] Though the outcome of their case is not of record, it must have made for some interesting conversation around the dinner table during Ballew-Gauntt family get-togethers.

The year 1919 was a time of death not only for Carter County, Oklahoma, but elsewhere in the Americas. On January 6, at the age of sixty years, former U.S. President Theodore Roosevelt died at his home on Long Island, New York. Three months later Mexican rebel and folk hero Emiliano Zapata was killed by government troops south of the border on April 10. Both of these deaths were topics of stern discussion among the populace of Carter County.

A member of the county clergy, the Rev. Dr. Brook, an itinerant evangelical preacher, had much to say about Carter's own manmade death rate at a weeklong revival meeting held at Ardmore's First Christian Church during the second week of April. His sermon of April 8, which came close to advocating vigilantism, made headlines in Ardmore. It perhaps best points up the strong feelings of a portion of the local population. Whether Bud Ballew felt himself included in the harangue is not of record. It is likely safe to say that those of the gun all felt the finger of accusation when Rev. Brooks exhorted that he:

. . . deplored the light value placed on human life in Ardmore. He referred caustically to our court record. He declared for the strict enforcement of the law and expressed himself emphatically in favor of capitol punishment. "The surest, quickest and only way to stop wanton murder," he said, "is to hang a few cutthroats and gun men. The rights and lives of the peaceful and the innocent should be protected. To assume any other attitude is to attack the very basis of society; for ours is a government of law.[8]

The following day Buck Garrett, accompanied by deputies Bud Ballew, Jim Carter, Early Young, and former Ardmore police officer John Dyer, now working as a special deputy sheriff, made a lightning raid on the blind tiger joints of Ardmore. Arrested in the dragnet were Battle Lindsey, King Lindsey, Tom Evans, May Thomas, Simon Keel, W. J. Frazier, Rose Kelly, Jim Moon, John Gernand, Jim Bouldin, Ernie Laster, Joe Bastine, and Frank Craddock, all old offenders. Assistant County Attorney J. L. Hodge found himself busy the next afternoon preparing the paper work against the bootleggers.[9] Only five days later Garrett and Ballew would experience what might have been the closest call in their law enforcement careers.

Late on the evening of Saturday, April 12, a well-known Ardmore resident and former county commissioner, James Taliafero, accompanied by his son and recently returned WWI veteran John Taliafero, and lumber-yard owner Alex Frensley, motored back to Ardmore following their attendance at a Masonic meeting held in Lone Grove. At the Hickory Creek Bridge three miles west of Ardmore, Taliafero was forced to come to a stop by the presence of a Ford automobile parked crossways on the road. Thinking the two men standing beside the car might need their assistance, the Taliaferos and Frensley approached the pair and inquired of their trouble. At this point the two reached into their pockets, pulled out .32 automatic pistols and ordered the trio of good Samaritans to "stick 'em up."

Jim Taliafero, his hands raised in the air, cautioned the bandits to "go slow with the guns and be careful that they did not kill somebody." Still with his ingrained army attitude, young John Taliafero at first refused to raise his hands. As one of the robbers continued to scream, "Put 'em up," the elder Taliafero finally convinced his son to comply with the gunman's wishes.

With their victims lined up along the side of the road, the smaller of the two highwaymen, described as about 145 to 150 pounds and sporting a head of red hair, handed his pistol to his partner. The second robber, a much larger man at around 6 feet tall and 200 pounds, held the pair of guns on the Taliaferos and Frensley while the smaller bandit went through the men's pockets. The take must have been disappointing. While the amount taken from Jim Taliafero and Alex Frensley was never disclosed, the robbers only realized $1.13 from the pockets of John Taliafero. Perhaps because of the paltry booty, the searching robber was tempted to lift the two elder men's watches, but was cautioned by his companion, "Take no watches. It's their damned money we want." The thief did later pilfer young John Taliafero's watch, which he found on the car seat where the young man had managed to toss it at the beginning of the affair. The bandits also grabbed a packet of deeds, mortgages, and other papers from the pocket of the elder Taliafero. Upon Taliafero's comment that the "papers were of value to him but could do them no good," the robbers returned them to him.

With the robbery now complete, the larger robber marched the three men a few yards down the road while his partner approached the Taliafero vehicle. Raising the hood, he busied himself cutting various wires to render the car inoperable. This done, the two highwaymen ran to their own auto, jumped in, and sped off down the road toward Ardmore.[10]

The three robbery victims had not been unobservant during their forced detainment. Besides the physical descriptions of the pair, they were able to observe the robbers' expensive dress and the large diamond ring sported on one of the fingers of the smaller man. They also took note of the pair's Ford automobile, which was a "one-eye," having only one headlight in working order.[11] All of this would be important later in identifying the highway robbers.[12]

As would later come to light, the smaller of the two bandits was a former state prison bird named Arthur "Rusty" Mills. His larger companion proved to be one Charlie Thomas, alias "Charlie Porter." Mills was a twenty-three-year-old[13] burglary specialist who had served two terms in the Oklahoma State Penitentiary. On March 30, 1915, Judge Oldfield of Oklahoma County sentenced the nineteen-year-old Mills to a two-year term in the prison for second-degree burglary.[14] He gained his release on June 28, 1916.[15]

Less than a year later, Mills was again arrested for burglary while working as an auto mechanic in Oklahoma City. Judge John W. Hayson of Oklahoma
County sentenced him to another two-year term at McAlister on March 4,
1917.[16] This term expired, and Mills gained his freedom on May 20, 1918.[17]

At this point Mills returned to Oklahoma City where he teamed up with
a twenty-nine-year-old felon from Lane, Atoka County, Oklahoma,[18] going by
the alias of "Charlie Porter" but whose real name was Charlie Thomas. The
pair more than once came to the attention of Oklahoma City lawmen and
became well known miscreants on the dockets of the Oklahoma City Police
Department.[19] Perhaps due to this perceived harassment by Oklahoma City
police, Mills and Thomas decided to move farther afield. They headed south to
start their own crime wave in the oil fields of Carter County. But they reckoned
without the team of Sheriff Buck Garrett and Deputy Bud Ballew.

Immediately following the robbery, the Taliaferos and Frensley walked
to the nearby general store of local bootlegger Frank Craddock. Here the robbery victims telephoned to the office of Carter County Sheriff Buck Garrett to
report the incident. The trio, retrieved to the sheriff's office, gave a report of the
robbery and a description of the thieves and their automobile.

Upon receiving as much information as possible concerning the hold-up,
Garrett and Ballew set out in separate cars in order to search for the perpetrators. Garrett at first considered the possibility that the highwaymen were some
of the many drivers for hire in town. Accordingly, the two lawmen toured up
and down the streets scanning the various nightstands in search of a vehicle
matching the description of the outlaw's Ford. Although this hunch failed to
pan out, the officers did encounter an old Negro who told them he had seen "a
Ford with only one eye" turning north off McLish Avenue.[20]

With this new information Garrett and Ballew decided the robbers
might have been headed toward Oklahoma City. Garrett drove northeast of
town toward the Berwyn road with Ballew following in his car a short distance behind. This lead-and-follow routine was a tactic the two lawmen had
developed over their years of working together. In this case it probably saved
Garrett's life.[21]

At about 2 a.m. Sunday, Garrett spotted a car and two wagons stopped at
the bottom of a hill around three miles northeast of Ardmore near a small stream

close to the John Griffith farm. The wagons belonged to Hall McClain and John Smith on their way home from Ardmore. Only seconds before, the two men had encountered the Ford with one headlight stopped on the side of the road and had halted in order to give the two troubled motorists assistance. McClain and Smith had been spared the experience of being the brigand's second victims of the night by the appearance of Buck Garrett's car topping the hill.

As the two unwitting farmers maneuvered their horses and rigs off to the side of the road, Garrett pulled to a stop beside the suspicious auto. Two men stood by the car, one tall and husky, and the other shorter and of slight build. Getting out of his car, Garrett approached the tall man standing at the rear of the other vehicle.

"What's the matter, old man, car trouble?" Garrett asked as he continued to advance.

At this point Charlie Thomas reached into his pocket.

Catching the movement Garrett yelled, "I am an officer," at the same time rushing forward. Garrett and Thomas slammed into each other as both men pulled revolvers from their pockets with their right hands and grabbed the other's gun with their left. Now a life or death struggle ensued between Garrett and Thomas, both attempting to wrestle free from the other's grasp. Garrett would later comment that Thomas was "about the toughest one to handle that I have ever tackled."[22]

As the sheriff and Thomas struggled for supremacy, Thomas continually screaming "stick 'em up, stick 'em up," Bud Ballew brought his car to a skidding stop behind Garrett's and dived out. Rusty Mills was just in the act of drawing his automatic pistol from his pocket to get a shot at Garrett when Ballew ran up to him.

Catching sight of the big diamond ring on Mills's finger Ballew knew they had encountered the highway robbers.

"I am an officer and will have to take that gun," Ballew ordered.

"You are not going to take anything from me," Mills barked, at the same time pointing his pistol at the onrushing Ballew and firing two shots. Mills's aim was off allowing Ballew, who had already pulled his own revolver, to fire a return shot. Ballew's slug splattered Mills's brains over the road, and the robber fell dead into the dirt.

In the meantime Garrett and Thomas continued their desperate fight for survival. Gradually Thomas began to work his pistol free while keeping a tight grip on Garrett's weapon. After the battle Garrett stated that he felt Thomas's trigger finger tighten and jerked his head to one side just as Thomas pulled the trigger. The bullet whistled past Garrett's ear. The bandit continued to squeeze the sheriff's fingers against the trigger guard of his own gun nearly breaking them but, as Garrett would later comment, "It was a sure enough fight by that time and there was no let up."[23]

Thomas managed to fire three more shots, all piercing Garrett's clothing but failing to puncture his body, when Garrett heard the gunfight between Ballew and Mills.

"Shoot, Bud, shoot!" Garrett shouted.

Ballew now turned his attention to Thomas and fired again. The bullet struck Thomas in the face, deflected off his jawbone, and exited beneath his eye. The force of the shot knocked the robber down. He dragged Garrett with him as they crashed to the dirt. Extracting himself from Thomas's grasp, Garrett quickly jumped to his feet. On his hands and knees, Thomas managed to fire one or two more shots to no effect. At this point Garrett and Ballew both blazed away at the downed man. Hit four more times, once in each leg, once in the side, the bullet breaking a rib and lodging under the skin in his back, and once under the shoulder, Thomas finally lay still. The desperate gun battle ended.[24]

Garrett and Ballew, with the assistance of the shocked McClain and Smith, loaded the dead Rusty Mills into the sheriff's car before hauling the badly wounded Charlie Thomas into Ballew's auto. Heading back to the city, Sheriff Garrett deposited the body of Mills at the Brown and Bridgeman Undertaking Parlor while Deputy Ballew took Thomas to the Hardy Sanitarium. Dr. Walter Hardy, by now an expert in the treatment of bullet wounds, thanks in no small part to Bud Ballew, had another patient on which to practice his skills.

Dr. Hardy's skills must have been well honed by this juncture. Despite his serious wounds Charlie Thomas quickly began to make what would eventually be a full recovery. Four days after the battle, John Thomas and Thomas's father, both from Lane, Oklahoma, visited the convalescing robber. At that time the local *Statesman* reported that he "seems to be getting along very well."[25] Unfortunately, the remainder of Thomas's career has been lost to history.[26]

Eventually Rusty Mills's family was contacted in Los Angeles, California. Through them arrangements were made for R. W. Hill, an uncle of the dead man from Dover, Oklahoma, to claim Mills's body. Mills had previously worked as a mechanic in his uncle's garage at Dover, and Hill made arrangements for his nephew's funeral.[27]

The *Ardmore Statesman* had high praise for the victorious lawmen:

> This is the first appearance of auto bandist (*sic*) in Ardmore. Most of the larger cities of the state have been infested with them recently, and many robberies have taken place in Tulsa, Oklahoma City and in the cities of the east. While it is regrettable that it was necessary to shoot these men up, yet it was undobltedly (*sic*) fortunate that this first attempt in the vicinity of Ardmore to practice what is becoming known as the profession of "Automobile robber" resulted in a victory for the officers. It is sincerely to be hoped that the incident will serve as a warning to the "fraternity" to give Carter County a wide berth when they start out in search of victims.[28]

At their preliminary hearing for the death of Arthur "Rusty" Mills held in the Carter County courthouse on April 18, the usual procedure played out for Garrett and Ballew. Following the waving of arraignment proceedings and the pleas of "not guilty" through the pair's attorneys, James Mathers and J. B. Champion, the parade of witnesses related their knowledge of the battle of five days previously. When all was said and done, Judge Winfrey expressed his opinion that the defendants "deserved the commendation of all good citizens" and should be discharged. As always, however, Garrett and Ballew demanded a jury trial. As a consequence the two officers were ordered held to a future sitting of the district court. Under a bail bond of $5,000 each, the two left the courthouse satisfied that their vindication was assured.[29] It was likely another case of allowing the information to die on the docket as no record exists of a trial from this incident.

CHAPTER 13

Victim #7–Johnnie Pierce

Although there were signs of the actual date of 1919, in some ways the Carter County seemed to be stuck in the 1860s or '70s. The area of Ardmore east of the Santa Fe Depot was known as "Black Town,"[1] where many Negro families had congregated to live separate from white citizens in an attempt to shield themselves from the obvious racism of many of the city's residents. Very few whites would venture into Black Town, especially after dark.

In August 1919 Bud Ballew would be involved in an incident with one of the habitués of Black Town. Although one can make a case for provocation and just cause (and admittedly these elements do exist), it is almost certain that, on this occasion, Bud Ballew, along with other officers, participated in an act of out and out murder.

City policeman Jake Williams happened to be patrolling through Black Town in the stifling hot early morning hours of Wednesday, August 27. At about 2 a.m. Williams spotted a suspicious-looking African-American man walking down the street near "The Dive," a notorious African-American gin mill and gambling parlor. Williams enquired of his business at such an early hour. Upon being surprised by the officer, the man tossed an object into the grass along the side of the street and slowly backed away.

Walking over to where the man had thrown the article, Williams discovered a broken bottle with the moonshine it had contained only seconds before seeping into the ground. Just as the patrolman bent down to pick up the broken glass, the man pulled a pistol from his pocket and fired a shot at Officer Williams, the bullet plowing a furrow along the policeman's back from shoulder to shoulder. As Williams fell to the ground, his assailant quickly spun on his heel and sprinted down the street.[2]

Responding to the sound of the pistol shot, Williams's fellow officers found him lying where he had fallen, loudly cursing his luck. Taken to the Hardy Sanitarium, the injured policeman was found to be painfully, though not seriously, wounded. Beyond the fact that his attacker was black, Williams was unable to give a detailed description.

The law enforcement community of the early 1900s was a close-knit fraternity of brothers. Everyone from Williams's companion officers on the Ardmore police force to the county sheriff's office and federal and constabulary peace officers were outraged at the shooting of the well-liked patrolman. Swiftly they joined forces in an effort to track down the gunman.

That same night and the next day a total of twenty-three African-American males were rousted from their haunts in Black Town by city police and deputy sheriffs and lodged in the county jail. Though none could be connected to the shooting of Williams, many were charged with gaming or various liquor offenses.[3] Eventually Sheriff Buck Garrett managed to ferret out the identity of the highly sought shooter.

In his interrogations Garrett learned that the man was Johnnie Pierce. Pierce proved to be an all-around bad character who was wanted for shooting scrapes in Texas and elsewhere in Oklahoma. Sometime in mid 1918 he had ventured to Ardmore, where he took up employment in a barbershop in Black Town. Even some of Pierce's associates were fearful of the man, claiming that he had taken a shot at one of them sometime previous. Others stated, "He was obsessed with the idea that he was a 'bad nigger.' "[4]

Garrett also managed to obtain the information that Pierce had friends in both Oklahoma City and Fort Worth, Texas, who were likely to provide him with succor. Deeming it likely that Pierce would seek refuge in one of these two places, Garrett notified the authorities in both cities with a description of the wanted man and a request to arrest him on sight.

Only two days following the shooting of Jake Williams, an officer in Oklahoma City spotted Pierce. When ordered to surrender, Pierce attempted to draw a revolver on the lawman. The weapon became entangled in his clothing, and, before he could bring it into play, the officer managed to collar the wanted man and drag him off to the Oklahoma City calaboose. Immediately Oklahoma City authorities telephoned Sheriff Garrett that his man was in their jail and that he should retrieve him as soon as possible.[5]

In the meantime Pierce made a statement admitting that it was he who had shot Officer Williams. He added that at the time of the shooting, he failed to recognize Williams as a lawman.[6] Whether Williams actually identified himself as an officer at the time he confronted Pierce has been lost to history.

That Friday night Garrett, accompanied by Bud Ballew and the sore but rapidly recovering Jake Williams, took the train to Oklahoma City. Staying the night, they arose early the next morning and made their way to the Oklahoma City lock-up. Oklahoma City officials promptly turned Johnnie Pierce over to the trio of Carter County officers. Without delay the lawmen hustled Pierce onto the southbound Santa Fe train for the return trip to Ardmore. The locomotive containing Garrett, Ballew, Williams, and their prisoner steamed into the Santa Fe Depot at Ardmore shortly before sunup that Saturday morning.

Then something happened. According to the story issued by the sheriff's office later that day and published in the *Daily Ardmoreite:*

> As they disembarked the Negro thought he saw a chance to make a get away and took it. That is where he made the last mistake of his life.
>
> No sooner had he taken the initial dive in his break for liberty than two guns cracked simultaneously [Ballew's and Williams's][7] and the Negro fell but a short distance from where he made his start.
>
> He was shot through the neck and through the right thigh. He was taken to the sanitarium where he died shortly before noon Saturday.[8]

Others had a different take on the events of that day. Walter M. Harrison, news reporter for the *Daily Oklahoman* in Oklahoma City, had known Buck Garrett and Bud Ballew for a number of years. In his book of memoirs published some thirty-five years later Harrison wrote:

These frontier types fascinated me in my early years. I had been their guest in and around Ardmore. On one occasion I wrote a feature story about Buck and Bud, which was printed in the magazine section of the *New York Times*. The innuendoes were highly uncomplimentary, but the way these two big ruffians cousined up to me after the publication of that story convinced me that they thought the New York publicity was the finest thing ever done for them.[9]

Perhaps in a move to keep the sometimes impudent Harrison under thumb with a show of force, Ballew telephoned the newspaperman before the three lawmen collected their prisoner Johnnie Pierce. Harrison continued:

It may have been in 1918 or 1919—I have not checked the date—one morning I received a telephone call from Bud Ballew. He asked me if I was busy and if I wanted to have a little fun. I queried him as to what type of fun he had in mind. Over the telephone, he said in substance, that he and Buck had come up to Oklahoma City to get a colored boy out of the county jail. He was an escaped murderer from the penitentiary at McAlester (*sic*). Bud said they proposed to take him down on the afternoon train. I said, "What's the fun about that?" Bud said, "He ain't a goin' to git there!"

I thanked the deputy sheriff and told him I was just too busy to take a day off. The next morning there was a brief item in the Oklahoman to the effect that the prisoner had made a break for liberty as the train stopped at the switch which entered the McAlester penitentiary (*sic*) and that Ballew had shot him dead on the right-of-way outside the day coach window (*sic*).[10]

Although Harrison misremembered some of the details many years after the event, there can be little doubt that he is referring to the Johnnie Pierce episode. Though it sounds illogical for Ballew to invite a newspaper reporter along on a planned killing, it was most likely a ploy designed to cow Harrison who had been known to publish some "highly uncomplimentary" material concerning

Bud and Buck, as he himself stated. The deputy sheriff probably wagered that Harrison would hesitate to reveal the true facts for fear of the Ballew revolver. He was right. Harrison waited until 1954, when all participants in the affair had long since gone to their final reward, to reveal the story in a chapter of his memoirs that he titled "Bud Ballew Scares the Wits Out of Me."

Everything points to Johnnie Pierce being the victim of what the Mexicans would call *la ley de fuga* (law of flight). When the train pulled into the Ardmore depot that morning, Pierce was likely told by the three lawmen to make a run for it. Garrett had the perfect pair with him for the mission. Bud Ballew would not hesitate to dispatch a man who had shot a fellow officer. Jake Williams was probably invited along to take his revenge on the man, a black man at that, who had attempted to take his life.

No one in Ardmore complained about Pierce's leave taking. Most wholeheartedly agreed with *Daily Ardmoreite* editor Sidney Suggs when he matter-of-factly stated at the conclusion of his report of the death of Pierce:

> His admission that he shot Williams and his sudden demise
> will save the county a whole lot of expenses in the final disposition
> of the case.[11]

Just as swiftly as it had occurred, the Pierce case quickly lost place in the interests of the public. By October 1919 Bud Ballew found his name recorded twice on the District Court calendar for two separate killings. Neither was related to the Pierce shooting. On October 23, along with Buck Garrett, Ballew would have a hearing in the case of the death of highway robber Rusty Mills.[12] This action would eventually be disposed of with the exoneration of the Garrett/Ballew team. The more hotly contested case would be developed in the matter of Ballew's killing of Dow Braziel in the previous January, to be commenced on October 31.[13]

Since Ballew was employed as one of Buck Garrett's deputies, the court disqualified Garrett from acting in his official capacity of summoning jurors to serve at Ballew's trial. As a result, local Ardmore banker Ed Sandlin agreed to act as "Special Sheriff" in bringing forth a venire of seventy-five potential jurymen.[14] Finally the case against Ballew could proceed. In what would be termed "the hardest contested case that has been tried in Carter County for some time" Ballew had his grievances against Braziel aired before the district judge and the people of Ardmore. With the aid of his ever-vigilant team of attorneys, Judge H. H. Brown and James H. Mathers, Ballew again rejoiced in a "not guilty" verdict on the afternoon of Tuesday November 4, the jury deliberating on this occasion for less than an hour.[15]

None but the most naïve were surprised by the verdict. Although the situation had the potential of volatility by Ballew's reaction before the many attending relatives and friends of Dow Braziel, the *Ardmoreite* reported: "The defendant, Bud Ballew, had no comment to make, going to his home immediately after the verdict."[16]

Though the outcome of the trial held no surprises, there did prove to be one development emanating from the proceedings that did cause many in Carter County to raise an eyebrow. As a result of certain testimony brought forth at Ballew's hearing, County Attorney Russell Brown filed information against Les Segler on a charge of killing Dow Braziel.[17] Despite the fact that Brown's reasoning is not of record, his decision to initiate charges against Segler may be a step toward suggesting a Ballew/Segler conspiracy in the death of Dow Braziel. Segler immediately made bond and had his case set for a future term of the district court. He would not live to see this court appearance come to pass.

On November 16, Sheriff Garrett and Deputy Ballew again made headlines in the local news media. As a result of the Williams shooting, demands had been raised for tighter enforcement of the laws over the dives on the east side of the Santa Fe tracks in Black Town. In response, Garrett and Ballew conducted a surprise raid on a large brick building located on East Main Street known to harbor illegal whiskey and a gambling layout. In spite of a physical confrontation in which Garrett sustained "a hand full of skinned knuckles caused by his fist coming in violent contact with an ebony skull of normal thickness,"[18] the two lawmen managed to gain entry and effect a number of arrests. The episode ended in a magnificent spectacle when "the sheriff and his deputy then took charge of everything in sight and soon had a big bonfire burning in the middle [of] the street fed by a conglomerate bunch of gambling paraphernalia which was soon reduced to ashes."[19] In spectacular fashion Garrett and Ballew were once again seen to be enforcing the laws of the land. The following month, the specter of Dow Braziel would return to haunt Bud Ballew's friend Les Segler in most devastating form.

Soon after his involvement in the Dow Braziel killing, Segler had resigned his chief of police position to go into the real estate business in Ardmore.[20] Buck Garrett's father-in-law, veteran lawman James Chancellor, replaced Segler in the office, giving the Garrett faction a monopoly on the law enforcement postings of the county seat.[21] Segler's wife had died sometime previous leaving him with three small children. Since that time his sister, Bonnie Love, often kept house for him and helped him raise the children.[22]

Early on the morning of Saturday, December 6, Les Segler left his children in Bonnie's care and boarded the train for Fort Worth on a business trip. At about 6 p.m. the former police chief was making his way back to the train station for the return trip to Ardmore when he met Dow Braziel's brother, Bob, near the corner of Fort Worth's Fifteenth and Main Street. Bob Braziel had been a resident of Fort Worth since shortly after his brother's death. Although no two witnesses gave the same story,[23] all that can be said for certain is that Braziel walked up to Segler with a drawn revolver and shot at Segler three times at almost point-blank range. Two bullets entered Les Segler's head. One slug punched through his left cheek and made its exit out the right side of his neck. The other penetrated his forehead almost dead center and entered his brain. The big man dropped to the sidewalk and died within minutes.[24] At the age of thirty-nine years, Les Segler had paid with his life for his involvement in the Ballew/Braziel feud.

After the shooting Braziel walked east to Commerce Street. Here he was taken into custody by Bob Bowles, a former deputy sheriff who still happened to have his badge in his pocket. Although no longer a commissioned peace officer, Bowles flashed his badge to Braziel, relieved him of his pistol, and escorted the gunman to the district attorney's office.[25]

Three days after Segler's death, Bob Braziel had his bond fixed at $10,000 to await the action of the Fort Worth District Court.[26] In short order W. H. Clark, R. L. James, S. H. Ellison, and B. F. Frensley all agreed to go on Braziel's bail, and he was released. Claiming, "I shot in self-defense," the killer of Segler could only bide his time and let the judicial process decide his fate.[27]

Despite the fact that Fort Worth officials set the date of Braziel's trial for the third Monday in February 1920,[28] due to various delays and legal maneuverings his day in court would not arrive for another nine months. Finally in September 1920 Bob Braziel went to trial in Fort Worth for the death of Les Segler. Braziel's defense team of Fort Worth attorneys Walter B. Scott and William P. McLean was successful in putting forward the claim that Segler had repeatedly made threats against Braziel's life and that Braziel acted in defense of his own well-being. Jim Craven, a former Ardmore resident who had previously been arrested by Les Segler for whiskey violations, claimed to have heard Segler state at one point that "he was going to bump Braziel off."

Taking the stand in his own defense, Braziel testified that he "was notified I would be killed if I stayed there [Ardmore], so I got up and left. I moved to Fort Worth." He claimed not to have known Segler was in Fort Worth the day of the shooting but met him by accident.

"I saw Sigler (*sic*) go for his gun," Braziel stated, "and I got mine[29] and shot him."

"Why did you shoot him?" questioned his attorney Walter Scott.

"Because I knew he would kill me if he got to his gun first," Braziel replied.[30]

On the evening of Saturday, September 18, 1920, the jury brought in a verdict of not guilty.[31] Bob Braziel left the Fort Worth courtroom a free man and lived the remainder of his life with his wife and children in relative obscurity. If Bud Ballew harbored any fears of Braziel's retribution against him, he kept them to himself.

Strangely enough, in the intervening one year between Ballew's acquittal in the death of Dow Braziel and the acquittal of Bob Braziel in the Les Segler case, Bud Ballew kept a fairly low profile. Though still employed as a deputy sheriff and continuing to perform the duties his position entailed, he engaged in no controversial incidents, and his name is rarely mentioned in the local Ardmore press. Perhaps because of the ongoing Ballew/Braziel feud, Buck Garrett desired to keep his chief deputy and good friend alive and well. At any rate, another major incident would prove to be lurking only one month away, which would give the Carter County law enforcement team of Buck Garrett and Bud Ballew national, and even international, press. Atypically enough, neither man would even have to draw his revolver.

CHAPTER 14

The Jake Hamon Affair

Despite the fact that a new decade was dawning, the Ardmore of 1920 could still be a dangerous place to work as an officer of the law. Sometimes this danger could come from the most unexpected sources. This point came violently to the forefront again with the events of May 20, 1920. At about 1:30 a.m. Claude Pruitt, brother of long time Deputy Sheriff Moses "Babe" Pruitt,[1] and Dick Crotzer drove up to the Ardmore police station on A Street South. In a frolicsome mood the pair laughingly released an opossum in the street in front of the station house. Ardmore Police Sergeant James Simms[2] chanced to be standing in the doorway of the station and spotted the prank. Angrily he ordered the two men to remove the offending animal forthwith. While Crotzer and another police officer carted the animal away, Simms and Pruitt fell into a loud exchange of words. After a few minutes Pruitt broke off the argument, jumped into his car, and drove off.

After going only a short distance down the street Pruitt turned his car around and drove back to the station. He resumed the disagreement with Sergeant Simms while remaining seated in the automobile. Suddenly Simms noticed that Pruitt held a pistol on the car seat in his right hand. Following Simms's demand that Pruitt relinquish the weapon, Pruitt raised it up and emptied the .32 automatic clip into Simms's body.

Pruitt would eventually be arrested and charged with the murder of James Simms.[3] Ten years later Claude Pruitt would be involved in another shooting death in Carter County. This time his victim would be one Semi Roberts, a man who was responsible for the killing of his brother, Babe Pruitt.[4]

On May 22, 1920, Garrett and Ballew were alerted to the presence of three suspicious characters lurking about Ardmore. The men appeared anxious to dispose of a seven-passenger Chalmers automobile and were also making numerous inquiries as to the whereabouts of Sheriff Buck Garrett and his deputy Bud Ballew, whom they apparently wished to meet.

That night Garrett and Ballew arrested the trio and took them to the county jail for questioning. Unaware that the two arresting officers were indeed Buck and Bud, the three men continually questioned their captors about their desire to be introduced to the two lawmen. They were quite surprised to learn that their captors were the famous pair. In searching the men's hotel room, officers discovered an automatic Remington shotgun, a .45 caliber revolver, and another smaller-caliber pistol. It was later discovered that the Chalmers car driven by the men had been mortgaged in Dallas, Texas. Garrett and Ballew were determined that they had "behind bars a pretty swift gang of highjackers, or else a band of toughs who came to Ardmore to 'bump' some one off."[5]

The actions of Garrett and Ballew make it quite obvious that they felt they themselves were the target. Unfortunately the true identity of the three men and their real mission in Ardmore is not revealed as the local press failed to mention the case again. It is not beyond the realm of possibility, given the activities of the two Carter County lawmen, that someone may have wanted to get rid of them.

There were a growing number of others in Carter County who wished to be rid of Garrett, albeit by more peaceful and legal processes. In the county elections of November 1920, Garrett, although once again winning the sheriff's race, saw his margin of victory greatly diminished from previous years. One who did fail to make the grade was County Attorney Russell Brown. He witnessed his defeat at the hands of well-known Ardmore barrister and previous county attorney, James Mathers.

The vote was declared "a protest against lax enforcement of the law again [sic] immorality . . ."[6] Immediately Garrett felt the need for a public display of law enforcement. In mid November he, according to the *Ardmore Statesman*:

. . . called his force together and issued the order that from thence hence forward the lid is on. That the Temples of Chance and Halls of Convivialty [*sic*] shall be decorated with a sign on the outer door bearing the word "closed," and closed thus used shall mean what it says. The booze boys[,] tinhorns, and nymphs of the "red light" section, shall be asked to choose a domicile beyond the borders of Carter County, and stick to their choice.

Continued the *Statesman:*

It is very doubtful if this edict of his can be strictly carried out overnight, but the advice of the *Statesman* to the citizenship of the county coming under the ban of the sheriff's order is that they "take due notice and govern themselves accordingly." To "buck Buck" usually spells to abide in jail.[7]

As usual the declaration and display of law enforcement was the main objective. In most cases the activities of the "booze boys, tinhorns, and nymphs" continued unabated. Relief of any pressure Garrett may have felt was in sight, however.

In only a week's time an incident took place in Ardmore that diverted the public's attention from the operations of the sheriff's department while at the same time bringing worldwide fame to Garrett and Bud Ballew.[8] The incident involved the death by gunfire of millionaire Carter County oilman, railroad magnate, and national Republican political power, Jake Hamon.

Born on June 5, 1872, in Grenola, Elk County, Kansas,[9] Jake Louis Hamon graduated from the University of Kansas law department in 1898.[10] That same year he was married at Sedan, Kansas, to Georgia Perkins.[11] During the opening of the Kiowa-Comanche lands to white settlement in 1901, the couple moved to Lawton, Oklahoma. Here Hamon became one of Lawton's first influential citizens, becoming the city's first city attorney and later serving as mayor.[12]

From the discovery of the first oil well in the Healdton field, Hamon became interested in the prospects of the Carter County area. Moving to Ardmore in 1913, the budding financier began dabbling in oil properties. With the advantage of being in on the ground floor of the oil boom, Hamon was able to buy various individual oil wells at extremely low prices from their cash-strapped owners. Later, at the height of the boom, he was able to sell the same wells at greatly inflated rates. Within five years Jake Hamon's oil enterprises had made him the area's first multimillionaire.

Although it was oil that made Hamon rich, his first love was railroad building. In partnership with Chicago financier and circus mogul John Ringling, he masterminded and eventually constructed the Ringling and Oil Fields Railway, commencing at the town of Ringling, Jefferson County. They received their charter in November 1916.[13] The railroad was a boon to the area, connecting Ardmore to the oil fields and providing an easy access for drilling components, building material, and men to reach the Greater Healdton Field. Eventually Hamon would own and operate various other railroad enterprises, which would add to the great wealth generated by his oil. With his millions, Hamon also decided to immerse himself in the political sphere. Quickly he became a power in the Republican party of Oklahoma. By late 1920 he had worked his way up to Republican national committeeman for Oklahoma. He became an intimate of Ohio Senator Warren G. Harding and Governor of Massachusetts Calvin Coolidge. When Warren Harding made his successful bid for the presidency of the United States on November 2, 1920, he and Coolidge, his vice presidential running mate, owed a great deal of their success to Oklahoma oil millionaire Jake Hamon. There was talk of Hamon himself harboring aspirations toward the White House.

Despite these successes there were cracks in the Jake Hamon façade. He is said to have been an expert at "dirty politics." Many felt his rise to power in the political arena was a testament to his proficiency at underhanded deal making and payoffs. As one Oklahoma observer has said, "Jake was as crooked as a snake."[14]

There was also scandal in Hamon's personal life. By 1918 or 1919 the wealthy oil tycoon had ensconced his wife Georgia and the couple's two children, a son named Jake Jr. and daughter Olive, in an opulent mansion in Chicago. By 1920 Hamon's constant companion was his secretary, Miss Clara Smith, a woman he had met some years before when she was only sixteen or seventeen years of age. Clara Smith was more than Hamon's secretary. Besides apparently being a shrewd businesswoman in her own right, she was also the oilman's mistress. In Ardmore she was known to one and all as Mrs. Clara Hamon. Indeed, everyone in town assumed that Clara was Hamon's wife.[15]

Apparently Clara Smith Hamon was a woman possessing both stunning beauty and irresistible charm. Bob Hutchins, former Ardmore chief of police who was hired by Hamon as his personal bodyguard, was obviously taken by Clara Smith's persona. He would record somewhat reverently that "the attractive Clara Smith" was "a girl of nineteen, with blues eyes and brown hair with a reddish glint, that looked golden in direct sunlight."[16]

Another of the Ardmore gentry to apparently be equally smitten with Clara Smith would be county attorney-elect and eventual Smith legal representative Jimmy Mathers.[17] Using the pseudonym of "Susan Hurley" for Clara in his 1954 published "recollections," Mathers would say of her, "She was a little girl—wouldn't weigh over one hundred pounds soaking wet—but she had brains and fire and drive . . . "[18]

Ironically, the reaching of his greatest stature in the political world would be the stimulus for bringing Jake Hamon's world crashing down. With the election of Warren Harding as president of the United States, Hamon became a serious contender for a possible cabinet post.[19] Neither he nor his political cronies, however, could see any success in the millionaire politico going to Washington, D.C., with a mistress on his arm. By late November 1920 Hamon was already planning to dump Clara and was making preparations for moving to the capital with his wife, Georgia.

Hamon and Smith made their headquarters at Ardmore's Randol Hotel on West Main Street. They occupied adjoining suites, and, as James Mathers later claimed, "they cut a special door between the two [suites], but I doubt if it was ever closed."[20]

On the evening of Sunday November 21, 1920, the patrons of the Randol Hotel cafe were suddenly startled by a loud pop, a sound strongly reminiscent of a pistol shot. Moments later Jake Hamon staggered into the cafe and up to the table of Dr. Cowles who had chosen the Randol for a late evening meal. Immediately Cowles recognized a gunshot wound in Hamon's abdomen. With the aid of Cowles, Hamon walked two blocks to the Hardy Sanitarium where he was quickly prepared for surgery.[21]

The bullet was found to have passed through the upper lobe of Hamon's liver and lodged near the spinal column in the muscles of his back.[22] In less than an hour physicians were able to remove the slug. In his hospital room after the operation, the oilman explained to associates the circumstances of his wound. According to Hamon he had accidentally shot himself while sitting in his hotel room carelessly cleaning and loading a small automatic pistol.[23] Others felt there was more to the story.

The very same evening of the shooting, Jake Hamon's mistress, Clara Smith, was quickly spirited out of Ardmore. Both county attorney-elect James Mathers and Hamon bodyguard Bob Hutchins would later claim in their respective memoirs to have been instrumental in the flight of Miss Smith, Hutchins claiming the assistance of none other than County Sheriff Buck Garrett.[24] The rumor swiftly spread through Ardmore that Hamon had been wounded by a shot at the hands of Clara Smith in a fit of jealousy over his planned shift to Washington with his legal wife, Georgia Hamon.

Following Hamon's seeming vigor and good health after the removal of the bullet, doctors Hardy and Cowles expressed their optimism in the patient's recovery. Being notified as soon as possible following the incident, Hamon's wife and daughter made a quick trip from Chicago to be at his bedside, a development that probably raised the eyebrows of many in Ardmore. Telegrams began to flood into the city enquiring of Hamon's condition. A message came from president-elect Warren G. Harding himself, at the time sojourning in Panama, asking for news of his good friend's health.[25]

Although his recovery seemed imminent, Hamon took a sudden turn for the worse on the evening of November 25. The next morning Georgia handed him a glass of water. "Thank-you," he murmured and closed his eyes in death.[26]

Immediately following Hamon's death, outgoing County Attorney Russell Brown issued a warrant for Clara Smith on a charge of murder. The gunshot death of the Republican committeeman threw a media spotlight on Ardmore, Oklahoma, the likes of which the city had never seen before and would never see again.

Following the lying-in-state of Jake Hamon at Ardmore's Convention Hall and his funeral on November 29, attended by many out-of-town dignitaries and newspaper representatives, the search for Clara Smith began in earnest. At length, following much intrigue, suspense, and media over-indulgence, authorities finally traced Smith to a small village in the Mexican state of Chihuahua.[27] In late December Buck Garrett traveled to El Paso, Texas, where the accused woman gave herself up to him as she detrained at Juarez, Mexico.[28] The sheriff and his prisoner landed back in Ardmore on Christmas Day.[29] The media circus was about to strike the Oklahoma city with full force.

Upon her arrival back in Carter County Clara Smith retained Jimmie Mathers and J. B. Champion, along with a Fort Worth firm, as her legal counsel. One who refused Smith's entreaties, however, proved to be star criminal defender and friend of Jake Hamon, Moman Pruiett, who termed Clara "a modern vampire."[30] Her case set for March 1921, the court granted her bail of $12,000.[31] At this point Smith retreated to her sister's home at Wilson to wait the coming court term.

As the court date neared, further developments continued to pique the interest of the ever-curious. Although County Attorney-elect James Mathers was to have taken office on January 3, he was given permission to demure until he could complete the defense of Clara Smith. Judge Tom Champion therefore appointed outgoing County Attorney Russell Brown as special prosecutor for the Smith trial. Brown would not be solely in charge of the proceedings. Deeming the case far too important, Oklahoma Governor J. B. A. Robertson appointed state Attorney General Prince Freeling as chief prosecutor.[32] It would not be the last time Freeling would be injected into Carter County legal matters.

Despite the seemingly endless media hype and public fascination with the Hamon murder case, Buck Garrett and Bud Ballew still had a county to police. In striving toward this goal, Garrett and Ballew, along with Gus Gaines, Jim Carter, and Earl Young, made another major raid against the illegal liquor distributors on the evening of Wednesday, February 2, 1921. Beginning at Dillard and swooping through Rexroat, Ragtown, Healdton, and Wilson, the five lawmen succeeded in confiscating over six hundred bottles of booze and placing twelve prisoners behind the bars of the county jail.[33] Despite this sterling performance, nothing could overshadow the anticipation of the trial of Clara Smith for the death of Jake Hamon.

As the March 10 trial date drew near, Ardmore was inundated by hundreds of newspaper representatives from all over the United States. This combined with the numerous other legal professionals, law enforcement officials, and the just plain curious caused Ardmore's usual population of just over fourteen thousand[34] to swell substantially in a matter of days. Along with the other newspaper reporters, both the Hearst syndicate from San Francisco and the Pathe Movie Company out of the budding motion picture capital of Los Angeles sent so-called "moving picture machines" to cover the trial.[35] Special arrangements had to be made at the Carter County courthouse to accommodate the crush of reporters and spectators expected for the proceedings.[36]

As Claude V. Barrow, former oil editor of the *Daily Oklahoman,* wrote in attempting to convey the circus atmosphere existing in Ardmore at the time:

> [The trial] was meat for the pavement pounders and the sobsters and the scandal writers. These birds of prey swooped down on Ardmore and hotel rooms were at a premium. Corn liquor was bought in fruit jars. Parties lasted all night and well into the morning. Gossip was grabbed as fact, anything for a new angle. The presses were running blood instead of ink again.[37]

In late February Sheriff Garrett appointed Bud Ballew as Clara's official bodyguard in her trips to and from the Carter County courthouse.[38] Decked out in a Stetson hat and cowboy boots and with two impressive looking .45 Colt revolvers strapped around his midsection, Ballew made quite an impression on the various newshounds. Looking for any possible angle of interest to report to the folks back home, a few decided to check into the backgrounds of the dangerous looking deputy sheriff and his boss. They were shocked and delighted to find in the personages of Ballew and Garrett two of the last vestiges of the gun-fighting Old West lawman.

Quickly feature stories began appearing in major newspapers throughout the country from San Francisco to Chicago to New York City concerning the two Carter County lawmen. Even the major dailies of such far-flung locales as London, Paris, and Peking ran articles on the Ardmore duo. One of the best of these actually appeared in the officers' own back yard.

In its issue of Sunday, February 20, 1921, the *Daily Oklahoman*, published at the state capital of Oklahoma City, ran a laudatory piece authored by Oklahoman staff writer and friend of Ballew and Garrett, William Krohn. In it Krohn spared neither verbiage nor aggrandizement in relating the careers of the two men. After detailing the battle waged by many officers of the law against banditry in early Oklahoma Krohn wrote:

> To combat such a spirit of antagonism required exceptional bravery, physical endurance, discreet power of deduction and almost perfect marksmanship among the men who composed the law forces. Oklahoma had many men who possessed some of these requirements, and also many who possessed them all. Those who did not number them all among their personal assets usually met death at the hands of those they attempted to apprehend. The others still live to relate the tales of their hair-raising adventures, and among these are Buck Garrett and Bud Ballew, two members of the sheriff's force of Carter County.

After a glowing rendition of Buck Garrett's "hair-raising adventures," Krohn introduced Bud Ballew:

> Buck's closest friend is Bud Ballew, one of his deputies. A great deal which has been said, concerning the bravery, judgment and personality of Buck, may also be applied to Bud. In reply to the question, "How did Bud and you form such a close friendship?" Buck replied, "Did you ever hear of love at first sight? Well, that is why I love Bud." It appears that the magnetic influence which makes such a great feeling of friendship spring up between some men when they get acquainted with each other, occurred in the case of Buck and Bud . . .
>
> Buck states that there are but two things he has against Bud, and they are the facts that "Bud won't smoke cigarets [*sic*] or go to a movie show." "Otherwise," says Buck, "he is O.K."

Krohn continued a bit later:

Bud has been in more dangerous places under more trying circumstances, during the past nine years, than perhaps anyone else in a similar profession. His duties required his presence very often in the oil fields which were the hot-bed of lawlessness at that time.

After a likewise praise-worthy telling of Ballew's many exploits Krohn concluded almost in a state of idolatry:

Buck Garrett and Bud Ballew are of a type of men whose memory the great cities of the southwest will serve as monuments.

With Bud Ballew close at her side, Clara Smith walked into the Carter County Courthouse on March 10 to face the charge of killing Jake Hamon. The trial would play itself out over the course of eight sensation-filled days.[39] The prosecution headed by Oklahoma Attorney General Prince Freeling attempted to prove that Smith's shooting of Hamon had been a willful act.[40] On the other hand the accused woman's coterie of defense attorneys, led by James Mathers, did all in their power to prove that the shooting had been a tragic, though unintentional, accident.[41] Mathers's strategy won out. On March 17 the jury pronounced Miss Smith not guilty.[42]

Clara Smith's acquittal proved to be an occasion worthy of celebration by her many supporters. That evening James Mathers and J. B. Champion invited everyone to a sumptuous dinner at an unnamed Ardmore restaurant in honor of the victory. Following the meal, the party got into full swing as liquid refreshments made the rounds. At one point, letting exuberance get the best of him, Bud Ballew suddenly pulled out his revolver and fired a number of holes into the restaurant ceiling.[43] After the shocked crowd realized that no one had been killed and that it was only Ballew letting off some steam, the party continued well into the early morning hours.

Subsequent to her release, Clara Smith drifted from the area. By August 1921 she had made her way to the burgeoning motion-picture capital of the world, Los Angeles, California. Here on August 22, she married movie director John W. Gorman. The couple planned to produce a film on the life of the new Mrs. Gorman.[44] If the movie was ever made, it perhaps lies somewhere in a vault of dusty old movie reels waiting to be rediscovered.

As for Bud Ballew, there were many who felt that the Jake Hamon/Clara Smith episode was the worst thing that could have happened to him. These were of the opinion that the laudatory publicity heaped upon him and Buck Garrett by the newshounds covering the trial went to the deputy's head. As one contemporary newspaper said of him concerning a perceived character change following the Clara Smith trial:

> The chief trouble with Bud Ballew was, that he would get drunk and ride thru town yelling and shooting off his gun. He never killed or hurt anyone in any of these tantrums, although he sure made the public nerves tingle. In fact, he never acquired this reprehensible habit to a marked degree until after the sob-sisters and sensation writers who reported the Clara Smith trial advertised Buck Garrett and Bud Ballew from Pekin [*sic*], China to London, England, as the "two remaining specimens of the 'wild west sheriff' of the movie reels and yellow back novels." Bud and Buck's pictures, underwritten as "the last of the wild west bad men," seemed to get under Bud's shirt, and he felt more or less called upon to live up to the character.[45]

CHAPTER 15

—— Bud "Ballew-izes" Ardmore ——

With the conclusion of the Clara Smith trial, all the newspaper reporters and various other strangers attracted by the affair quickly faded away. Soon Ardmore returned to normal, or as normal as Ardmore was wont to get. With his heightened notoriety Bud Ballew continued to perform his regular duties as a Carter County deputy sheriff. For a while Ballew had familial accompaniment in Ardmore law enforcement circles. Half brother Scott Ballew hired on as an officer with the city police force under Chief Jim Chancellor.[1] Scott's service proved short lived, as he soon moved on to other endeavors.

Bud Ballew's first major case of 1921 would be the Charles Dixon murder investigation. In March of that year Ballew and fellow deputy sheriff, Horace Kendall, were dispatched to explore the facts surrounding the apparent accidental death of Dixon in a single automobile mishap on the road between Berwyn and Ardmore. Following various inconsistencies in the stories told by the driver of the car, Newt Ashcroft, and various other suspicious evidence at the scene, Ballew and Kendall decided to arrest Ashcroft for the death of Dixon. At Ashcroft's preliminary hearing held in Ardmore on March 23, Deputies Ballew and Kendall were the main witnesses. Evidence seemed to suggest that Ashcroft had been involved with Mrs. Dixon. Charles Dixon attempted to blackmail Ashcroft, the two struggled, whereupon Ashcroft brained Dixon with the auto jack. Placing Dixon inside the car, Ashcroft attempted to make it look like an accident by pushing the vehicle over an embankment.[2] Ordered held for trial, Newt Ashcroft eventually was convicted in the death of Charles Dixon.

In May Carter County took another giant step toward the advanced technology of the twentieth century. Late that month Buck Garrett decided to employ the services of an airplane in the search for hidden whiskey stills in the wilds of the county. It would be a first for the Carter County Sheriff's Department. For this historic occasion Garrett chose Bud Ballew as the candidate for the honor of being the first county law enforcement office to take to the air. Apparently Garrett felt that Ballew, being the old cowboy that he was, would back out of the assignment. He jokingly placed a bet with an acquaintance that Bud would not take wing. The sheriff had to pay up, however, when Ballew took his place behind the pilot. The *Daily Ardmoreite* of Sunday, May 29, 1921, reported the episode:

"BUCK" LOST BET WHEN "BUD" HIT BREEZE
IN LOCAL SHIP OF THE AIR

While friends and foes alike betin' heavy and light according to the size of the roll, "Bud" Ballew, one of Ardmore's most popular officers, took the "air" like a real sport yesterday afternoon and in Plane Ardmore,[3] with Pilot Askew at the control traveled "over" Criner mountains on the first official trip for the air hunt for stills and other outlaw joints said to flourish in the inner recesses of the mountains.

"Bud's hair did not lose its curl nor color, nor did he get cold feet," Pilot Askew reports.

"This is great!" Bud said, as he got out of the plane, "and it is something the officers need in helping them with their work."

The trip consumed something like an hour's time.[4]

Bud Ballew returned to earth triumphant. In a strange quirk of fate, airplanes would play a pivotal part in the later life of Ballew. As opposed to the first, his second, and last, flight would be a matter of sorrow rather than joy.

In spite of Carter County's obvious progression into the contemporary world, as displayed by such developments as the sheriff department's use of aircraft surveillance, the area could still suddenly fall back in time as if it had never departed from the era of the wild and wooly Old West. Such proved to be the case on July 6, 1921, at the oil field town of Rexroat. That afternoon Rexroat night marshal and special deputy sheriff, George Pollock, encountered a drunken oil driller name Bill Williams on Main Street. Williams was having trouble with his two brothers-in-law and had been conducting himself in a threatening manner when Pollock confronted him. In a scene reminiscent of a Hollywood western, the two men faced each other on Main Street. When Williams reached for the revolver in his right hip pocket, Pollock beat him to the draw and fired two rapid shots. Shot in the right arm and left side, the latter bullet penetrating a lung, Williams collapsed in the dusty street. His death followed shortly afterward. Sheriff Garrett dispatched Ballew to Rexroat; however, Pollock drove himself to Ardmore and surrendered at the county jail.[5] The days of shoot-outs and death by gunfire were not over in Carter County.

Bud Ballew himself was not averse to falling back on the "old ways" from time to time, especially, as some would claim, after the publicity garnered by the Clara Smith trial. One day during the third week of September, Ballew, apparently for no other reason than a feeling of ardor, unlimbered his revolver at the corner of A and Main Streets and fired a number of shots into the air. Although startling a number of pedestrians and business owners along Main Street, this "Ragtown stunt," as the *Ardmore Statesman* termed it, ended harmlessly enough.[6] It would, however, be the cause of a new word entering the Carter County lexicon.

One week later Deputy U.S. Marshal Ben Bedford, in the city attending the fall session of federal court, repeated Ballew's stunt. Exiting the H. & H. Cafe on Main Street the evening of September 27, Bedford pulled his pistol and fired a few rounds into the sidewalk. In reporting the incident later, the *Statesman* lamented, "A good deal of indignation was expressed by the people doing business along Main Street over the growing inclination to make a shooting gallery out of that thoroughfare." The newspaper headlined the piece "A 'Ragtown' Stunt" and further blared in bannerline, "A Hayseed Deputy U.S. Marshal Butts In On The Local Shooting Gallery . . . And 'Ballew-izes' City Thoroughfare."[7] The press had now created a new word incorporating Ballew's name to describe the shooting of guns on the Ardmore streets. One can only wonder at Ballew's reaction.

In a week's time dissent was once again running rampant throughout Carter County against the office of County Sheriff Garrett. This time the impetus would be an incident that took place in downtown Ardmore on November 4. It would spell the beginning of the end for the Buck Garrett regime in Carter County, accomplishing what no outlaw's bullet could.

On the day in question, Mrs. George W. Casey leisurely walked along the sidewalk of East Broadway in Ardmore. Suddenly, four armed denizens of the city's active underworld attacked her.[8] While attempting to assail Mrs. Casey physically, the four thugs were quickly apprehended and jailed, eventually facing charges of assault with intent to kill.[9]

The attempted assault on Mrs. Casey stemmed from an earlier incident of October 21. Being newly arrived residents of Ardmore, Mr. and Mrs. Casey booked lodging at the Palace Hotel pending more permanent residency. In the course of settling in, they became aware of the fact that they were unable to lock the door to their room due to a missing latch but thought nothing of the matter. Later, while George Casey was absent on an errand, a strange woman entered the room and offered Mrs. Casey a "bracer," bootlegged booze. Refusing the proffered liquor, Mrs. Casey was attempting to oust the woman when a man entered and continued to harass the hapless newcomer. Encountering more belligerents in the hallway, Mrs. Casey fled in search of an officer.

According to her account Mrs. Casey found Sheriff Garrett most reluctant to take action in the matter. It seems that Garrett's hesitancy in the affair originated with the fact that the ne'er-do-wells were friends of Ardmore businessman Jake Bodovits, a friend of Buck Garrett. Eventually the Caseys prevailed, however. Late in October the Palace Hotel roughs received various charges in the Ardmore courts including possession of illegal liquor and other violations dealing with the harassment of Mrs. Casey. As the trial dates drew near, the thugs even went so far as to offer Mrs. Casey a bribe not to appear as a witness against them. The outraged woman severely rebuked this and testified against the group at the subsequent court hearings. Thus the retaliatory strike against her on November 4.[10]

This act of violence against a respectable lady of the city, combined with the seeming lack of vigorous law enforcement, outraged many in Ardmore. Led by former county attorney Russell Brown, a mass meeting of citizens was called for the evening of November 8. That night the people packed Convention Hall. The animated throng listened with alternate periods of hushed silence and raucous cheering and applause as such county leaders as Judge Tom Champion, Rev. C. C. Weith, Judge R. McMillan, and Russell Brown spoke on lawlessness in Carter County in general and the Casey case in particular.

Former county attorney Brown had steeled himself for this meeting. As reported the following day in the *Daily Ardmoreite*:

> In a speech which did not attempt oratory but which reflected both firmness and kindness Mr. Brown stated that such meetings had been held in Ardmore always, but they had done nothing. That there is a remedy but the people do not use it. He spoke of Garrett and Champion and congratulated them upon their ability, but said both of them knew that he knew they were not enforcing the law. That Garrett does not think the county wants the law enforced. He explained the Attorney General act in which he said in counties where the laws are violated that it is presumptive evidence against the sheriff, that it is a charge against the sheriff. He stated that the law required the attorney general to come and prosecute, but he said he knew Prince Freeling would not come because he had declined to do so when he (Brown) was county attorney.[11] The next remedy, said Mr. Brown, was to appeal to the governor. He stated that after an investigation, the case would have to be tried, that it should be tried by a judge who was not prejudiced. He said it should not be tried before Champion because he was afraid to do what Garrett did not want him to do.[12]

Courageous words, indeed, with Buck Garrett, Bud Ballew, Deputy Earl Young, and Tom Champion sitting in the audience. As Brown concluded, Champion stood up and "denounced the words of Brown as being false." A chorus of boos and calls for him to "sit down" prompted the judge to return to his seat.

Dr. Ashley Chappell, a member of the Ardmore clergy broke the tension and added some levity to the proceedings when he related his experiences at attempting to help other communities deal with their local morality issues. At one point he related of traveling to the rip-roaring oil town of Ranger, Texas, "to help build up the morals of that town." When he told them he was from Ardmore, Oklahoma, however, the people of Ranger all laughed at the irony of someone from a city worse off than theirs in the lawlessness department attempting to tell them how they should live.

Seriousness soon returned to the conference. Following various other speakers, Mr. and Mrs. George Casey stood up and related the facts of their ordeal. This caused feelings to rise once again and many in the crowd began calling for Buck Garrett to answer the charges against him. In his usual reticent style Garrett drawled, "The hotels involved in the injunction petitions were closed and those who assaulted Mrs. Casey have been arrested."

With County Attorney James Mathers being a somewhat ineffective official during most of 1921 due to illness,[13] Assistant County Attorney Hodge was left to answer for the county officials. When his turn came Hodge claimed defensively, "The county officers have rendered every service to Mr. Casey. I myself and two deputy sheriffs went out on the case. Statements have been taken and the same attention was given this case that would have been given a murder case."

One of the aforementioned deputies, Earl Young, added, "Only three witnesses were indorsed on the complaint, but there will be fifteen to twenty summoned!"

Most in the audience were unconvinced, especially with Deputy Young. When called to make his comments, former Deputy U.S. Marshal and current Ardmore Chief of Police Dick Hignight, who had taken over the position from James Chancellor earlier in the year, stated, "There was perfect co-operation between city and county officers. Mr. Hignight named only one deputy sheriff who he said did not co-operate as well as he might and named Earl Young as the deputy."

City Manager Kirk Dyer caused a sensation to run through the assemblage when his turn at the podium came. "Delegations have asked me not to prosecute further closing [of businesses in violation of the various liquor and gambling laws, etc.]. That it hurt business, I have a petition of business men to open a pool hall," he continued. "The women should look to their own husbands and clean them up. Somebody has to support bootleggers or they could not do business."

Although this chastisement brought some people to attention, the biggest rise came when Judge Rutherford Brett got to his feet and called out, "Gentlemen, there are some things that the officers of the law can not get at and if the Ku Klux Klan will do its duty I'm for them!" This brought deafening cheers and stamping of feet from "almost every person in the audience."[14]

This proved to be the first public mention by someone of authority of the Ku Klux Klan in Carter County. Despite its onerous reputation today, it is little wonder that many in the Ardmore of the time applauded the mention of the organization. Though its repulsive policies of racism and religious bigotry have always been a part of the Klan, these were far less evident in the 1800s and early 1900s than they are today. By the 1920s the Ku Klux Klan pushed a forum of moral reform and opposition to lax law enforcement. They would be one of Buck Garrett and Bud Ballew's most implacable enemies.

The period of greatest growth for the KKK occurred following the First World War. Setting up their Oklahoma headquarters in the oil capital of Tulsa, the Klan quickly began to infiltrate every institution in Tulsa County. As Carter County Attorney Mathers later claimed:

> . . . the Klan membership permeated the entire population [of Tulsa County]. I think it safe to say that a large majority of the so-called middle and upper-class men belonged to it; at least ninety percent of government officials and community leaders were Klansmen. The sheriff and his deputies, members of the police department, county commissioners, city councilmen, the county attorney, even most of the judges and court attendants belonged.[15]

The presence of these elements led to one of the worst race riots in American history in Tulsa on June 1, 1921. The day before, Tulsa police had arrested an African American bootblack on a charge of attacking a white woman. By that evening the rumor had made the rounds to the effect that the Klan planned a lynching. Quickly a group of some five hundred African Americans armed with rifles, shotguns, pistols, knives, and clubs surrounded the Tulsa jail in an attempt to protect the suspect. After failing at an attempt to disperse the mob, Tulsa police threw a cordon around the building in an act of containment. Suddenly someone fired a shot and the battle became general. Gunfire echoed throughout the streets of Tulsa all that night and into the next morning. By dawn of June 1 gangs of heavily armed whites were making sorties into the black section of the city. By the time the fighting had been brought under control, eighty-five people of both races had been killed with hundreds more injured.

At around this same time Ku Klux Klan members were establishing a firm foothold in Carter County answering the clarion call of county residents for aggressive law enforcement. Again according to Mathers:

> Paid organizers went about the country recruiting members and establishing units of organization at all levels, and they were skillful in their sales presentations. They could make the Klan sound like it was only a step below the church—maybe even half a step at that—in the promotion of goodness and light, and the Klan was at liberty to do things the church couldn't do—practical things which supplemented the church's teachings.[16]

Oklahoma commentator Claude V. Barrow would concur with Mathers's assessment adding in his irreverent manner:

> Then came the Ku Klux Klan supported by some misguided folk who were willing to risk anything for a change. Bed sheets were paraded and burning crosses topped the hills. Whispers became open talk and threats but the bootleggers, auto thieves and petty criminals continued.[17]

With all this tension swirling around Carter County, it was felt someone had to act. Following the mass meeting of citizens on November 8, the people had elected a committee composed of Russell Brown, Rutherford Bret, Guy Cobb, R. McMillan, and R. L. Disney. The purpose of the committee was to take the concerns of the populace regarding nonenforcement of the laws to the governor asking for investigation followed by prosecution.[18] This time the powers that be would be listening.

Bolstered and encouraged by the favorable reaction of a large majority of attendees at the meeting of November 8 with the invocation of their name, the Klan made its next move ten days later. In the *Daily Ardmoreite* of November 18 they sponsored a full-page ad declaring their objective that "the black stain of shame be forever wiped from the good name of . . . Carter County." They professed this to be a "first, last and only warning to: Gamblers, bootleggers, hijackers, gunmen, loafers, lawbreakers of every description, black and white alike . . . the unseen eye is upon you always by day and by night. . . . You can not escape us, we know who you are what you are; where you are . . . Change your ways this hour lest you be stricken as with a lightening bolt from a clear sky . . . We have given fair warning beware."[19]

While the Klan threatened, Russell Brown and his citizens committee took decisive action. Soon after the mass meeting in Ardmore, the appointed representatives confronted Oklahoma Governor Robertson directly. Recognizing the distasteful state of affairs in Carter County, Robertson responded by sending state Assistant Attorney General Elmer Fulton to investigate the state of the county. Fulton returned to Oklahoma City with the recommendation that the state empanel a Grand Jury to investigate the Carter County officials. Attorney General Prince Freeling agreed with Fulton's assessment of the situation.[20]

One of the first tangible signs of state involvement in Carter County law enforcement occurred on the afternoon of November 19. Without so much as a word to the county office of Sheriff Garrett, federal officers conducted a major raid on suspected bootleggers holed up in the northwest portion of the county. Arrested in the federal sweep were moonshiners Elmore Johnson; Will Hooks; Jack Simpson; Clyde Sykes; Lloyd, Jim and Bud Austin; Fred Morris; and Will Womack. The men were carted to Chickasha to be arraigned before a United States commissioner on charges of contravening federal liquor laws.

The feds also claimed to have captured twelve stills and numerous gallons of "white lightning."[21]

Outraged at the federal "invasion" of his territory and insulted at the snub of not being consulted by the U.S. officers, Buck Garrett at first denied the story told by the feds. Garrett claimed there had been only five stills confiscated and most of these had actually been taken in neighboring Stephens County. Quoted later in the local press the sheriff defensively stated:

> I do not wish it understood that I desire to start a controversy with anyone over this matter. I know that whisky has been made and sold in Carter County the same as any other county in the state, and I also know that it will be made and sold long after the incidents covering this raid have been forgotten. I do not think it fair to the name of Carter county that the stigma of other counties' wrong doing should be shouldered off on Carter County when it is not a fact as these affidavits [issued by federal authorities] set forth.[22]

Slowly but surely the power of Buck Garrett's hold on Carter County, and as a consequence Bud Ballew's prestige as well, was gradually being eroded away. Attacked from three sides by the KKK, the state government, and disgruntled and exasperated citizens of the county, Garrett and his supporters dug in for a stubborn defense.

CHAPTER 16

——Gun Battle at Wilson ——————————

O ne of the more active members of Carter County's law enforcement community when it came to the suppression of bootleggers and auto theft rings was C. G. Sims, plainclothes detective of the Ardmore Police Department. Born ca. 1879,[1] Sims relocated to Ardmore via Dallas, Texas, about the year 1909.[2] Upon his arrival in Ardmore, he entered the horse and mule business, opening a livery stable at 222 A St. N.E.[3] In 1916 the married man and father of an adopted boy went to work as a policeman under Chief Bob Hutchins. Sims continued to work sporadically as an officer. By 1921 he was serving under Police Chief Dick Hignight, a man to whom Sims had lost in the most recent city elections. With the victory of Hignight, Sims remained with the force as a plainclothes man.[4] He was called "fearless as an officer, showing a degree of bravery which has never been surpassed."[5]

There was another side to C. G. Sims, however—a secret clandestine side, a side shared with many other prominent Ardmore civic leaders and businessmen. Although statements are conflicting, evidence suggests that C. G. Sims was a member of the Ku Klux Klan.

Sims displayed his evident zeal to enforce the liquor laws on November 25, 1921, with his arrest of veteran bootlegger Gus Key, owner of the Diamond A Drugstore on East Main Street.[6] There were other plans afoot at this time as well, grander conceptions designed to make a concerted effort at combating lawless elements in Carter County. For C. G. Sims it would amount to a case of being hoist by his own petard.

Sims and his partner on the Ardmore force, fellow plainclothes man C. C. Hathcock, planned to make a raid on a known whiskey joint on the afternoon of Thursday, December 15. Unable to get together until late, Sims convinced Hathcock that the approaching darkness would make such an undertaking extremely hazardous.[7] The pair agreed to call off the raid but decided to meet later that evening to do investigative work on another case they were involved in. Sims failed to appear. Hathcock again missed Sims the next morning at the station house. Hathcock waited until just after 11 a.m. At that time he received word that his partner's dead body had been found in a field some two miles north west of the town of Wilson.[8]

Facts would later come to light revealing that officer Sims and several other leaders of the local Klan or "Business Men's League" as they sometimes preferred to term themselves, planned a major expedition for the evening of December 15. The target of this raid would be the Wilson bastion of Walter and Joe Carroll, believed to be the leaders of a large gang of whiskey ped-dlers and car thieves. To say the least, the operation would not go according to plan.

A distillation of the facts and various later testimony suggest that on the evening of December 15 Sims and other leading lights of the organization recruited as many local men as possible in sympathy with their cause. Travel-ing to Healdton, the Ardmore lawman managed to convince former bootleg-ger and friend of the Carroll family, Jeff Smith, to accompany the men. Late that night Sims and his companions drove to a prearranged meeting place, a vacant field near the village of Joiner City, just northwest of Wilson. Soon upward of thirty or forty cars and some two hundred men were congregated at the meeting place.

Apparently, the plan was to use Jeff Smith to help convince his brother, John, also a friend of the Carrolls and a former bootlegger, who resided in Wil-son, to lead the Sims party to the Carroll home. It was hoped John Smith would be able to lure the Carrolls out to facilitate an easy capture. They then planned to bring the Carroll brothers to the Joiner City meeting place. Here the alleged kingpins of organized crime in Carter County could be made to talk and reveal valuable information concerning their nefarious operations.[9]

In pursuance of this design, shortly before midnight two carloads of men, including C. G. Sims and Jeff Smith, left the others and headed for Wilson. In Wilson the men managed to coerce John Smith to guide them to the Carroll house. About 12:30 a.m. Friday, with masks covering their faces, the men drove up to the house. Moving to the front door, John Smith knocked and called out for Joe Carroll. Opening the door and peering outside into the dark, Carroll reacted to the sight of the masked men on his doorstep. Reaching into the front pocket of his overalls, he jerked out a revolver. One of the mob grasped the arm of Carroll and began grappling with him.[10]

At this point the still night air began to reverberate with the crackle of gunshots as the firing became general. Joe Carroll fell dead on his hearth with at least one bullet in the face. Jeff Smith received a slug in the leg. He managed to drag himself back into one of the mob vehicles and out of the way of bullets fired by Walter Carroll and family friend H. A. Hensley from inside the shack. Not so lucky, Jeff's brother, John Smith, staggered back with a gunshot wound to his side. Quickly the attacking force, save the wounded John Smith, piled back into their vehicles and sped away from the scene. Walter Carroll and Hensley fired after the retreating autos, striking them with a number of rifle and pistol bullets but otherwise doing little other damage. In all some thirty-five to forty shots had been fired in the wild gun battle.

The severely wounded John Smith stumbled away from the Carroll house and down the street until encountered by an acquaintance named Hall. Mr. Hall assisted Smith into his car and sped the injured man to the Wilson Hospital. With his wife, who had been informed of events, by his side, Smith reportedly stated that "the Ku Klux Klan had got him." He then told officers that Joe Carroll had shot him.[11] Shortly after the shoot-out, John Smith expired from the effects of his wound.[12]

Soon after the affray Buck Garrett received a telephone call at his Ardmore office informing him of events. Gathering together Bud Ballew, Will Ward, Horace Kendall, and Jim Carter, along with Assistant County Attorney John Hodge, the lawmen motored to Wilson to initiate an investigation early Friday morning. Obtaining information concerning the meeting grounds northwest of Wilson, the officers drove out to the area shortly before noon. Near the road and inside the pasture the sheriff's party found the dead body of Officer C. G. Sims. He had sustained three gunshot wounds to the chest and had also apparently been beaten about the face. He had obviously been dead a number of hours before being found. He was dressed in what were described as dark brown "unionalls," his mask still around his neck.[13]

The death of C. G. Sims has always been, and still remains, shrouded in a cloak of mystery. The most logical supposition, and the theory of both Garrett and Ballew, was that Sims had been shot in the fight at the Carroll residence, carried back to the group's meeting place and left on the field in a dead or dying condition.[14] There were other factors that throw doubt on this hypothesis, however. The evidence of Sims's chest wounds having been apparently delivered at point blank range, his bruised and beaten face, and an apparent attempt to cut his throat[15] were troubling. Officer Sims's brother, Claude Sims, would later make the claim that his brother had actually been "tied, or handcuffed, and murdered in cold blood."[16] How Claude Sims reached this conclusion is unknown, but it nonetheless caused further doubt to be thrown on the Ardmore peace officer's death.

Garrett and Ballew were convinced that the local Ku Klux Klan had precipitated the Wilson fiasco. It even gained report that the "unionalls" the dead Sims had been wearing were identical to those worn as a uniform by the Klan. This was countered by the statement that the garb was nothing more than a standard pair of overalls such as worn by most auto mechanics.[17] Evidence would seem to point to the fact that the attack against the Carrolls was a maneuver of the KKK. At any rate Garrett and Ballew found this the perfect opportunity to strike back at their implacable enemies in the Klan.

Immediately following the melee, Deputy Sheriff Will Ward arrested the wounded Jeff Smith along with the Smith brother's cousin, Healdton butcher John Smith. Earl Young brought in J. D. "Curley" Smith, no relation to the other Smiths. All were locked in the Carter County jail.[18] Soon two more, Healdton Baptist minister Rev. Leon Julius and Ardmore oilman and former sheriff's candidate J.A. Gilliam, would be added to the ever-growing list.[19] Walter Carroll and H. A. Hensley were also brought in and held for investigation.[20] The arrests were only beginning.

By Sunday, December 18, Sheriff Garrett had locked up nine more prominent county men. These included Dr. E. C. Harlow, Ardmore optometrist; Frank Cardwell, insurance agent; W. L. T. Hilton, local rancher; Ray L. Beede, auto dealer in Ardmore; Tom Hailes, oil lease broker; Clifton Whitchurch of the Whitchurch Supply Company, an Ardmore oil field equipment dealership; Bill Ratliff and John Murray, oil field workers; and Dan Ridpath Jr. Ardmore building contractor.[21] Within a day J. A. Pitts of the Ward Motor Company would join the others at the county jail.[22] All would have their complaints signed and filed by Bud Ballew.[23] Many in Ardmore were shocked at the turn of events, which saw their friends and neighbors placed behind bars on charges of the murder of Joe Carroll.

Perhaps the *Daily Ardmoreite* expressed the feeling of the community best when it editorialized:

ON A POWDER KEG

The most perilous time in the history of Carter County is at hand. Literally we are sitting perched upon a powder keg. The tiniest bit of indiscretion will plunge this county into a vortex of deathly hell. It must not come.

For the sake of the lives of good men, for the sake of the women and children of today and for the sake of the future of this section, the Ardmoreite *appeals for calm judgment and cool headed action.*

Men on the streets are making threatening remarks. They are breeding trouble. A certain pawn shop, we understand, is practically sold out of guns and revolvers. That calls for immediate action from the city and county forces.

Some are agitating a raid on the county jail. No more foolhardy thing could be contemplated.

Sane, common sense points unwaveringly to a policy of careful deliberation.

*Some of the best men in the commu-
nity have been arrested. Their friends and
acquaintances are naturally aroused to the
highest pitch. But still, constituted law must
be respected.*

*If the immediate future develops the fact
that these men have been arrested unjustly; if
their arrests are the result of political perse-
cution, as it is openly alleged, then time will
disclose it. We can well afford to wait.*

*If these men are the victims of retaliation,
as has been charged, then a long-suffering public can act so decisively as to leave no stigma
upon the men themselves. These men's reputation will not be hurt by a few days in prison.
Rather, they will be martyrs to a good cause.*

*On the other hand, if the unbelievable
is true, and they are accessories to a murder
plot, the sheriff is within his right. Justice will
not be gained either way by violence.*

*Gunplay on the part of good citizens
will place them in a class with those they are
trying to rid the county of. Attempts to go
through any other route other than that of
the courts of the land is not worthy of this
community.*

*The parting of the ways has come, it is
true. The future of Carter County depends
upon the outcome of this Wilson affair. There
must be no more open lawlessness in Carter
County. The day for that is past.* [24]

One who failed to heed the *Ardmoreite*'s advice in respect to the need
for a cooling off period was Presbyterian pastor Charles Weith. That Sunday
Weith officiated at the funeral of police officer C. G. Sims conducted by the
local Masons, of whom Sims had been a member of long standing. Rather than

simply presenting a service to honor the life of the fallen lawman, Weith used the occasion as a platform for his radical ideas on county reform.

At one point in the service, said to have been one of the largest ever held in Ardmore, Rev. Weith got a rise out of the mourners when he boomed from the pulpit, "Is the death of your brother Mason going to be in vain?" Since Weith was an old political enemy of Buck Garrett, many people interpreted this as a call for the sheriff's removal from office.[25]

Events began to unfold rapidly, everyday bringing new developments in the tense situation. On Monday afternoon another of the seemingly perpetual mass meetings of Carter County citizenry took place at Ardmore's Masonic Hall. Rumors had floated through the city since the arrest of the men held for the Wilson fiasco that the prisoners were being held by Garrett incommunicado. The idea of the men being caged without benefit of either legal council or family support sent a wave of indignation rippling through the hall. Threats of removing the prisoners by force if the situation was not remedied were widely expressed.

Once again Rev. Weith took the opportunity to vent his spleen against Sheriff Garrett, at one point declaring, "Nothing short of the removal of Sheriff Buck Garrett and all his deputies will relieve the situation!" Weith was not the only Garrett basher at the gathering. Dr. R. L. Davidson, Baptist clergyman, and Ardmore Mayor R. A. Hefner were amongst those prominent in the denunciation of Garrett. Hefner was of the opinion that his city police force was "powerless to act with the sheriff's force" and that the fault lay entirely with the county lawman. Davidson alleged that in the year and a half that he had resided in Ardmore he had officiated at the funeral of fifteen individuals as a result of the gambling and bootlegging activities of Ardmore's underworld. He placed the blame squarely in the sheriff's lap.

The close of the meeting saw the formation of two citizen committees. One headed by Mayor Hefner and *Ardmore Statesman* owner and editor Roy Johnson was assigned the task of repairing at once to the county jail to enquire into the welfare of the Wilson suspects. They found that the situation had been greatly exaggerated and that, indeed, the prisoners had been receiving visits from legal representatives and concerned family members. This cooled the fires somewhat but failed to douse the flames totally. A second committee, led by Ardmore City Bank president A. H. Palmer and composed of forty other prominent Carter County residents, was appointed to travel to Oklahoma City and lay their concerns before Governor J. B. A. Robertson. This committee would be responsible for hammering a large fist full of nails into the coffin of the regime of Sheriff Buck Garrett.[26]

Early the following day the trainload of Carter County men had their audience with Robertson. In the governor they found a most sympathetic ear. After listening to the delegation and consulting with Assistant Attorney General Elmer Fulton, who had conducted an investigation into Carter County affairs a short time previously, Governor Robertson concluded immediate action was necessary. "The situation in Carter County is serious," he told the group. "I doubt if Russia in its palmiest pre-war days ever had such a situation in a community where there was supposed to be an established government. . . . Efforts have been made to get me to call off the investigation, but I have put my hands to the plow, and there will be no turning back."

Many in the throng implored the governor to call out the National Guard. This Robertson refused to do, cautioning them, "I would invoke martial law in the county regardless of the cost if I thought it would save one life, but as long as there is any other way around the difficulty, I think it best not to call out the guards. Nothing would give the established court system a greater blow than to admit that it has failed." Although the National Guard company stationed at Wilson was notified and placed on a heightened state of readiness, true to the governor's word, they would not enter into the Carter County difficulties. Governor Robertson did promise, however, to send Attorney General Prince Freeling to Ardmore to take full charge of the case involving the Wilson killings.

The Carter County committee received its greatest encouragement from the words of the assistant attorney general. In adding to Robertson's general tone, Fulton commented forcefully and to the point, "There is not doubt about criminals being protected by the sheriff's force. . . . " Fulton continued, "A large number of officials, not one or two or three or four, but a large number will face ouster proceedings just as soon as arrangements can be made to get their cases before a fair jury."[27] No doubt Weith and the rest left Oklahoma City rubbing their hands with glee.

Later that same day Buck Garrett was given his chance to give a rebuttal and defend himself from his many attackers. Published in the *Daily Ardmoreite* in the form of a statement to an Ardmore reporter, Garrett expressed himself in his usual straight forward and brusque manner:

> You can tell them that I emphatically deny remarks attributed to Mayor Hefner, who was quoted as saying that the city police here are powerless to act with the sheriff's force. If his men can't get along with us, why don't he fire the police?
>
> Regarding the ouster proceedings, I will gladly face a speedy trial, if they have reference to my department and you can tell them all that I'm ready and rarin' to go!
>
> In answer to the Rev. Mr. Weith's statement that nothing short of my removal will relieve the situation, my opinion is the Rev. Weith is an agitator of mob law. This is the course Rev. Weith has pursued since I ran and was elected for office. He has no grievance against me as an officer, but only because he and I do not agree in politics.
>
> Dr. R. L. Davidson told a falsehood when he said attorneys had been refused admittance to the county jail to interview their clients, "who are my prisoners in connection with the killing of three men at Wilson Thursday night." In answer to Dr. Davidson's statement that in the year and a half that he has been in Ardmore, he has officiated at fifteen funerals growing out of gambling and bootlegging activities in the underworld of Ardmore, I say that he should instruct the people here not to patronize bootleggers.[28]

While Garrett defended himself at home, County Attorney James Mathers paid his own visit to Governor Robertson at Oklahoma City to plead the case of the county officials. It was most likely as a result of Mathers's talk with Robertson that the local National Guard unit stationed at Wilson received notice of heightened awareness. Ordered to keep at least fifteen men on duty at the armory at all times, Lieutenant Colonel William Hutchinson assured everyone that the order was simply a precautionary measure.[29] Despite Robertson's earlier promise, however, it was a clear signal that the unit would be ready if called upon.

Developments continued to unfold rapidly keeping the community "stirred up to a degree that the city has never before experienced. More of its people were excited and wrought up, and were worse wrought up, than the oldest inhabitant can recall, in even this city of exciting experiences," the newspapers claimed.[30] The next sensation came that Tuesday night with the release from the sheriff's office of the first sworn statement by one of the arrested suspects in the Wilson killings of the previous Thursday. The statement of J. A. Gilliam, witnessed by Deputy Sheriff Bud Ballew, Assistant County Attorney John Hodge, Homer Hinkle, Otis Smith, F. E. Tucker, and O. H. Wolverton, gave most people in Carter County their first real account of the doings in the affair.[31]

The next afternoon, Wednesday, December 21, Attorney General Freeling notified Mathers that he would arrive in Carter County later that day to take full charge of the hearings of the accused Wilson raiders, as well as conduct a full investigation into county affairs. That morning all the Wilson suspects held in the county jail were allowed to make a bail bond of $2,500 pending a preliminary hearing set for the next day. The one exception proved to be Bill Ratliff who was given his outright release as no evidence could connect him with the killings.[32] Both Garrett and Ballew probably saw the writing on the wall when Freeling declared, "No citizen or officer who is interested will be done an injustice and no citizen or officer who is guilty will be whitewashed; I will not be stampeded or excited in the matter but will make a thorough investigation."[33]

Public sentiment continued to be fomented on Wednesday with the release of statements from the widow and brother of the deceased C. G. Sims. "I want to see justice done," stated Mrs. Sims. "I do not want to see any innocent suffer, but the guilty must be brought to justice. We must await until the facts are established, the facts which will reveal the hotbeds of crime which must be wiped out."[34]

Claude Sims concurred: "I want to see right done . . . I want to see that my brother has not died in vain . . . two thousand women of Ardmore—women who have been aware of the clean, righteous and worthy character of my brother—are aware of matters and are aiding in bringing to light facts, which, although they have been of a more or less mysterious nature, nevertheless will be revealed when their efforts are moulded into form."[35]

Despite Claude Sims's optimistic outlook and the help of the "two thousand women of Ardmore," whoever they may have been, he would learn little more of his brother's death. Neither he nor the widow Sims attained much satisfaction. The death of Officer C. G. Sims would remain a mystery and an unfortunate incident in the history of Carter County.

On Thursday, December 22, Attorney General Freeling began the preliminary hearing of Dan Ridpath, Ray Beede, C. G. Whitchurch, Tom Hailes, Frank Cardwell, W. L. T. Hilton, John Smith, and J. H. Pitts in the Wilson affair before Justice of the Peace D. W. Butcher at the Ardmore courthouse. The other defendants managed to have their cases postponed to future hearings. Freeling's first matter of business was to introduce a letter signed by Governor Robertson directing the attorney general to take charge of the prosecution of the case in place of County Attorney Mathers. The edict also stipulated that neither Mathers nor Assistant County Attorney John Hodge were to have any involvement in the case. Freeling also requested that the court appoint court officials other than members of the county sheriff's department or Ardmore Police Department.[36] This being accomplished, the hearings went forward.

The first day saw the examination of three witnesses, the widows of John Smith and Joe Carroll and Carroll's brother, Walter. The biggest sensation of the day occurred when Freeling questioned Walter Carroll concerning who shot his brother Joe as he lay on the doorstep during the Wilson gun battle. Without hesitation Walter Carroll pointed to Ray Beede seated amongst the defendants. "That is the man," Carroll proclaimed. At that point Mrs. Ray Beede jumped up from her seat just behind her husband. "He didn't," she cried, and then fell away into a faint. It took several minutes to revive her before court could be resumed.[37]

With large crowds flocking to the courthouse the preliminary hearing continued the following day. In addition to the questioning of many more witnesses the day was marked by a pointed exchange between Freeling and defense attorney H. H. Brown in which, for all intents and purposes, Brown called Freeling a liar.[38] Once this dispute had been ironed out the proceedings continued.

The most controversial aspect of the day came when the court placed Franklin Bourland on the stand. In the face of a barrage of questions from

Freeling concerning his alleged involvement with the local Ku Klux Klan, Bourland held fast and refused to answer. Exasperated, the attorney general finally requested an adjournment until Tuesday, December 27, in order to give him time to study the various statutes on whether Bourland could be compelled to answer the interrogatories.[39] He would later decide not to press the witness in this regard.[40] The end of this day's session would see the outright release of Healdton butcher John Smith by order of Freeling due to lack of evidence.[41] Likewise, the other defendants would have little more to worry about.

To the surprise of many people, Tuesday's court session brought the preliminary hearing to an abrupt end. Along with releasing Rev. Leon Julius and John Murray, Freeling ordered all other defendants to be held on a bond of $10,000 each to await trial at the January term of court.[42] The Wilson defendants had nothing to fear from the court process, however. They would see their various cases delayed and nolle prosequi'd through multiple court terms until, eventually, all gained their outright release. No one would ever stand trial for the deadly shoot-out at Wilson.[43]

Before the case could cool down to any measurable degree, certain developments stoked the fires again on December 29 and 30. The first of these proved to be a pair of statements issued by Walter Carroll in reference to which the *Ardmore Statesman* quipped they "had a decided flavor of liquid inspiration."[44] On December 29 Carroll issued a statement witnessed by Wilson businessman W. E. J. Wren and *Wilson Gazette* editor Jesse Lewis and published in the *Gazette*. In part of this presentment, probably prepared by Wren and Lewis, Carroll made a denial that he could identify any of the men involved in his brother Joe's death.[45]

The next day Carroll experienced a change of heart. Traveling to Ardmore the twitchy bootlegger (or former bootlegger as he wished everyone to believe) repudiated his first signed statement. "The testimony I gave in the trial of the men charged with killing my brother is absolutely true . . . " Carroll backtracked. "I never stated that notwithstanding any former statement I may have made that I cannot identify any person or persons who were in any way connected with the above mentioned shooting affair at Wilson in which my brother, Joe Carroll, was killed."[46] Since he was reported as looking "unshaven and very nervous from the events of the past two weeks,"[47] many people likely passed off Walter Carroll as a man out to save his own hide. There was a good chance, however, that he was indeed being harassed and intimidated by members of the Klan hoping to dissuade him from testifying against their brothers in the Wilson killings.

The second item to set Carter County tongues wagging was the parting salvo of C. G. Sims's brother, Claude Sims, before his bowing out of the scene and return to Wichita, Kansas. In the *Daily Ardmoreite* of December 30, Sims lambasted Buck Garrett, Bud Ballew, and the rest of the county sheriff's department. Sims began:

> "I write these facts without question, direction or suggestion
> of any man or woman and with positive knowledge that it is at the
> risk of my life."

He then waded in:

> "Under natural conditions I would have turned to your law and
> officers for investigation, but as my brother was killed in the county
> instead of the city I found the county officials and sheriff's force had
> charge of all investigations. Before I reached your city, while yet on
> the train, I was forewarned through general comment of the incident
> (the Wilson gun battle); my informants not knowing that I was in any
> way related to C. G. Sims, or knowing who I was, said that there was
> a tough bunch in charge of your county affairs."

Sims went on to declare that he knew he had no hope of ever getting justice for the life of his brother. "In this charge," the newspaper stated, "he names the county attorney, assistant county attorney, justice of the peace, the sheriff and his force."

Sims did not save all of his invective for the county officials. He also vented his spleen against Attorney General Freeling for not taking into consideration his own investigations and "permitting armed men at the door of the court room during the preliminary trial last week." Of the city police Sims ranted, "They either belong to the same element, or have not nerve enough to be called men if they allow such to go on." No one, it seemed, could escape the obviously bitter man's wrath.

Despite the fact of his having enough bile for everyone, Claude Sims gave a special dose to Bud Ballew in his final declaration to the folks of Carter County. Sims alleged that during the Wilson preliminary hearing Deputy Sheriff Ballew visited the hotel room of Prince Freeling carrying with him a satchel containing bottles of whiskey. Sims further alleged that following his visit with Freeling, Ballew spotted a man, said to have been involved in the Wilson affair, in the hotel lobby. "Hey Ku Klux!" the deputy called out, inviting the man to have a drink with him. With that Ballew apparently reached into his satchel, removed one of the bottles of whiskey, uncorked it, and took a long pull on the contents. When another man touched Ballew's satchel, Sims claimed, Ballew growled at the fellow not to be so free with his fingers or he would "pop a cap" under him. Sims went on to assert that the day following this incident, the deadly deputy stopped him on the street and gave him a thorough cursing out.[48]

If nothing else, the incidents show Bud Ballew to be a man of brass and gall if not subtlety and discretion. If true, the occurrences must have done little to smooth the already ruffled feathers of the state officials. With the Wilson matter already fading from the picture, the momentum it had generated continued to gain force. State representatives could not back down from their promises. The county cabal of Sheriff Garrett would be their next target.

CHAPTER 17

Ouster

As 1921 drew to a close, the allegations of corruption and protection schemes in Buck Garrett and Bud Ballew's county cabal not only continued unabated but gained pace considerably. Although no one source unequivocally supports the "dirty cop" scenario, a strong circumstantial case can be made, however misleading this may be, that something was not quite right in the county sheriff's office. One example of this is the written reminiscences of Harrell McCullough, grandson of U.S Deputy Marshall Selden Lindsey.

Harrell McCullough spent his teenage years in the late 1920s in Ardmore, Oklahoma living across the street from the family of Garrett deputy, Earl Young,[1] and his wife, Grace. Earl Young's son, Doss, and McCullough became best friends during this time. According to Mr. McCullough, at one point Doss Young revealed to him some very shocking details concerning Garrett's regime as county sheriff. Although McCullough would refuse to reveal the specifics of Young's knowledge for fear of the effect it may have had on certain living relatives, he himself termed the information "surprising."

As a small child Doss Young often accompanied his father, Deputy Sheriff Earl Young, to weekly meetings conducted by Sheriff Garrett with Bud Ballew and various other deputies. As little Doss crawled over the lap of his father, the lawmen would discuss assorted situations and problems affecting the county that particular week and their possible solutions. Although too young at that time to understand the importance of what was said, years later, during his friendship with Harrell McCullough, Doss Young remembered what was said and did understand.

In his Selden Lindsey book, McCullough revealed that prior to Buck Garrett becoming Carter County sheriff he and Lindsey had been close personal friends. After Garrett was elected to the sheriff's office, Lindsey eventually broke off their friendship. McCullough wrote that after he heard what Doss Young had to tell him years later about the workings of Garrett's office, he finally realized why his grandfather had ended his relationship with Garrett.[2]

Oklahoma Assistant Attorney General Elmer Fulton had his own strong suspicions and amassed evidence from his weeklong investigation into the doings of various Carter County officials in late 1921. On January 1, 1922, with the support of Governor Robertson and Attorney General Freeling, Fulton announced his intention of filing ouster charges in civil court against four Carter County officials.[3] The four named by Fulton proved to be Carter County Sheriff Buck Garrett; Ardmore Chief of Police W. R. "Dick" Hignight; Mayor J. H. Langston of Healdton; and Healdton Chief of Police N. A. "Lem" Bates.[4] The state was also considering charges against two additional Carter County officials, District Judge Thomas Champion and County Attorney James Mathers. These two managed to avoid the predicament of their colleagues, however, when Fulton decided his investigation did not warrant pressing charges against them.[5] Everything points to Buck Garrett being the main target of the state probe.

Prince Freeling gave his assistant free rein in the Carter County proceedings. Fulton jumped in with both feet. In an interview with the press, the assistant attorney general declared unequivocally that his investigation ". . . shows that houses have been run openly for selling liquor and for purposes of prostitution. These conditions are laid directly at the doors of those who have the enforcement of the law in their hands."[6] Quickly the county began to take sides. Although imperceptible at first, this juncture can be pinpointed as the beginning of the slow evaporation of Buck Garrett support.

From his Oklahoma City office on January 3, Fulton announced that his assistant in the upcoming prosecutions would be none other than former Carter County Attorney Russell Brown.[7] The work this implacable enemy of the Garrett regime had done in the initial investigation assured him of his place beside Fulton. No doubt Brown wished to be on hand to witness the desired toppling of the mighty sheriff. The Supreme Court appointed Judge E. D. Oldfield of the Oklahoma County Court as trial judge for the hearings scheduled for January 16.[8]

Arriving in Ardmore on the evening of the January 4, Fulton made his way to the Carter County courthouse bright and early the following morning. At 9 a.m., Thursday, the state official filed ouster petitions against Garrett, Bates, and Langston. The three were each charged with one count apiece of failure to enforce the prohibitory laws; failure to enforce gambling laws; and failure to enforce the laws prohibiting the operation of immoral resorts.[9] In addition to these charges, Fulton would add two further counts against Garrett. One dealt with a charge of assisting certain accused individuals in their criminal trials. This charge related most specifically to the case of Ernest Ford and his wife, Red Jones, and Lula Cobb in their trial of an assault against Mrs. George Casey within which Garrett had been accused of paying a portion of the Fords' legal expenses. The other additional charge against Garrett was a case of releasing certain county prisoners before the expiration of their sentences.[10]

The circumstances surrounding the absence of Ardmore Police Chief Dick Hignight in the list of accused would be a permanent dilemma for Fulton. Hignight and his direct supervisor, City Manager Kirk Dyer, contested Fulton's proposed petition on the grounds of the state lawyer's lack of jurisdiction. As Fulton himself admitted:

> "My authority is limited to filing charges against officers who fail to perform duties enjoined upon them by the laws of the state. The duties of the chief of police of Ardmore are enjoined, I find, not by statutes of Oklahoma, but by the charter of the city of Ardmore. In my tentative plans I did not reckon with the fact that Ardmore was being operated under the commission form of government."[11]

Though delayed in his decision, Fulton did decide to go ahead with ouster proceedings against Hignight by the second week of January. Hignight, however, would continue to be successful in dodging the assistant attorney general's efforts. At any rate Fulton's main task was in another arena. His power punches were to be saved for the county sheriff.

As reported in the local press, the specific petition against Garrett was a document both straightforward and revealing:

The petition against sheriff Garrett states that he became sheriff on January 1, 1921. The first count relative to the prohibitory laws states that Garrett, "willfully, knowingly and consciously failed, neglected and refused to perform his duties as sheriff of Carter County and has failed, neglected and refused to enforce the laws of the state of Oklahoma relating to the unlawful manufacture, sale, barter, giving away and otherwise furnishing of intoxicating liquor in Carter County."

The petition lists the following rooming houses as places where liquor was sold or given away in Ardmore. The Palace, the Jordan, the Travelers, The Phoenix, the Main Rooms. In Wilson, the Lunar and a place not named but operated by the Carroll brothers and Frank Jones, a gambling place known and operated by Cork Lunsford and Roy Profit in Healdton, the Ruth rooms, the Palace, the Elks, the Alemeda and a "gambling joint" over the Southern cafe. The petition says there were additional places in the towns of Dillard, Rexroat, and Wirt, all in Carter County.

The petition, under the first count, further states that there are in Carter County a large number of stills where whiskey is manufactured and lists twenty-six men alleged to be prominently engaged in the business. It is alleged that these stills were run "openly without pretense of concealment," and that their operation "was a matter of common talk and general knowledge." The petition alleges that Garrett permitted "and still permits the said persons to operate in open violation of the law."

Under the second count, relating to gambling, it is alleged that "almost continuously since his (Garrett's) induction into office, men with the common and general reputation of gamblers have openly conducted in diverse places . . . games of poker, roulette, craps and other banking and percentage games."

A number of these places are listed.

The third count against Garrett concerns the alleged attack on Mrs. Casey and lists the attackers, besides Mrs. Ford, Mrs. Lulu Cobb and "Red" Jones. It relates that when an intent to kill was filed against the defendants in the case, it became the duty of Garrett to assist the state in the prosecution but that "instead of so doing, said defendant and his deputy, Bud Ballew, openly advised with and assisted said defendants and in addition, thereto, said defendant (Garrett) furnished money to pay the fees," of an attorney. For this reason, the petition declares the state says Garrett "has been guilty of official mis-conduct and has willfully failed and neglected diligently and faithfully to perform the duties enjoined upon him by the law and should therefore be removed from his said office."

The fourth count charges that during Garrett's tenure of office there have been in operation "large numbers of houses of prostitution, run openly and notoriously to the extent that it was a matter of common talk and public knowledge."[12]

Despite all of this the attorney general's office stated that no evidence of criminal corruption had been found during the investigation into Garrett's conduct.[13] The prosecution would thus leave this angle alone and attempt to gain a victory with the lawman's removal from office on the civil court charges.

In an interview with the *Daily Ardmoreite,* Garrett expressed his opinions with the tone of a persecuted man.

"The only thing I regret," Garrett said, "is that charges have been filed or contemplated against any other officer in Carter County. I feel that the whole works was aimed at me, and I want to take all the blame, if there is any blame to be placed." Continued the beleaguered sheriff, "A lot of people will believe me guilty anyhow, and have always blamed me for everything that has happened, and a lot that never took place, so why need they bring in others at this time? It would please me a whole lot better if they had left others out of this."[14]

Garrett's attempt at martyrdom would have no effect on the attorney general's office.

Another interview in the same issue of the *Ardmoreite* would create a mini-controversy in the midst of the sensational developments. In answer to an inquiry regarding the relationship between himself and Sheriff Garrett, the paper quoted Police Chief Dick Hignight as stating "that he and the sheriff always co-operated with each other, and any statement to the contrary was wrong."[15]

Perhaps wishing to distance himself from the sinking ship that was the Garrett regime, Hignight felt compelled to release a signed statement to the following day's issue of the *Daily Ardmoreite*:

> I deny emphatically that I said Sheriff Garrett and I always co-operated together.
>
> Moreover, I gave out no interview whatever Thursday regarding the matter and have made it a point to refrain from making any statements for publication.
>
> I am sorry to have to break into print, but it is the only way I can get the matter right.
>
> I have said in the past that I had always co-operated and had received co-operation from some members of Sheriff Garrett's force, but as for giving the impression that all had been well between the sheriff's office and the city police office, I had no such intention.
>
> I want the *Ardmoreite* to quote me as re-affirming the statement made at the first mass meeting, which is my position in the matter exactly. That stands.[16]

This statement made by Hignight only confirmed most people's belief in the discord between the city and county law enforcement organizations.

Through his bevy of no less than fifteen attorneys, which included J. B. Champion and Guy Segler, Buck Garrett filed his answer to the ouster charges on January 6 and expressed himself ready to stand trial while denying all accusations.[17] Hignight, Langston, and Bates followed suit on January 10, and likewise denied all charges filed against them. [18] In his usual modes operandi, Garrett expressed his desire for a speedy trial. [19] Judge Oldfield granted this request when he scheduled the sheriff's hearing to commence on January 16. [20] Although slightly delayed by the legal wrangling of both sides, Buck Garrett's fate would be decided by mid-February.

On Tuesday, January 17, Elmer Fulton appeared before Judge Oldfield with a motion that Garrett be suspended from office pending his upcoming trial. Oldfield sustained the motion. After a committee of Carter County civic and church representatives failed to agree on Garrett's temporary replacement, Garrett attorneys, along with Fulton and Russell Brown, jointly recommended a young Ardmore insurance agent named Ewing London. A veteran of World War I and commander of Ardmore's George R. Anderson Post, American Legion, London had the respect and good will of most people in Carter County. At first reluctant to accept the appointment, London finally yielded to pressure from all sides in the affair. [21]

On Thursday, January 19, Ewing London became the new sheriff of Carter County. [22] Meant to be only a temporary appointment until the outcome of Buck Garrett's ouster trial was known, the reluctant law officer quickly warmed to the job and showed signs of wishing to make it a more permanent position. That morning at 9 a.m., by order of the court, all Garrett deputy sheriffs were required to resign their commissions at the sheriff's office.[23] Bud Ballew's state of mind must have been in a turmoil of anger and despair as he, along with Bill Ward, Earl Young, Horace Kendall, and all of Garrett's other deputies, handed in their commissions to London that morning.

That same afternoon London appointed his own deputy-sheriff force consisting of Undersheriff Ernest I. McCann and Deputy Sheriffs Robert P. Short, Thomas Smith, George White, Oscar Johnson, E. J. Cowles, and Dave Wright. Joe Kemp and C. F. McComas received appointments as day-shift jailers. Jailers on the night shift would be J. A. Nicholson and Van Worley.[24] While delving into the intricacies of former Sheriff Garrett's books and ledger reports, the new sheriff also issued an order:

> To all persons holding special commissions as Deputy Sheriffs, or permits to carry arms:

Under the order of the court appointing me sheriff, pro tem, all commissions were revoked.

I hereby request all men holding county commissions to see me at once about their renewals.

E. C. London,

Sheriff.[25]

Following much wrangling over jury selection,[26] Buck Garrett's ouster trial finally got under way before Judge E. D. Oldfield in the Carter County courthouse at Ardmore on February 7. That same day, in an unrelated but surprising move that shocked many people in Oklahoma, Attorney General Prince Freeling tendered his resignation to the governor in order to represent certain interests before the Supreme Court in Washington, D.C., in the so-called "Red River Boundary" case.[27] Garrett put his fate in the hands of his army of legal talent, with a jury consisting of D. M. Langley, John Heartsill, and W. R. Palmer of Lone Grove; H. Hammond, Henry Lloyd, F. L. Blackburn, Will Farthing, and J. E. Cruce of Ardmore; J. S. Reed of Wilson; J. W. Cleventer of Reck; G. C. Porter of Brock; and J. L. Berryhill of Berwyn.[28]

With the local citizenry packing the courtroom to a standing-room-only capacity, the preliminaries of the first day paled in comparison to what was to follow. On February 8, federal Prohibition officers P. E. Brents, C. F. Buzzi, and J. J. Sims, along with various deputy sheriffs from Stevens and Comanche Counties testified concerning the raid near Tatum in December 1921, which resulted in the seizure of a number of stills and illicit whiskey.[29] At one point one of the lawmen quoted one of the individuals arrested on that occasion as saying, "Mr. Garrett left the impression that they would not be bothered."[30]

A sensation ran through the courtroom during the questioning of a resident of the town of Dillard relative to the number of drinking and gambling establishments allowed in the city. The witness related that "he had seen Bud Ballew and Bill Ward, deputy sheriffs of the county frequent these places, and that the operators of the joints were their associates."[31] As for Garrett, however, he had never seen him around any of these places.

A further ripple of excitement ran through the court with the testimony of George Deems, Creed Fraley, Pete Smith, and Dave Wright, all former members of the Ardmore Police Department. Apparently the quartet had been involved in a raid on the Jordan Rooming House on East Broadway in the fall of 1921. The patrolmen said they were confronted in one of the rooms by Deputy Sheriff Earl Young, who sported a drawn revolver and ordered them from the scene claiming he was in charge of the situation.[32] The sensational testimony of Gus Key concerning his various bootlegging activities with apparent impunity in and around Carter County capped the day's hearings.[33]

The following day the press of the crowd in the courtroom to witness proceedings had not diminished in the slightest. Former Garrett deputies continued to come under fire for their conduct during the trial's third day. This time it would be Horace Kendall's turn to take the heat. According to one J. L. Warburton, a traveling salesman for the Pennington Grocery Company, whose duties demanded that he visit the various joints in Dillard, Healdton, and other towns in the oil fields, he often witnessed Deputy Kendall drinking and gambling in the dives.

While various witnesses testified to the openness of the liquor, gambling, and prostitution business throughout the county, one, Dr. O. R. Gregg of Rexroat, also zeroed in on Kendall. As the *Daily Ardmoreite* told it:

> He was called to a place (in Dillard) which had been termed a bawdy house to treat a woman. When he arrived he said Horace Kendall and another were there with the woman.
>
> One of them was wanting to put hot water on the woman's stomach, while the other was wanting to put cold water on her stomach, the doctor said.[34]

The fact of whether Kendall was the hot-water or cold-water man and the merits of his doctor skills was a moot point. The tactic of Fulton and the prosecution was to paint Garrett's deputies, and through them Garrett himself, as frequenters and supporters of the criminal element in Carter County.

That afternoon Fulton brought the questioning around to the workings of the sheriff's office. Assistant Carter County Attorney John Hodge was forced to admit that one prisoner, a bootlegger named W. B. Wright, had been released from the county jail by Garrett prior to the expiration of his sentence following the order of county physician, Dr. J. C. McNeese.[35]

On hearing this testimony, Judge Oldfield interjected, "This was assuming too much authority. That the governor alone had the authority to pardon prisoners when they had been sentenced by a court."[36]

This would weigh heavily upon the jurors and may have eventually played a major part in the outcome of the hearings.

The testimony of current Sheriff Ewing London further damaged Garrett. According to London's perusal of the jail records, there should have been forty-five prisoners behind bars at the time of his takeover. In actuality only thirty-three inmates were there to greet London when he took over the office.[37] As London put it, "some of the missing men are still unaccounted for."[38]

The testimony of Friday, February 10, continued in the same vein under the direction of the state attorneys, the prosecution attempting to show that illegal joints ran wide open throughout Carter County without any interference from Buck Garrett and his deputy force. At one point Garrett attorney J. B. Champion attempted to discredit one of the state's witnesses and show his prejudice by asking the man, Rupert E. Martin, Healdton building contractor, if he were not a member of the Ku Klux Klan, sworn enemies of Garrett. "I am," Martin answered, the first time anyone had freely admitted to such membership in Carter County court.[39]

Again the beleaguered Horace Kendall became the focus of the proceedings. Various witnesses swore that Kendall had been in charge of a stud poker game in the gambling rooms over the Southern Cafe at Healdton during his tenure as a deputy sheriff. Another witness testified to having seen Sheriff Garrett hanging around in front of the Southern and other known illegal establishments. Bud Ballew and Bill Ward again came in for their share of the spotlight when Rupert Martin swore to having seen them drinking in Jack Farrar's booze and gambling parlor in Dillard. Under cross-examination from Champion, Martin admitted, "He did not know the contents of the receptacles from which they were drinking."[40]

With the close of testimony on February 10, the state rested its case. It would now be the defense's turn to attempt an effective rebuttal to the damning testimony of the past four days. Elmer Fulton was determined not to make it easy on the opposition. With the beginning of the defense case on February 13, Fulton began a routine of objecting to almost every question put forward by Garrett's legal council.[41] As the trial bogged down to a snail's pace, Garrett's attorneys pressed on.

Witnesses such as Assistant County Attorney John Hodge, Wilson merchant M. J. Carrigan and Gilmer Oil Company superintendent W. H. Dawson spoke of the general good conduct and efficiency of Garrett's force. At one point Dawson mentioned that, as far as he knew, the laws in Ragtown were generally enforced. In his testimony he gave out that once or twice a year cock fights were held in Ragtown. Under cross-examination from Fulton, Dawson said, "I do not believe a law covering chicken fights could be found on the statutes."[42]

This provoked a smile from Fulton as he returned to his seat.

The next day the defense carried on in its attempt to show that Garrett and his department did their best at enforcing the various laws. One witness, store owner E. W. Davis of Wilson, testified that Bud Ballew and Bill Ward brought prisoners before the local Wilson justice of the peace "almost every morning."[43] The following day Garrett's beleaguered former deputies were called to his defense. Bud Ballew, Bill Whitson, Earl Young, Gus Gaines, and Jim Carter all spoke of their enforcement of the laws in Carter County, Whitson claiming, "Garrett had instructed all of his men to go after the law violators and 'give them hell.'"[44]

One witness, O. C. Orr, provoked a round of laughter from the spectators when he claimed that Wirt was devoid of illegal establishments through most of 1921.[45] It was almost impossible for the citizens of Carter County to believe in a sanitized Ragtown.

As Buck Garrett's trial entered its last day of testimony on February 16, at least one other Carter County official could breathe easier to be out of the mess. Healdton Mayor J. H. Langston had announced his resignation that morning. In response, Elmer Fulton decreed that the charges against Langston would be dropped upon the receipt of the necessary paperwork.[46]

In the meantime Garrett's ordeal continued. That Thursday morning the defense team resumed its usual tactics with former under sheriff George Leeman, suspended jailer William Bishop, District Judge Thomas Champion, and County Judge Millard F. Winfrey giving their testimony. The most pertinent information may have been elicited in the questioning of Bishop concerning the release of certain prisoners. In reporting Bishop's attempted explanation the *Daily Ardmoreite* wrote:

> Jailor Bishop testified that four men were released by him, one white man and three Negroes. He also stated that two men, whom it is charged were released without authority were serving time and were trusties at the time the new sheriff took charge of affairs. He named the men.
>
> The three Negroes were released on orders of the county attorney, Bishop said. He said that he left the jail at 4 o'clock on the afternoon of January 19th and while Sheriff London had been to the jail he had not counted the prisoners. [47]

The jury would prove hard to convince on this point.

The defense of Buck Garrett finally concluded just before noon with the placing on the witness stand of Garrett himself. In his own defense the former sheriff denied all charges against him and attempted to explain away the various points brought forward during the course of the trial by the prosecution.[48] Though his final pleas may have had some effect on the jurymen, it would not be enough to save the harassed lawman.

Following a final rebuttal by the state, both sides decided to wave final arguments. The case finally went to the jury late on the afternoon of Thursday, February 16.[49] Deliberating overnight, the jury panel returned to the courtroom at 10:30 a.m. Friday. Before a sparse crowd, many spectators having yet to arrive at the courthouse following the disappointment of the jury not returning the day before, the court body presented its verdict. On the counts of failure to enforce the prohibitory laws, failure to enforce the gambling laws and failure to enforce the laws regarding so-called "immoral resorts,"[50] the jury found Garrett not guilty. On the charge of releasing prisoners before their terms had expired, the jury returned a verdict of guilty. Although he was found guilty on only the one count, it was enough. That Friday morning, February 17, 1922, Buck Garrett was ousted as Carter County sheriff.[51]

Of the four men brought up on ouster charges, Buck Garrett would be the only one convicted. The Monday following his conviction, the case against

Chief of Police Dick Hignight went before a jury in Carter County court. Despite the negative evidence of self-declared "former bootlegger" Gus Key, in which Key accused Hignight and his now dead former partner, Dow Braziel, of various protection schemes and payoffs, a verdict of not guilty was returned against him after a two-day trial.[52] With the charges against Healdton City Marshal Lem Bates having been dropped on February 16 following his resignation from office,[53] that left Buck Garrett the only convicted official. All things considered, Assistant Attorney General Elmer Fulton, Special Prosecutor Russell Brown, and everyone in the state attorney general's office most likely felt this lone conviction a successful outcome of the entire proceedings. Getting Buck Garrett out of the sheriff's office had, after all, been the primary goal.

Though he was the object of the wrath of the state of Oklahoma and various political enemies in Carter County, Buck Garrett professed himself as happy concerning the outcome. The *Daily Ardmoreite* reported at the conclusion of the court process:

> In speaking of the verdict which resulted in his forced resignation, Garrett stated that he was proud of the manner in which it resulted, pointing out that he and his department have been vindicated as far as the charges of lack of enforcement of the liquor, gambling and immoral resort laws were concerned, and have been found guilty of but one count, namely, that of permitting prisoners to come and go from the jail before their sentences had expired.
>
> Garrett stated further that he bears no ill feeling towards any of the jurors or anyone else interested in the case. "I'm glad the case resulted as it did, rather than with a hung jury," said the former official, "for vindication of the efforts of my department in the enforcement of its duties has resulted with the verdict as turned in by the jurors."[54]

Garrett's chief council, J. B. Champion, added: "None of the charges of the original petition stood up and it was only that charge that he turned prisoners loose that stuck to him. If you want to know the truth about it, Buck Garrett let those fellows out of jail through the kindness of his heart, and he knew when he did it that they would come back and finish their terms when he said the word." Champion added that he would be appealing the conviction within the next day or two. [55]

With this pronouncement by Champion of Garrett as a kind-hearted fellow perhaps acting as a campaign kickoff, the former sheriff took the opportunity to announce his intentions to run for Carter County's top law enforcement position again at the next primary.[56] It was to prove a fleeting hope on his part. Indeed, if Garrett considered the outcome of his trial as some sort of victory, it must have been a hollow one at that. When all was said and done, Buck Garrett had been ousted as sheriff. Ewing London was the new sheriff of Carter County. In fact Buck Garrett had performed his last duties as a lawman in Carter County or anywhere else. Likewise, Bud Ballew had also seen the end of his career as a law-enforcement officer.

CHAPTER 18

──Shoot-out at the Courthouse ──

With the dismissal of Buck Garrett as Carter County sheriff, the problem of who would be his permanent replacement until the next county elections now needed to be addressed. Almost immediately various groups throughout the county began lobbying for their favorite candidates. The very afternoon of Garrett's eviction from office, members of the American Legion began circulating a petition in support of sheriff pro tem Ewing London.[1] Just as quickly former Garrett deputy William Brooks, who had retired as a lawman back in early 1921 to go into the oil business, declared himself a candidate for the unexpired term.[2] Though both men had their adherents, by this time the anti-Garrett sentiment in Carter County had nearly reached its peak and it was abundantly clear that London held a wide majority of county support. As the *Ardmore Statesman* expressed it:

> The good women of the town, thru their various clubs, also the Kiwanis, Rotary and Lions Clubs, endorsed the recommendation of London. The Ministers Alliance of the city endorsed him. Legionnaires, ladies, businessmen, countrymen and men and women from practically every walk of life started out with copies of the petition and before the commissioners met on Monday, thousands of names had been added to the petitions (in favor of London).[3]

The three county commissioners under whose jurisdiction fell the dubious honor of appointing the next county sheriff to serve until the August primaries must have felt the pressure of their positions most keenly. But two of these had also unequivocally made their choices. County Commissioner Marion Pierce, a good friend of Bud Ballew, Buck Garrett, and various other former county officers, declared himself for Bill Brooks. Commissioner Roy M. Johnson, *Statesman* owner, oil millionaire, and stalwart of Ardmore business and social circles, announced himself squarely in the Ewing London camp. The one holdout, Commissioner Joe T. Taylor, professed himself undecided until the county commissioners could meet to discuss the matter.[4] The meeting was scheduled for Monday afternoon, February 20, 1922, to be held in the county commissioners' rooms on the second floor of the Carter County courthouse in Ardmore. It would be a meeting quickly overshadowed by what was to follow.

In an attempt to influence the county commissioners' decision, the London supporters, with delegations from almost every town in Carter County, met en masse in Ardmore's Convention Hall that morning. The usual speeches and harangues ended with the throng naming Mrs. Walter Young, secretary treasurer of the county Democratic Committee, as their representative "to go before the commissioners meeting at 1:30 that afternoon, and demand the appointment of London in the name of the American Legion, the women's clubs and other civic clubs that had endorsed him, as well as in the name of law, order and public decency."[5]

With the expectation that the county commissioners would appoint the permanent sheriff that afternoon, some three thousand people crowded in and around the courthouse in anticipation of developments. Even before the meeting got under way, the Ku Klux Klan again made its presence felt with the delivery of three letters, one each to commissioners Pierce, Johnson, and Taylor. Printed on official Klan stationary and signed by the "King Kleagis of Ardmore Chapter No. 7,"[6] the letters demanded that the county commissioners bow to the so-called "will of the people" and appoint London to serve the rest of Garrett's unexpired term.

"This is not time to antagonize a set of people," the letters cautioned. "The people have demanded that London be made sheriff, and you should be judged accordingly. London has made good."[7]

Despite this unexpected and somewhat threatening development, soon after the meeting commenced the commissioners came up with a surprise of their own. A letter from Assistant Attorney General Elmer Fulton was presented which was destined to disappoint almost everyone. As the *Statesman* explained it:

> [Fulton] gave it as his opinion that the commissioners should not and could not legally proceed to the appointment of a sheriff to fill out the unexpired term of Buck Garrett, because, Mr. Garrett, thru his attorneys, had moved for a new trial, and the motion would have to be disposed of by Judge Oldfield who heard the case. That until the motion was disposed of the appointee pro tem, Ewing C. London, would hold office, and there would be no vacancy. Thereupon, the commissioners adjourned to the first Monday in March, leaving things in status quo.[8]

While many people disappointedly drifted off toward their homes, many others continued to mill about the courthouse and grounds discussing these new conditions. Shortly after the adjournment of the county commissioners' meeting, Bud Ballew met Ewing London in the corridor between the county attorney's and sheriff's offices. According to witnesses, the pair engaged in a friendly conversation and walked together into the county attorney's office, closely followed by former Garrett deputy, Bill Whitson, and former jailer, Ike Byrd. County Attorney James Mathers was out of town this day and would miss what was to follow in his office.

As Ballew and London continued their casual conversation, W. T. "Skeet" Martin, Carter County livestock inspector, entered the office. Standing silently for a few minutes, Martin suddenly began to make disparaging remarks toward London.

At length Martin finally walked up to London and confronted him with, "Do you have your pistol?"

The surprised London answered, "I do not. I never carry one."

"Then," Martin snarled, "I am going to give you a damn good licking."

Tossing his own revolver onto a nearby table, Martin waded into London with fists flying. At first taken aback by the unexpected turn of events, Sheriff London quickly recovered. For a few minutes the two men traded punches in a classic one-on-one punch-up. While the fistfight progressed, someone, it was never learned who, locked the door of the county attorney's office.

All at once two pistol shots rang out. It never became public knowledge who had fired the two shots,[9] but they would prove to be the precursor of a major gun battle in the Old West tradition.

Hearing the pair of gunshots, a number of London's deputies burst forth from the sheriff's office and ran down the corridor toward the county attorney's office. In the meantime, as London would later admit, Bud Ballew jumped between the two combatants and, attempting to act as peacemaker, threw his arms around Martin, pinning Martin's arms to his sides.

To shouts of, "They are beating Ewing up!" the first two of London's deputies to arrive on the scene proved to be E. J. Cowles and Bob Short. Finding the way blocked by the locked door, Cowles smashed the glass panel on the upper half of the door with his revolver.

This proved to be the signal for a dangerous firefight to commence as all hands presented revolvers and began shooting. A number of bullets smacked into Ballew's chest. Apparently saved by his bulletproof vest, Ballew was knocked off his feet by the force of the shots. Jumping up, Ballew blazed away with his own revolver, inflicting wounds on Cowles and Short. Observers later estimated some fifteen to twenty shots flew through the air within the confines of the office. During the battle Bud Ballew received two slugs in the left leg; Bill Whitson took two bullets in the arm and a third in his leg; E. J. Cowles suffered a bullet wound to one leg and another in his foot; and Bob Short had one slug cut a furrow along one of his arms. Ike Byrd, who somehow managed to cut his finger to the bone on the glass shattered from the office door, sustained the only other injury in the melee. By some strange miracle no one had been mortally injured in the close-quarters shoot-out.[10]

As the gunfire died away and acrid gun smoke began to drift throughout the courthouse, the combatants began to make their exit from the building. The first to emerge was Ballew who stepped warily out the west door of the courthouse onto the steps. He waved his pistol above his head warning all within earshot to keep their distance. At the start of the gun battle, Buck Garrett had been standing on the sidewalk north of the courthouse. Hearing the gunfire he ran toward the courthouse and arrived just in time to meet Ballew on the west side steps after the fight.

As Garrett attempted to relieve his former deputy of his revolver Ballew yelled, "Don't take my gun; they are trying to murder me!"

Catching the tone of Ballew's exclamation and the hard glint in his piercing eyes, Garrett, perhaps for the first time, backed away from the menacing gunman allowing him to go on his way. Warily scanning the surrounding area, Ballew hobbled some half a block to the Hardy Sanitarium to attain treatment for his leg wounds. Slowly, singly and in pairs, the other wounded gunfighters followed him to the hospital. Skeet Martin managed to make himself scarce.[11]

The county attorney's office showed the ravages of the battle that had played out within its walls. According to the *Ardmoreite*:

> Blood spots make a shaky path from the front of the door into the big outer room of the county attorney's office, and many persons have been following up this to hedge a possible conclusion. The officers are disregarding the blood spots on the floor.

BULLET HOLES ARE INSIDE

> *Five defined bullet holes have been located thus far, and four of them are in the door of the office, ranging from the inside.*
>
> *One bullet hole is through the glass facing on the right side of the door about 13 or 14 inches from the floor. Two are in the right facing, about three and a half feet up, going straight through, and the other glancing in the side. A fourth bullet hole is found almost in the center of the door, a few inches below the glass, while the fifth is in the left wall of the room, and apparently glanced.*[12]

Six additional bullet holes would be discovered later, three more in the office and three in the walls of the corridor outside.[13] It is likely that more than one of these shots fired toward the door from the inside came from the revolver of Ballew shooting at Cowles and Short.

The courthouse gun battle had various repercussions in Ardmore. The most immediate of these came in the postponement of Police Chief Dick Hignight's ouster trial. Although the trial was in progress the very day of the imbroglio, it was decided to suspend proceedings to the following day due to "the effect that the situation created by the shooting was such as demanded the attention of the chief on the streets for duty."[14]

The following day the county attorney's office contemplated its first actions in light of the affair. Once again displaying his waning interest in the position, his lack of good health, or both, exasperated James Mathers initially turned the entire investigation over to his assistant, John Hodge.[15] Hodge, though intimating that charges may be filed in the affair, reserved judgment until he could meet with Sheriff London.[16] By Wednesday February 22, Mathers, unable to dodge the press, gave out to a reporter for the *Daily Ardmoreite* that he would be seeking a "compromise" in the case. In his view of the situation the county attorney had decided, "The shooting was caused by (a) 'mistaken conclusion' of Deputy Sheriff Cowles, who is said to have fired the first shot through the door . . . No charges have been filed to date, and it is doubtful whether any will be filed, (Mathers) said."[17]

This would be James Mathers's last word on the subject, or indeed, on any official subject dealing with Carter County. One day later, on Thursday, February 23, a tired and disgusted James Mathers tendered his resignation as Carter County attorney to Oklahoma Attorney General George Short.[18] On March 6, 1922, a well-known Carter County lawyer named J. E. Bristow would replace him.[19]

By Thursday everything seemed to have calmed down somewhat, the *Statesman* editorializing:

> As this is written (Thursday afternoon) peace reigns and things are entirely normal. All of the injured are said to be "getting along as well as could be expected,' all but Whitson and Cowles having returned to their homes. Ballew is said to be suffering considerably from his wounds, but is at his home in Wilson. Short was not

hurt enough to put him off duty. Byrd's finger is said to be doing well, and what became of Martin is occasioning but little concern.[20]

The Statesman tempered this bit of optimism by ending with the cautionary sentence, "The next chapter will be written when the players get into action again."[21] For, in Carter County, one never knew.

Despite the seeming lack of interest in the whereabouts of Skeet Martin, he would be the only one to face any sort of charges in the courthouse battle. On February 23 the belligerent "tick inspector" appeared in county court to face a charge of assault and battery resulting from his attack on London. Found guilty, he received a fine of $50, which he promptly paid and gained his release.[22]

All the wounded in the February 20 shoot-out would eventually make a full recovery. Bob Short, his injury being the least serious, returned to duty the day following the fight.[23] Deputy Sheriff Cowles was released from the Hardy Sanitarium three or four days after being shot.[24] He would return to duty by March 9, though sporting a pronounced limp from his injuries.[25] Perhaps the most seriously injured, Bill Whitson would spend two weeks in the hospital. There was some fear at first that his arm, broken by one of the slugs, might have to be amputated. The healing process took over, however, and on March 8 he gained his release from the sanitarium to further convalesce at his home in the country near Ardmore.[26] At length he too would be up and around again.

But Bud Ballew was not having an easy time of it with his serious and painful leg wounds. Released from the Hardy Sanitarium a few days after the gun battle, probably as a result of his insistence to be allowed to go home, Ballew continued his recovery under the care of Fannie at the couple's home in Wilson. After two weeks he continued to have problems when a painful abscess formed in his wounded thigh.[27] Still, it could have been worse for Ballew. According to certain eyewitnesses to the courthouse firefight, he probably owed his life to his ever-present "steel jacket" or bulletproof vest. Again, according to further eyewitnesses present in the hospital immediately after the fight, when Ballew removed his upper garments the "bullets dropped out of his clothes 'like buckshot out of a bucket.' Although none of the bullets penetrated the steel jacket, the force was sufficient to knock him down . . ."[28] Once again the innovative vest had proved its worth. Leg wounds could eventually heal. Chest wounds would have been infinitely more serious.

With the arrival of early March, three weeks after the ouster proceedings against Garrett, the ex-sheriff had yet to file a petition for a new trial.[29] Though this would eventually come to pass, for the time being Garrett bided his time and held his counsel. Other matters temporarily took precedent. The Garrett-Ballew duo had moved on to other fields of endeavor.

At this point in their lives both Buck Garrett and Bud Ballew needed a legitimate reason to carry firearms. Both men had made far too many enemies in their respective law-enforcement careers to be caught in some dark corner without weapons of protection. Partly as a result of this need, soon after being removed as sheriff, Garrett formed the Southwestern Anti Car Thief Association, with himself as president and Ballew as his main operative.[30] With this quasi-official enforcement group behind them and the collusion of the properly placed state officials, the pair was able to obtain legal permits to carry firearms. There was also talk the two former lawmen were recruited by former Oklahoma City mayor and budding gubernatorial candidate John Calloway "Jack" Walton as muscle for his alleged strong-arm squad.[31] Such has been suggested, but Walton would not be elected governor until January 6, 1923. Much would have changed by then.

The forced confinement of over a month while his bullet wounds healed could not have been a pleasant experience for the usually active and gregarious Ballew. Even the local newspapers seemed to miss reporting on his interesting and unpredictable doings, prompting the *Ardmore Statesman* to comment:

> Ever since the shootfest in the county attorney's office several weeks ago, when Bud Ballew was shot in the thigh and laid up for a month or so, he has failed to figure very importantly in the news columns of the local papers. But he is now out and getting around nicely.[32]

Just how nicely manifested itself in an incident that took place in Healdton on Monday, April 24. As it happened Ballew got word that a gang of men had been arrested by the Healdton police on a charge of loitering. With the trial slated to come off this particular Monday, the slightly limping Ballew decided to pay a visit to the justice of the peace court to witness proceedings.[33] Almost unquestionably, he partook of some liquid refreshments before he ventured forth to the place of trial, taking his seat near the jurors' box.

At this point the *Statesman* picks up the story:

> The testimony seemed to rouse the ex-deputy's risibles, and his sonorous laugh resounded thru [the] courtroom and surrounding community with old time resonance. The local dailies report that these vocal expressions of amusement so got on the nerves of the court and jury that the case was dismissed, and the ubiquitous Bud wandered forth into the streets where he mounted his gasoline Pegasus and proceeded to "take in the town' and afford excitement by bombarding the air with his .45.
>
> On being informed of the facts and appealed to for succor, our new county attorney, Judge Bristow, wended his way toward the oil metropolis to find out the whys of the wherefore. As this is written he has not returned to his office in the courthouse, and no word has come in from him. However, the Wednesday morning paper tells of Bud having called at Wilson Tuesday morning and "got funny with his gun," and that later in the day he returned to town and coughed up $20.00 as compensation for the pastime.
>
> One of the attaches of the Ringling railroad told the *Statesman* of another entertainment—or encore—Bud pulled off. Monday evening after having laughed the case out of court at Healdton, he evidently started for his home, but his car stuck in the mud. Not being able to get 'er goin' again, he leaned back in the seat, took a nap until some one came along and pulled him out, leaving him to snooze on by the roadside. Evidently he waked up for the next morning he was doing things at Wilson.[34]

With Bud up and around again things could now get back to a state of normalcy in Carter County. What a difference eleven days would make—the difference between life and the end of an era.

E. C. London Sheriff of Carter County and his department, circa 1920

1915 explosion, Ardmore, Oklahoma

Ardmore Police Chief Bob Hutchins *(on left with pipe)* and unidentified people

Sidney Suggs, owner and
publisher of the *Daily
Ardmoreite*, circa 1934

Main Street, Ardmore, 1913

Buck Garrett, Chief of Police, Ardmore, Oklahoma

Ardmore officers on horseback, circa 1911: Roy Thorton *(third from left)*, Bob Rodgers *(fourth from left)*, and Dow Braziel *(fifth from left)*

The former Denver Hotel building in Wichita Falls, Texas, is now the Somewhere in Time Antique Mall.

The present-day upstairs level of the Denver Hotel building shows rooms where Bud Ballew stayed on the night he was killed.

Present-day photo of Ballew home at Lone Grove, Oklahoma

Bud Ballew monument in Lone Grove, Oklahoma, cemetery

CHAPTER 19

——— Victim–Bud Ballew ———

Death was far from the mind of Bud Ballew this early May 1922. He had survived another near-fatal encounter in the courthouse gunfight of February 20. It has been argued that each successive shoot-out produced a stronger sense of invincibility in the veteran gunman's mind. Although he apparently often talked of wishing to "pass out with his boots on,"[1] he may have thought that day would never come.

Though Ballew most likely begrudged the loss of his deputy sheriff's commission he was not financially strapped by any means. His ranching operation at Lone Grove, comprising three sections of a total of over 332 acres on which he ran hundreds of horses and cattle, both for himself and others, had been a paying operation for years. His fine-bred Durham cattle were considered of the highest quality.[2] Ranching was not his only source of income. He had also taken advantage of the oil boom and made considerable money buying and selling various oil leases.[3] Though working as a lawman along with Buck Garrett had been his first love, he was now definitely financially able to pursue a sidekick-free course along with his wife Fannie and son Dorris. There was also time for amusement.

May was rodeo time in The Falls. Just as today, when the folks of Ardmore wished to get away to the "big city" many headed straight south ninety miles to the twin metropolises of Dallas/Fort Worth. However, those people who wished a change of pace but also the same down home flavor as Ardmore itself, with the same excitement of a growing, lively community, would travel some seventy-five miles southwest to the city of Wichita Falls, Texas. Like Ardmore, by the mid teens The Falls had exploded in the throes of a raucous oil boom. Cashing in on the same bonanza that struck nearby Burkburnett, by 1919 the city was home to some of the largest-producing oil wells in the country where tracts of land were selling for as much as $25,000 an acre.[4] As one contemporary source described it:

> While there seems to be an ebb and flow in the crowded condition of this city there is nothing in the building activity that indicates a decline of the wave of prosperity that is lifting Wichita Falls out of class of a county seat towns (*sic*) and sweeping it on to the class of a thriving, ever-growing city. In all parts of the business district substantial buildings are being moved or razed to make room for skyscrapers, or other modern buildings.
>
> Wichita Falls is surrounded by tent towns. In one quarter there are 75 or more army tents pitched so that it resembles an army camp. Everywhere you go, in the outskirts of the city, are tents and board shacks of every description. Tents that have been circus tents, side show tents, teepees, everything imaginable; big and little. Even wagons and autos are used for sleeping quarters. And yet, the hotel and rooming house keepers, when you ask for a room look at you with scorn and grunt "full up." Big new rooming houses are planned, and some of them have been started . . .
>
> Crowds of men and women visit the oil exchanges here day and night, where they buy and sell stocks in the various companies organized here. Some of these stocks sell for five and six for one, and the same stocks are traded back and forth every day.[5]

Wichita Falls had deeper connections for Bud Ballew. A pair of his distant relatives, William and Dave Ballew, uncles of early Ardmore gunman Bill Ballew, were two of the earliest settlers of the community in the early 1880s along with such men as Judge Thomas Barwise, merchants Thomas Williams and John Converse, blacksmith F. M. Wattenburger, and Dr. E. J. Perego. Dave

Ballew and Tom Williams operated one of the first stores on Wichita Falls' historic Ohio Avenue as early as 1881.[6] Bud's own uncle, Joseph Ufrates Ballew, the sixth son of Harvey and Pernette Ballew, along with his wife, Martha Ann Cundiff Ballew, and their children, were permanent residents of Wichita Falls. The couple would live and die in the city being buried there in 1933 and 1947 respectively.[7]

In late April 1922, organizers of the fourth annual Wichita Falls Round-Up, led by Tom Burnett and managed by famous rodeo personality Fred M. "Foghorn" Clancy, invited Bud Ballew to appear as one of their special guests at the three-day affair scheduled to begin Wednesday, May 3. While invited to serve as a judge at some of the rodeo events, Ballew and his eighteen-year-old son, Dorris, also took the opportunity to enter some of the roping and riding contests.[8] Bud may have decided this would be a perfect excuse to leave the strife of Carter County behind for a few days of fun and frolic in The Falls. He may also have intended to pay a visit to his uncle Joe and aunt Martha while in the Texas city.

Thus, with Fannie Ballew deciding to visit relatives at Nash, Oklahoma,[9] while her men were away rodeoing, Bud and Dorris, along with their friend from Healdton, Bert Tucker, set out for Wichita Falls on Tuesday, May 2. Bud planned to meet his former fellow deputies, Bill Whitson and Horace Kendall, at the Texas city the following day.[10]

By the time of Ballew's arrival Tuesday afternoon, Wichita Falls presented a carnival atmosphere as cowboys, hucksters, various hangers-on, and hundreds of visitors roamed the streets and sidewalks. Despite the rainy conditions, a number of special events were held Tuesday as a kickoff to the roundup. One of these was the arrival of cowgirl Nan J. Aspinwall after a thirteen-and-a-half-day horseback ride across Texas from her Laredo home. A large throng headed by a welcoming committee of city dignitaries, rodeo officials, and newly hired Chief of Police J. W. McCormick met the young lady at the city limits and escorted her to rodeo headquarters. Although her "horse was lame and she was a tired young woman . . . glad that the journey was over,"[11] she also appeared proud of her accomplishment of endurance.

The next days' *Wichita Daily Times* proudly proclaimed the headline: "Big Crowd Attends As This City's Fourth Round Up Is Opened."[12] With the clouds having subsided and the sun presenting a warm glow over the grandstand, a standing-room-only crowd was on hand to enjoy the first day's events. Preceding the first competitive event, a number of dignitaries and special guests were introduced to the audience. When it came Bud Ballew's turn, the announcer presented the ex-lawman as "the man who stuck by Garrett through thick and thin and who is glad he did!"[13]

It may be safe to speculate that in Bud Ballew's mind no truer words were ever spoken.

The first day's events proved a rousing success, both for the cowboys and cowgirls participating as well as for the enthusiastic spectators who were given some expert performances and some thrills and spills to gasp over. In the bronc riding, Dave White on Triangle Paint and Kenneth Cooper aboard Headlight gave the crowd their money's worth. Cowboy Ben Johnson scored the fastest time in calf roping with a mark of thirty-one seconds. Though Slim Caskey, a good friend of Bud Ballew, and Roy Quick disappointed in the bulldogging, there was other excitement in store for the crowd. Future silent movie stunt man and cowboy actor Yakima Canutt gave a rise to the throng when the steer he attempted to throw broke away and charged the arena fence, almost smashing into the stands. Quick managed to get trampled while Dick Kirnan broke the horn off his steer causing the animal to bleed profusely. Many in the crowd thought the cowboy had been badly gored until they realized that the blood covering the arena floor belonged to the steer and not Kirnan. When all was said and done, Fred Atkinson managed to come out on top, tying his steer in a time of thirteen and two-fifths seconds.[14] More entertainment of the same style would follow on Thursday and Friday before large, enthusiastic crowds. The results of Bud Ballew's sorties into the arena are not of record. As usual it would be his extracurricular activities that would draw attention and overshadow the final day's events.

As usual where large crowds of humanity gather in search of entertainment and frivolity, the Wichita Falls police had their hands full with assorted ne'er-do-wells. In the period between Thursday and Friday mornings the lawmen, led by Wichita Falls Chief of Police J. W. McCormick, made a total of sixty-eight arrests of various thieves, vagrants, pickpockets, and prostitutes. The local press called it "the busiest day and night the department has had since the boomdays."[15] In one raid alone Chief McCormick, accompanied by Night Sergeant Bebout, City Detectives Shook, Johnson, and Belcher and Texas Ranger Koonsman, managed to collar twenty-one offenders in a local hotel. The raid boosted city coffers by $465 in paid fines.[16]

McCormick was no novice when it came to law enforcement and was well able to handle the extra work brought by rodeo week in Wichita Falls. Having enlisted on March 27, 1920, in Texas Ranger Company B under Captain Tom Hickman, McCormick rose to the rank of sergeant in the state force.[17] Not known strictly as a gunman, he had been forced to use his gun on occasion to quell bad men. On one particular instance he had been compelled to shoot a bootlegger in a successful attempt to prevent the man's escape during a raid in the oil fields near Wichita Falls.[18] Luckily for the bootlegger, he survived his wound and had his day in court. Ranger Captain R. W. Aldredge, in charge of the headquarters company at the state capitol in Austin, would speak of McCormick as a "fearless, upright man and in every word a gentleman."[19]

McCormick wished to further his law enforcement career. Offered the post of chief of the Wichita Falls police force in late April 1922, Texas Ranger Sergeant McCormick received his discharge from the Rangers on April 23.[20] Almost immediately the ex-Ranger began his service to the people of Wichita Falls. At the time of the May 1922 rodeo, he had been in the police chief's office for fewer than two weeks.[21]

There is reason to believe that McCormick, or more likely his former captain in the rangers, Tom Hickman,[22] felt there was a strong possibility of some sort of trouble with Bud Ballew sometime during the course of the Wichita Falls Round-Up. Sometime on Tuesday or Wednesday McCormick accompanied Hickman to rodeo headquarters. Though McCormick had never met Bud Ballew, Hickman was acquainted with the fast-shooting Oklahoman. At length Hickman found the opportunity to introduce the police chief to Ballew. The two men shook hands "but nothing was said beyond the formal words of greeting."[23] This was most likely an opportunity for Hickman, perhaps at the request of McCormick, to allow the chief to recognize Ballew in the future in case of possible trouble. On their next meeting McCormick would have no difficulty in instantly recognizing the stout, redheaded former deputy.

According to an old rodeo performer named E. M. "Nevada Dick"

Dickey, who got the details from Foghorn Clancy, himself a participant in the events, Ballew was in his usual jocular mood while attending the Wichita Falls rodeo. Apparently Tom Hickman felt Ballew's antics could be the beginning of trouble ahead. Going to Chief McCormick, Hickman warned him that Ballew was wandering the streets drinking heavily and carrying two revolvers. Since both men knew Ballew was no longer a lawman, McCormick decided to telephone Oklahoma authorities to check on the former peace officer's right to bear arms. Informed that Ballew had been issued a "special" permit by the state of Oklahoma allowing him to carry revolvers, McCormick decided to simply keep a close watch on the man and hope major trouble could be averted.

On Thursday evening[24] one of the larger hotels of The Falls hosted a cowboy dance. As the evening progressed, Ballew continued his heavy drinking. At one point amidst the revelry, the intoxicated gunman pulled a revolver from the shoulder holster under his coat and fired two shots through the ballroom ceiling. Several friends quickly disarmed him and escorted him to his room to sleep off the intoxicants of the night. For now, an encounter with the Wichita Falls police had been averted.

The next day, Friday, May 5, found Ballew once again on the streets imbibing freely and celebrating in grand style. Wishing to avoid a possibly serious confrontation, McCormick telephoned the rodeo ticket office and asked the ticket agent, Ray McKinley, if he could not get some of Ballew's friends to get him off the streets. Activity at the office resulted in McKinley neglecting the Ballew situation until, about one half hour later, McCormick phoned again. The chief of police stated that he had begun receiving complaints from various residents about the activities of the celebrating Ballew. He needed him off the streets now.

In response to McCormick's urgent telephone call, McKinley asked Ballew's cowboy friend Slim Caskey to round up the carousing man and escort him to his room. Assenting, Caskey located Ballew at a nearby bar. After a few more drinks Ballew insisted on going to a restaurant for a meal before heading back to his hotel. In order to humor his inebriated friend, Caskey agreed. Making their way to a diner about a block from the ticket office, the pair sat themselves at a table. Suddenly Ballew drew his revolver, stood up, and told Caskey he would go back into the kitchen to inform the cook how he wished his meal to be prepared. With that he disappeared into the kitchen.

A few minutes later, after having given the cook his cooking lesson and probably the fright of his life, Ballew returned to the table and began a conversation with Caskey. Gradually Ballew's voice and trademark laughter became measurably louder. Receiving complaints from his other customers, the restaurant proprietor ventured over to Ballew's table and asked Ballew if he could not be a little quieter as a courtesy to the other patrons. According to Caskey, as he told it later, a strange expression suddenly came over Ballew's face. Pulling his six-gun, Ballew presented it under the restaurateur's nose with the growled warning: "Get back to your cash register before I blow your head off!"

The man hastened to obey.

After finishing their meal, Ballew and Caskey left the restaurant. On the sidewalk they met Foghorn Clancy who called out to Ballew, "How are you, Bud?"

"All right, Clancy," Ballew replied, "but I'm awful drunk."

Still unable to get Ballew to return to his hotel room, Caskey accompanied him back to the rodeo office. Here they joined other cowboys in the makeshift lounge in the backroom, telling stories and discussing the day's events. Once again Ballew's laughter boomed through the building. Here, however, it was not only accepted but also expected, and all enjoyed the rowdy conversation.

In the meantime the restaurant owner who had previously had trouble with Ballew telephoned the city police station to make a complaint regarding Ballew's behavior. About the same time Caskey finally managed to convince Ballew to return to his room at the Denver Hotel at 617 Ohio Avenue. Once again, however, the troublesome Ballew was not quite ready to go off to bed. He insisted on stopping at the Domino Parlor run by Paul Adams, a former resident of Ardmore, located on the main floor of the Denver Hotel building. Here Ballew and Caskey had a few more drinks, a few more stories, and ribald fun. The time was shortly after one o'clock in the afternoon.[25]

By this time Chief McCormick had received three or four additional telephone calls dealing with Bud Ballew's disruptive conduct. He decided he could ignore them no longer. Recruiting Chief of Detectives Jack Miller and another unidentified officer, McCormick led the way in search of Ballew. By 1:30 the trio was able to track the wanted man down to the Domino Parlor.

As McCormick and his fellow officers entered the Domino Parlor, they spotted Ballew leaning against the bar talking loudly to Caskey, Adams, and two or three others. McCormick motioned for his men to split up, one each taking a wide route and approaching Ballew from either side while McCormick walked straight up to him.

"Bud, you're under arrest. Give me your gun," the police chief commanded.

At this point Ballew froze. "Put up your hands and I'll get it myself," McCormick said while Miller reached in to find Ballew's revolver.

According to the later testimony of McCormick and Miller, at this point Ballew turned half way around. "Oh no, buddy, you've got the wrong man this time," a smiling Ballew snarled. "You're out of luck."

At the same time Ballew reached to his side in an apparent attempt to draw his revolver.

McCormick either had his Smith & Wesson .38 in his hand or made a quick draw that beat Ballew. At any rate, before Ballew managed to draw his pistol, McCormick began firing at him. Miller jumped back, his right hand powder-burned by one of the chief's shots as he reached for Ballew's gun. Two bullets slammed into Ballew's chest just above the heart. One shot exited out his back while the other deflected off a rib and lodged just under the skin behind his left shoulder.

According to McCormick, when Ballew remained on his feet, the thought flashed through the police chief's mind that his opponent might have been wearing a bulletproof vest. Aiming the revolver at Ballew's head, McCormick squeezed the trigger again. The slug entered the right corner of Ballew's mouth, plowed through his skull and smashed its way out behind his left ear. Though Ballew neglected to don his "steel vest" this time, the shot to the head made that a moot point. As the fatally wounded man finally began to topple to the floor, McCormick fired two more shots at him. These two bullets struck Ballew high up on the left side and emerged from his chest. Bud Ballew fell to the floor beside a domino table, a dead man at the age of forty-four. Not only had he failed to fire a shot, he had not even drawn his gun.[26]

Immediately following the shooting, authorities examined Bud Ballew's body as it lay on the floor of the Domino Parlor. Two fully loaded revolvers were found on his person, one a silver mounted and engraved Colt .45 with what appeared to be six notches carved under the barrel, the other a .44 Smith and Wesson.[27] This examination also confirmed the fact that the former deputy had failed to don his bulletproof vest.[28] In short order authorities summoned an ambulance, and the dead man's remains were taken to the G. W. Hines Undertaking Parlor. After Ballew's body was removed, Paul Adams locked the doors of his establishment in order to clean the gore from his floor. Curious onlookers peeked in the windows as someone washed up a large pool of blood near one of the tables.[29] Soon Adams would again open his door and be back in business.

Shortly after his shooting of Ballew, McCormick surrendered himself to his former superior with the Texas Rangers, Company B Captain Tom Hickman. Accompanying McCormick to the county courthouse, Hickman went through the duly constituted procedure of filing a murder complaint against the police chief. After telephoning his wife to let her know he was all right, McCormick placed a call to his attorney, Judge C. C. McDonald. On McCormick's behalf, McDonald waived a hearing and bail was set at $10,000. According to the *Wichita Daily Times*, McCormick "was rather pale as he waited at the courthouse for his bond to be fixed, but maintained his composure."[30] Eventually he managed to round up a number of sureties to sign his bond. By mid afternoon McCormick had gained his release.[31] It would now be up to a future sitting of the grand jury to decide if further action should be taken.

At the mortuary, G. W. Hines made a thorough examination of Ballew's corpse. He determined that all five of McCormick's shots had entered the body and scored vital wounds. He also found that all the bullets had exited the body except the one he pulled from under the skin behind the left shoulder. It was Hines's judgment that all the wounds originated from front entry to back exit. Justice of the Peace R. V. Gwinn, who also examined the body, corroborated this conclusion. There is no record of an officially designated physician or medical examiner scrutinizing Ballew's body while it lay in Wichita Falls. Hines also found something that may almost be considered symbolic. In one of Ballew's pockets, he discovered a large quantity of shattered glass, apparently the remains of a whiskey flask broken when Ballew fell to the floor of the Domino Parlor. After his examination the undertaker had his embalmer, John T. Burris, prepare the body for burial.[32] Here Ballew's remains lay until instructions from relatives were received.

There is no record of Dorris Ballew's reaction to the news of his father's death. Dorris contacted Buck Garrett back in Ardmore soon after being informed of the shooting. While a shocked Garrett attempted to get in touch with Fannie Ballew, he also proceeded to make arrangements for Bud's body to be brought back to Ardmore.

After contacting the Harvey Funeral Home, Garrett placed a call to the Hardy Sanitarium who made available their unique "flying ambulance." The airplane, especially constructed with a canvas stretcher hung in the fuselage behind the pilot's seat, was used by Dr. Hardy to transport patients—and, on occasion, bodies—quickly and safely to his treatment facility. Late Friday after-noon Herbert Harvey, with Pilot Askew behind the controls, took off from Ard-more on the doleful mission of retrieving Bud Ballew's mortal remains from Wichita Falls.[33]

G. W. Hines had Ballew's body transported to Wichita Falls' Call Field airbase. The air ambulance from Ardmore arrived in The Falls about 6 p.m. Before a large crowd of curious onlookers, attendants transferred the body from the hearse to the aircraft.[34] As the Wichita newspaper reported the scene:

> (Ballew's corpse) was dressed in ordinary civilian clothes and was not encased in a casket or other container. The Ardmore plane is constructed with special care and is so arranged as to per-mit the easy transportation of persons stricken with illness. In the fuselage back of the pilot's seat a canvas stretcher is securely hung and in this the body of the man was placed.
>
> A metal covering, held by heavy straps, covered the silent figure and thus, with no chance of its falling, it was conveyed back to be greeted with varying emotions to Ardmore.[35]

For the second time the pilot, Askew, took Bud Ballew up over the Okla-homa grasslands. For Bud it would be his second and final trip in a "ship of the air." Dorris Ballew declined the airplane ride. Shortly before the aircraft took off for Ardmore, he boarded the train for his lonely ride back home.[36]

CHAPTER 20

Aftermath

Little twelve-year-old Allie, the future Mrs. Allie Gardner, heard the low drone of the approaching aircraft as she played in the front yard of her family home near Ardmore early on the evening of Friday, May 5, 1922. Stopping in the midst of her amusement, Allie stood up and turned her eyes skyward toward the sound. Sure enough, an airplane, louder now, drifted in front of the clouds as it passed over her house. Airplanes were rare in Carter County, Oklahoma, in 1922, as in most rural areas of the country at that time. At the noise the rest of her family ran out to join her in the yard, gazing up at the uncommon sight.

"Must be bringing Bud Ballew back to Ardmore," her father said as the plane slowly disappeared into the northern dusk.

To the day of her recollection in her ninetieth year, Mrs. Gardner would remember exactly where she was on the day of Bud Ballew's death;[1] so it would be for many people in Carter County. While he had lived, Ballew had definitely carved his niche in the area, and his demise proved a major event.

At about 8 p.m. Askew landed the air ambulance on the racetrack just north of the city of Ardmore.[2] Oddly enough, the place where Bud Ballew had experienced some of the most enjoyable times of his life would be where his body was received. Quickly the body was taken in a hearse to the Hardy Sanitarium for examination.

Dr. Walter Hardy's autopsy of Ballew would be the source of initial bitter, and potentially dangerous, acrimony. Following his examination, Dr. Hardy concluded that more than one gun had been involved in the shooting of Ballew. Applying the infant technology of x-ray photography, the physician found what looked like a large-caliber bullet lodged in the body under the dead man's left arm. Apparently he made no attempt to remove the slug. In Hardy's estimation two other wounds found on the corpse had been inflicted by smaller-caliber bullets. He also felt that at least one or two of the fresh wounds had been inflicted from back to front.[3] Soon after Hardy's examination Ballew was moved to the Harvey Brothers undertaking establishment.

Following his immediate inspection of the mortal remains of his former chief deputy and close friend, Buck Garrett reportedly emerged onto the sidewalk with "tears welling in his eyes."[4] Deferring to give a long interview with reporters at that time, Garrett did lament, "He didn't have a chance. Five shots and all from the back." Shaking his head, Garrett stated that "the law should be allowed to take its course" and despite his personal feelings "no feud would arise across the border as a result of the slaying."[5]

It had been a bad two days for Garrett in more ways than one. The day before Ballew's death, Thursday, May 4, the district court, under the direction of Judge E. D. Oldfield, denied Garrett's appeal for a new trial in his ouster case.[6] The following day, the very day Ballew was killed, Garrett's attorneys announced their intention of appealing his case to the Supreme Court of the United States.[7] Though hopeful, Buck Garrett would have as little luck in the courts as he would in getting perceived justice for the death of his old friend.

Back in Wichita Falls, J. W. McCormick vehemently denied the accusations of his Ardmore detractors. "He faced me all the time," the police chief adamantly stated. "There's not a one of the shots that went in from behind."[8] Other witnesses to the shooting corroborated the chief's statement. Beyond this McCormick refused to comment except to say, "I'm sorry it happened."[9]

As Bud Ballew lay in state at the Harvey funeral parlor late Friday night and into Saturday, scores of people flocked to get a glimpse of the notorious gunman. The *Daily Ardmoreite* vividly recounted the scene:

THOUSANDS VIEW BODY

Many eyes were wet as they looked upon the form of Bud in Harvey brothers' undertaking parlors Friday night and Saturday. Thousands streamed in during the time it lay under a silken coverlid in the reception room.

Whispered remarks were made; no one lingered long except close friends of the deceased. Buck Garrett was present most of the time and shook hands in condolence with hundreds.

Men and women in profusion, young girls and boys were included among the visitors, many of them bringing floral offerings, tokens of friendship.

Visitors in the city who had heard of Ballew in the past were anxious to view his body and pause a moment while looking upon his features. Thus did some of them see the man they had heard so much about.[10]

Although Garrett had a hard time tracking down Fannie Ballew, he finally was able to notify her of her husband's death. Friends met the bereaved widow at Waurika and escorted her to Ardmore where she arrived late Saturday afternoon. Fannie repaired immediately to the Harvey Funeral Home where she viewed the body of her departed husband.[11] After almost twenty-one years of marriage to the unpredictable Ballew, Fannie's life would now have to take a separate course.

Rumors continued to multiply concerning J. W. McCormick. The general public could not fathom that any one other than a "super gunman" could have bested Bud Ballew in a gunfight. It became general gossip that McCormick had killed a number of men in his career, one dispatch claiming that Ballew was his thirteenth victim and that the lawman was somewhat perturbed concerning the unlucky number. McCormick and those who knew him well attempted to assure the press that, in fact, Ballew was the first man he had ever killed, his only other shooting victim being the unlucky bootlegger he had winged in the raid near Wichita Falls some two years previous.[12]

While busy with his police duties and not wising to make any statements while his case was still in the courts, McCormick continued to garner unwanted publicity from the shooting. The *Wichita Daily Times* did its best, however, to be supportive in its reportage:

> Chief McCormick's attitude since the killing has certainly not been that of a man accustomed to taking life. He believes that he shot in line of duty, if not to save his own life, and that there was justification of his course, but it has been evident that the affair has been weighing heavily upon him. The very loyal support of his friends and of many who, though knowing him only slightly, have felt it something of a duty to uphold his course, has been a big factor in sustaining him. The chief is deeply appreciative of the sentiments that have been expressed to him since the affair.

The paper went on to describe the effect of the shooting in the city the following day:

> McCormick was kept busy throughout all of Saturday dodging inquisitive visitors who wished to discuss the affair with him. Around the city hall the shooting was the chief topic of conversation, while many and varied were the stories circulated as to the prowess and accomplishments of Ballew. Efforts to settle on how many victims had fallen before his gun were futile, but old timers who knew the man and who had followed the development of the Oklahoma territory in which Garrett and Ballew established their reputations recounted many thrilling tales of border warfare in which Bud always proved to be the quicker on the draw.
>
> Police Commissioner (J. B.) Fitts and other city officials expressed regret that the chief was compelled to resort to such heroic measures but all declared their intention of standing behind the chief in whatever legal fight he may be forced to make.[13]

A large portion of the residents of Wichita Falls stood firmly behind their new police chief as is made evident by the letters of opinion sent to the local newspaper.[14] Despite the fact that, as the *Ardmore Statesman* put it, "it is undoubtedly the belief of Bud's friends here that he was shot in the back,"[15] many citizens of Ardmore also supported McCormick's actions in the affair. Over the course of the days following his killing of Ballew, McCormick received many telegrams and messages from Ardmore residents assuring him that they did not believe the stories of his "gunman" reputation or the rumors of his having backshot the dead man.[16]

With the help of Buck Garrett, Fannie and Dorris Ballew made arrangements with the Harvey Undertaking Parlor[17] to hold funeral services for Bud on Sunday, May 7, at two p.m. at Lone Grove. Interment was to follow in the little Lone Grove cemetery where Ballew would be buried beside his father, Bryant, and son, Buster.[18] Torrential rains had inundated the Lone Grove and Ardmore area, however. When the hearse containing Ballew's body and cars of friends and relatives arrived that afternoon, they found that the heavy downpour had washed out a bridge situated between the town and the graveyard.[19] Thus it was decided to postpone the funeral to the next day and everyone, along with the deceased, returned back to Ardmore.

That evening, his best friend still unburied, Buck Garrett opened up a little more to reporters. According to the United Press International release, the former sheriff took Ballew's death both philosophically and bitterly.

"Just one of those things that come sometime or other in every man's life," Garrett sighed. "Ballew was shot in the back. He never had a chance, but perhaps it had come his time to die. Bud saved my life on several occasions. I wish I could have been present to save his. The memory of Bud Ballew will always be a tender one to me,"[20] the grieving ex-lawman concluded as he turned and slowly walked away. Perhaps along with the death of his friend, Buck Garrett also recognized the demise of his own persona as a force in Carter County. Without question the end of an era had arrived.

With the heavy rains showing no sign of abating, Ballew's funeral was again postponed on Monday.[21] Finally, on Tuesday afternoon, May 9, 1922, the weather relented enough to allow the overdue funeral rituals to take place. Services at the Lone Grove Methodist Church conducted by Rev. John F. Young, the father of Ballew's former brother, deputy Earl Young, and Rev. Charles W. Clay, were delivered to an overflow crowd of mourners. Following a rousing rendition of "Rock of Ages,"[22] the solemn cortège made its way to the Lone Grove cemetery north of town.

With the casket borne by pallbearers Buck Garrett, John Harrell, and former Carter County deputy sheriffs Fred Williams, Jim Carter, Bill Ward, Bill Whitson, Horace Kendall, and Earl Young,[23] Bud Ballew was laid to rest in a grave next to his father and son. Those notables giving floral offerings included Buck Garrett, who gave two, one in his own name and another along with his wife, Ida; Bud's own son, Dorris Ballew; ex-deputies Jim Carter, Fred Williams, and Jake Williams and wife; Bud's brother, Scott Ballew, and wife; former county attorney James Mathers and wife; lawyer J. B. Champion; the notorious Mr. and Mrs. Earnest Ford; Bob Key of the well-known Key family; and Mr. and Mrs. W. T. Martin, cattle inspector and former courthouse battler along with Ballew. Others included the "Ladies of Wilson," the Baptist Church, the Carter County Sheriff's Department, and the Budd Hoard Co.[24]

With Bud Ballew dead and buried, the only thing left to be settled in the case was the fate of his killer, J. W. McCormick. Rumor and gossip quickly developed around Wichita Falls to the effect that Buck Garrett himself would set out to conduct a personal investigation of the shooting.[25] Rumor and gossip it would prove to be, however, and nothing more. Garrett would stay out of the case, and it would be left to the Wichita County Grand Jury to decide any consequences devolving on McCormick. Most were doubtful of any action being taken. When the grand jury of the 30th District Court met in Wichita Falls in June 1922,[26] the august body failed to find an indictment against McCormick for his killing of Bud Ballew. The jury decided that the chief had fired strictly in the line of duty, and no action need be taken. Some rejoiced while others, most likely Buck Garrett amongst them, bemoaned the decision. But, as he said he would, Garrett "let the law take its course" and sadly moved on.

McCormick would continue to be a fractious chief of police at Wichita Falls. On June 27, 1922, well-known Wichita Falls notary public J. Orville Bentley became embroiled in an argument at city hall with Police Commissioner J. B. Fitts. At length Chief McCormick became involved. Pushing Bentley outside, McCormick began a violent fistfight in which both men received damage in the form of black eyes and split lips.[27] Charged with assault, McCormick had his day in court on July 3 at which time a jury found him not guilty.[28] McCormick would go on to complete a successful term as police chief at Wichita Falls. Never again would he experience as close a call as he had on May 5, 1922, when he mixed it up with Bud Ballew.

As the days and weeks passed since the demise of Ballew, many theories and speculations arose concerning the gunman's death. Some felt McCormick had been part of a conspiracy to get rid of Ballew. Others charged that Ballew had been involved in various extortion schemes, including extorting money in the form of "a percentage on the winnings" from the cowboys at the Wichita Falls rodeo,[29] and that this was the reason for someone wanting the man dead. Ballew had made many enemies over the years of his lawman career. Perhaps one of them had found a means to put him out of the way.

Another theory evolved within certain factions of the Ballew family itself. According to Norman Flowers, a descendant of one of Bud Ballew's cousins, the story was that Bud had encountered J. W. McCormick previous to their meeting in The Falls. It was told within the family that the pair had come together at a convention of area lawmen a few months before the Wichita Falls roundup. At this gathering a disagreement broke out between some of the Oklahoma officers and their Texas counterparts. As a result hot words passed between Ballew and McCormick. Thus, on May 5, 1922, McCormick found the perfect opportunity to settle his score with Ballew. As Mr. Flowers himself would say, "That's the story, whatever it's worth."[30] Indeed, it was one of many stories, conjectures, and tall tales.

One of the most absurd narratives concerning the Ballew shooting was passed to the author by Ardmore historian Sally Gray. As related by Ms. Gray, an old rodeo cowboy named Floyd Randolph told her that Bud and a couple of his cronies traveled to the Wichita Falls rodeo in order to conduct a rendezvous with some rodeo cowgirls. As Ballew and his friends sat in a bar with the women, a jealous husband of one of the ladies strode in and shot Bud to death.[31] The stories have continued to multiply over the years, each one more dramatic or outlandish than the last.

Despite all the conspiracy theories and tales of sex and intrigue, evidence suggests that Bud Ballew's death at the hands of Wichita Falls Chief of Police

J. W. McCormick was nothing more than a simple arrest attempt gone bad. Liquor and male machismo caused a dangerous situation to turn deadly. The *Daily Oklahoman* newspaper based in Oklahoma City may have summed it up best when it stated, "Bud Ballew, idolized by many as a hero and hated and feared as a killer by others"[32] was now a matter of history.

AFTERWORD

—— Future Lives, Future Times ——

S ubsequent to the death of Bud Ballew, Buck Garrett's career was somewhat anticlimactic. No longer chasing after the criminal element, the ex-sheriff decided to try his hand in the oil business full time, a pursuit he had been delving into on a part-time basis for a number of years. Setting up office space in Ardmore, he is alleged to have accumulated a considerable amount of money out of the endeavor.[1]

Garrett may have felt some small measure of satisfaction in 1925. That year the grand jury indicted Sheriff Ewing London, who had been officially elected to office, on a charge of "allowing prisoners to roam at large."[2] London was temporarily removed from the sheriff's desk and a man named James Cruce was appointed to serve in his place. Cruce holds the distinction of serving the shortest term of any Carter County sheriff, a mere thirty days.[3]

In 1928 Buck Garrett ran for reelection as sheriff of Carter County. He was defeated in the race, however, by Republican Walter Colbert.[4] From this point on it would be uphill for Garrett. Stories of Garrett's supposed philandering were commonplace around Ardmore. Finally Ida Garrett decided she had had enough. Sometime in 1928 the couple separated, although Ida would refuse to give her husband the divorce he wanted.[5]

At this point Garrett moved to Oklahoma City. Shortly after this move, he suffered a crippling stroke at his Oklahoma City home. Still harboring tender feelings for her estranged husband, Ida brought him back to Ardmore where she cared for the partially paralyzed man. On May 6, 1929, at the age of fifty-seven, former Carter County sheriff Buck Garrett suffered a major heart attack and died at Ardmore.[6] He was buried in Ardmore's Riverside Cemetery while an overflow crowd of mourners looked on. Ida would live until 1958. The Garretts' only child, son Raymond, would die in 1965.[7]

Not all of those who had been associated with Bud Ballew suffered such hardship in their later years. Former Carter County Attorney James Mathers, for one, went on to a successful career and enjoyable old age following his Carter County days. Eventually Mathers moved his wife and family to Oklahoma City where he engaged in a prosperous private practice. After serving as a county judge for a number of years, he retired to a ranch near Ada, Oklahoma, following the death of his wife. Despite his advanced age, Mathers gained an appointment as an associate district judge for the area encompassing Coal and surrounding counties.[8] In the early 1950s he related his various reminiscences to author Marshall Houts. The result was *From Gun to Gavel: The Courtroom Recollections of James Mathers of Oklahoma* published by William Morrow & Company of New York City in 1954. His book would relate many of the incidents of early Carter County and Ardmore, Oklahoma. In order to "protect the innocent," he changed Bud Ballew's name to Bud Brent." He was one of the first to reveal various Carter County incidents to the world. Death ultimately claimed the pioneer jurist in 1967. His son would follow in his father's footsteps and go on to a successful career as a lawyer in Oklahoma.[9]

As the years passed, Carter County and Ardmore, though slowing down some with age, continued to be, on occasion, dangerous places where violence could strike without warning. On December 10, 1930, Carter County Deputy Sheriff William "Con" Keirsey and Undersheriff Vernon D. Cason attempted to arrest two auto thieves named Colquitt and D. I. Davis in Wirt, Oklahoma. In the ensuing gun battle, Keirsey was killed and Cason wounded. On the day of Keirsey's funeral, December 12, D. I. Davis was killed in a shoot-out with police in Wichita, Kansas. Colquitt Davis was later arrested and sentenced to life in prison.[10]

A few months later, in 1931, Carter County Deputies Bill Guess and Cecil Crosby stopped a car on E Street N.W. in Ardmore following a traffic violation. Inside the vehicle was the nephew of Mexican President Rubio. In the confrontation that followed Guess shot Rubio's nephew to death. The affair made its way all the way to the White House. An international incident was finally averted when U.S. President Herbert Hoover sent a letter of regret to the Mexican president.[11]

Over the subsequent years four members of the Ardmore Police Department would be killed by gunfire in the line of duty. On January 31, 1931, Officer Elmer "Buddy" Moorehead was shot and killed by armed robbers while on patrol near Ardmore.[12] On January 3, 1952, Assistant Chief Oscar Wilkes was shot to death while investigating a domestic dispute on Hargrove Street.[13] A little over six years later, on April 28, 1958, Officer Charles Washington would be mortally wounded while attempting to arrest a drunk in the Veterans Cab Company on East Main Street.[14] Finally, on December 22, 1960, Officer Bobby Rudisell received fatal gunshot wounds while investigating a burglary in progress on Ardmore's North Washington Street.[15] Though scenes like these, reminiscent of the old days, would occasionally play themselves out, year by year Ardmore and Carter County left the "wild old days" behind them and headed toward the future with hope and promise.

By 1925 oil activity in Carter County had begun to level off. The fields were a major supplier of oil, however, during the frenetic times of World War II. After 1940 the agriculture sector began a shift away from cash-crop farming and began a return to the industry that had been the reason for the area's settlement in the first place, cattle ranching.[16]

Ardmore's population had reached almost 17,000 by 1940.[17] Caddo Street would continue to be a rough section of town well into the 1950s. By the late 1960s, however, the street had abandoned most of its gin mills, gambling joints, and call-girl cribs. In 1966 the *Daily Ardmoreite* signaled this decline in an editorial entitled "Death Rattles from Caddo."[18] Ardmore had proven its ability to exist and prosper without Caddo's vices.

Today Ardmore, Oklahoma, is a beautiful city of some 23,000 people, a major stop on the highway between Oklahoma City and Dallas/Fort Worth. Cattle ranching and oil drilling and refining still combine to make the area a prosperous and growing community. The Goodyear tire factory is another booster to the city's economy. The days of Bud Ballew are long gone but, perhaps surprisingly in this modern technological age, not forgotten. A little of Bud Ballew's Wild West will always be a part of Ardmore and Carter County, Oklahoma.

Over four years after her husband's death, Fannie Ballew married Dr. John Tidmore at Lone Grove on December 2, 1926.[19] Fannie Ballew Tidmore would spend the rest of her life living in the Wilson/Lone Grove area. Called by her granddaughter-in-law a "lovely lady—very much the lady,"[20] Fannie would live to once again become a widow following the death of Dr. Tidmore. Living to her seventy-second year, Fannie died at Lone Grove on April 15, 1955.[21] After thirty-three years Fannie finally rejoined Bud when she was buried beside him in the Lone Grove cemetery.

Bud and Fannie's only surviving son, Dorris Letcher Ballew, had already begun shaping his own destiny. Soon after the death of his father in 1922, Dorris began to make a serious vocation in the Oklahoma oil business. At length he made a success in the oil fields and soon owned and operated his own oil-drilling company.[22]

Despite the press of business matters, Dorris Ballew also found time to start a family. He married Mildred Wright, in Stroud, Oklahoma, April 17, 1926.[23] April 17 had also been the date of his parents' wedding day in 1901. A little over two years later, the couple's only child, son Dorris Eugene, always known as Eugene or "Gene," was born at Beardon, Oklahoma, on August 17, 1928.[24]

During the mid 1940s the states of Louisiana and Mississippi began to experience an oil boom. By now a prominent force in the oil industry of Oklahoma, in 1945 Dorris Ballew moved his family to Mississippi, eventually settling in Natchez. Within a few short years, Ballew attained considerable success in his oil endeavors. His many positions of status in oil affairs included being owner of his own company, Ballew Drilling Company; director of the Mississippi-Louisiana Division of the Mid-Continent Oil and Gas Association; president of Oil International; and chairman of the board of Tulsa, Oklahoma-based Loffland Brothers, an oil-drilling firm.[25]

Harboring a love of horses, cattle, and ranching, in common with his father, Dorris purchased a large spread near Natchez. Here he found time to indulge in many other activities outside the oil industry. Eventually he became one of the major movers and shakers in the history of Natchez and one of its most prominent citizens. His numerous accomplishments included being president of the Mississippi Cattlemen's Association; founder and president of the Mississippi Quarter Horse Association as well as the Mississippi Cutting Horse Association; director of the Louisiana Quarter Horse Association; and director of the American Quarter Horse Association.[26]

Dorris Ballew was a man who gave both willingly and generously to his community and fellow citizens. A multitalented individual of boundless energy, Dorris was also president of the Natchez Baseball Association. One of the baseball diamonds in Natchez still bears his name. He was a member of the State Coliseum committee and, in 1949, was voted Natchez's "Outstanding Citizen of the Year."[27]

On May 2, 1962, while en-route to Franklin, Tennessee, to act as a judge at a quarter-horse show, Dorris Ballew died of a heart attack at Tupelo, Mississippi.[28] He was fifty-eight years old. His good friend and secretary-manager of the American Quarter Horse Association, Howard K. Linger, memorialized him thus:

> Dorris contributed much in the years he was associated with the Quarter Horse industry; his words of hope and material gifts to children and adults alike enriched the lives of many. Dorris was generous, honest, and considerate. Those of us who knew him and cherished his friendship can only pay our respects to his beloved memory.[29]

Following his death, the newly constructed wing of the Mississippi State College was dedicated as the Dorris Ballew Animal Science Building and a yearly scholarship begun in his honor.[30] Dorris' wife, Mildred Ballew, would live until 1988, dying in Jackson, Mississippi.[31]

Dorris and Mildred Ballew's son, Eugene, continued in his father's footsteps. In 1951 Eugene married Ann Louise Lum, a native of Vicksburg, Mississippi.[32] The couple would eventually add four girls to the Ballew family.[33] Following a stint in the Korean Conflict, Eugene returned to Natchez and worked along with his father in the family enterprise. Subsequent to the death of Dorris Ballew, Eugene continued to oversee his father's many and varied business ventures. At one point he operated the Natchez Auction Commission, the expansive headquarters being another accomplishment of his multifaceted father.[34] Tragically, while still a productive member of society, Eugene Ballew would die at Natchez on April 2, 1951 at the age of fifty-eight.[35]

At this writing all of Bud Ballew's descendants, great-grandchildren and great-great-grandchildren, still live and flourish in the Natchez area. One example of the many accomplishments of the current generation is that of Bud's great-great-granddaughter, Margaret Paige Carlton. The beautiful twenty-one-year-old received featured space in the *Natchez Democrat* in early 2000 when she was chosen as Queen of the 2000 Natchez Confederate Pageant.[36] Always a lover of family pride and a believer in putting one's best foot forward and doing one's utmost, devil-take-the-hindmost, Bud Ballew would have approved.

To this day Bud Ballew is still a legend in Carter County and Ardmore, Oklahoma. He has been the subject of bard and playwright. In the intervening years since Ballew's death, his tombstone—like those of Billy the Kid, Wild Bill Hickok, and Wyatt Earp—became the victim of souvenir hunters and vandals. In later years J. B. Ponder, owner of Ponder's Restaurant in Ardmore and a Ballew family friend, replaced the chipped and chiseled grave marker with a new, impressive monument. This is the current memorial that graces Bud Ballew's grave today. As one enters the tiny Lone Grove cemetery, the memorial looms over the other graves like a symbol of retribution and justice. In death, as in life, Bud Ballew dominates his fellow man, casting his imposing shadow over all around him. The man may be gone, but his legend marches on into the future.

Notes

BEGINNINGS

1. Ancestor Chart courtesy of Malcolm R. Dixon, San Antonio, Texas, great-great-grandson of George Ballew, compiled May 19, 1990. Family Chart courtesy of Ann Ballew Carlton, Natchez, Mississippi, great-granddaughter of Bud Ballew.

2. Telephone interview with Malcolm R. Dixon from San Antonio, Texas, August 16, 2001. Mr. Dixon asserted that George accompanied his son Harvey to Kentucky where he stayed when Harvey moved to Texas. Marriage Bonds, Book 1, p. 10, Russell County, Kentucky. Pernette's name is also spelled variously in the records Pernettee, Pernetta, and Purnette.

3. Federal census of the United States, 1850, County of Russell, State of Kentucky, Dwelling #208, family #208. The 1850 census lists Pernette as being born in Kentucky. It also lists her age in 1850 as thirty-five giving her a birth year of ca. 1814; Ancestor Chart courtesy Malcolm R. Dixon, San Antonio, Texas, compiled May 19, 1990; Family Chart, courtesy of Ann Ballew Carlton, Natchez, Mississippi.

4. Family Chart, courtesy of Ann Ballew Carlton, Natchez, Mississippi.

5. Ibid.; Federal Census of the United States 1840, County of Russell, State of Kentucky; Ancestor Chart courtesy of Malcolm R. Dixon, San Antonio, Texas, compiled by Mrs. Douthitt McKay, San Antonio, Texas, great-granddaughter of Harvey Ballew, March 9, 1978.

6. Family Chart courtesy of Ann Ballew Carlton, Natchez, Mississippi.

7. Federal Census of the United States, 1860, county of Fannin, state of Texas; Post Office, Garnetts Bluff, enumerated on 17 August, page No. 181. Dwelling #1191, family #1212.

8. Family Chart courtesy of Ann Ballew Carlton, Natchez, Mississippi. There is some confusion as to the dates of Bryant Ballew's two marriages and the offspring of each marriage.

9. Copy of page from Ballew family bible provided courtesy of Ann Ballew Carlton, Natchez, Mississippi. Federal census of the United States, 1880, county of Eastland, state of Texas, enumerated on the 22 of June, page No. 36, Supervisors Dist. No. 3, Enumeration Dist. No. 174, Dwelling #346, Family #346.

10. Family Chart courtesy of Ann Ballew Carlton, Natchez, Mississippi; Ancestor Chart courtesy of Malcolm R. Dixon, compiled by Mrs. Douthitt McKay, San Antonio, Texas, March 9, 1978; Federal Census of the United States, 1880, county of Eastland, state of Texas, enumerated on 22 of June, page No. 36, Supervisors Dist. No. 3, Enumeration Dist. No. 174, Dwelling #346, Family #346.

11. Federal Census of the United States, 1880, county of Eastland, state of Texas, enumerated on 22 of June, page No. 36, Supervisors Dist. No. 3, Enumeration Dist. No. 174, Dwelling #346, Family #346.

12. Soundex of Federal Census of the United States., 1900, Indian Territory, Chickasaw Nation, Vol. 10, E.D., 176, Sheet 6, line 87; Family Chart courtesy Ann Ballew Carlton, Natchez, Mississippi.

13. Family Chart courtesy of Ann Ballew Carlton, Natchez, Mississippi.

14. Texas Land Title Abstract, Ancestry.com.

15. Larry S. Watson, ed., *Smith's First Dictionary of Oklahoma Territory for the Year Commencing August 1, 1890* (Guthrie, Oklahoma Territory: James W. Smith; reprint, Histree, 1989), 229, (231). Smith's dictionary for 1890 lists a David "Ballou" living at S E Section 15, Township 16, Range 2. This may be Bud Ballew.

CARTER COUNTY GENESIS

1. *The Daily Oklahoman*, (Oklahoma City), February 20, 1921; *Daily Ardmoreite*, May 5, 1922; *Wichita Daily Times*, (Wichita Falls, Texas), May 5, 1922; *The Ardmore Statesman*, May 11, 1922.

2. Ardmore Junior Chamber or Commerce, *The History of Carter County* (Fort Worth, Texas: University Supply and Equipment Company, 1957), n.p.

3. Ibid.; Paul N Frame, *A History of Ardmore, Oklahoma* (Masters Thesis, University of Oklahoma, 1949).

4. Telephone interview with Sally Gray, (Ardmore historian), from Ardmore, Oklahoma, September 9, 2000.

5. Marshall Houts, *From Gun to Gavel, The Courtroom Recollections of James Mathers of Oklahoma* (New York: William Morrow & Company, 1954), 6.

6. Ardmore Junior Chamber of Commerce, *The History of Carter County*, n.p.; Paul N. Frame, *A History of Ardmore, Oklahoma.*

7. Ibid.

8. Ardmore Junior Chamber of Commerce, *The History of Carter County*, n.p.; Paul N. Frame, *A History of Ardmore, Oklahoma.*

9. Ardmore Junior Chamber of Commerce, *The History of Carter County*, n.p.

10. Ibid.

11. The town of Berwyn, Carter County, in 1941 changed its name to Gene Autry in honor of the cowboy film star who purchased a ranch in the area. Kenny A. Franks, *Ragtown: A History of the Greater Healdton-Hewitt Oil Field* (Oklahoma City: Oklahoma Heritage Association, Western Heritage Books, Inc., 1986), 3–4.

12. *Fort Worth Gazette*, April 20, 1895; Ardmore Junior Chamber of Commerce, *The History of Carter County*, n.p.

13. *Daily Ardmoreite*, June 9, 10, 11, 1894; Harrell McCullough, *Selden Lindsey, U.S. Deputy Marshal* (Oklahoma City: Paragon Publishing, 1990), 97–132.

14. Elizabeth A. Long, *Songs Unsung* (Lakeville, Minnesota: Galde Press, Inc., 1997), 69–72; Elmer LeRoy Baker, *Gunman's Territory* (San Antonio, Texas: The Naylor Company, 1969), 288–290. Both cite *Ripley's Believe It or Not.*

15. Ardmore Junior Chamber of Commerce, *The History of Carter County*, n.p; Roy M. Johnson, John P. Gilday, and Mark H. Salt, eds., *Oklahoma History, South of the Canadian, Historical and Biographical* (Chicago: S.J. Clarke Publishing Co., 1925), 448–449.

16. Ardmore Junior Chamber of Commerce, *The History of Carter County*, n.p.

17. Federal Census of United States 1900, Indian Territory, Chickasaw Nation, Lone Grove, Vol. 10, Enumeration District 126, Sheet 1, Line 4.

18. Ibid., Sheet 6, Line 87.

19. Copy of page from Ballew Family bible, "Family Record," "Births." Copy provided courtesy of Ann Ballew Carlton, Natchez, Mississippi. William Harper was born in Kentucky on October 22, 1840; his wife, Ana Eliza, on June 26, 1842. Their nine children born prior to Fannie were Lycurgis born February 7, 1864; John Byrd, March 9, 1866; Annie, December 1867; William Martin Jr., 1869; James Evret, March 21, 1872; Adah Burnes, April 24, 1874; Thomas Letcher, March 13, 1876; Joseph Robert, November 6, 1878; and Lucian Lembert, December 19, 1880.

20. Ibid., "Marriage" page. Probably completed at a later date the year of the marriage in the family bible was entered incorrectly as "1900." Mary Turner Kinard, "Chickasaw Nation Groom Index, 1895–1907"; *Marriage Record Book E,* Indian Territory, Southern District, p. 393, Marriage License No. 502.

21. Copy of page from Ballew Family bible, "Family record," "Births." Copy provided courtesy of Ann Ballew Carlton, Natchez, Mississippi; Bud Ballew Family Chart, also courtesy Ann Ballew Carlton.

22. Ibid.

23. Federal Census of U.S., 1910, State of Oklahoma, County of Carter, Lone Grove Township, Enumerated on April 20, 1910, Dwelling #62, Family #62. Although he was apparently close to Bud and family at this point in time, it would appear Scott was not on the best of terms with some members of his family. The photo (passed down through some members of the Ballew family, apparently originating with Fannie Ballew) in which the face of Scott has been scratched out is perhaps testimony to this rift with Scott.

VICTIM #1—PETE BYNUM

1. The outcome of the Epperson affair is unknown.

2. Robert Hutchins was born September 8, 1871, and raised in Texas. After working as a cowboy as a young man, he gained a deputy U.S. marshal commission in the Indian Territory. His career, which involved many outlaw chases and gunfights, brought him often to the Ardmore area. Hutchins was elected police chief of Ardmore in 1915 and served until 1917. Following his stint as police chief, he worked as a bodyguard for millionaire oilman Jake Hamon and then moved to El Paso as a border guard along the U.S.-Mexico line. The veteran lawman died at the age of eighty on April 29, 1951, and is buried in Ardmore's Rose Hill Cemetery.

3. *Ardmore Statesman,* October 2, 1915; Elmer Le Roy Baker, *Gunman's Territory* (San Antonio, Texas: The Naylor Company, 1969), 290–295; Kenny A. Franks, *Ragtown: A History of the Greater Healdton-Hewitt Oil Field* (Oklahoma City: Western Heritage Books Inc., Oklahoma Heritage Association, 1986), 71–79; Mac McGalliard, *Reporter's Notebook, Number One,* scrapbooks in the collections of the Greater Southwest Historical Museum, Ardmore, Oklahoma, October 15, 1969, n.p.; Ardmore Junior Chamber of Commerce, *The History of Carter County* (Fort Worth, Texas: University Supply and Equipment Company, 1957), n.p.

4. *Ardmore Statesman,* November 20, 1915.

5. Ibid.

6. Ibid.; *Daily Ardmoreite*, November 19, 1915; *Daily Oklahoman*, February 20, 1921.

7. *Ardmore Statesman*, November 20, 1915; *Daily Ardmoreite*, November 19, 1915.

8. *Daily Ardmoreite*, November 21, 1915. John Gauntt would eventually go on to marry Bud Ballew's sister.

9. *Ardmore Statesman*, December 11, 1915.

10. *Wichita Daily Times*, May 6, 1922.

11. *Ardmore Statesman*, December 11, 1915.

RAGTOWN AND MIGHTY OIL

1. Kenny A. Franks, *Ragtown: A History of the Greater Healdton-Hewitt Oil Field* (Oklahoma City: Western Heritage Books, Inc., Oklahoma Heritage Association, 1986), 10–17.

2. Ibid.; Ardmore Junior Chamber of Commerce, *The History of Carter County* (Fort Worth, Texas: University Supply and Equipment Company, 1957), n.p.

3. Ibid. By the 1920s the Wheeler Field would eventually become part of the greater Sho-Vel-Tum Field and a major oil producer.

4. Ibid.

5. Kenny A. Franks, *Ragtown: A History of the Greater Healdton-Hewitt Oil Field*, 18–29; Ardmore Junior Chamber of Commerce, *The History of Carter County*, n.p.; McGalliard, Mac, *Reporter's Notebook* (Ardmore, Oklahoma: Sprekelmeyer Printing Company, 1973), 117–118.

6. Kenny A. Franks, *Ragtown: A History of the Greater Healdton-Hewitt Oil Field*, 33–35; Ardmore Junior Chamber of Commerce, *The History of Carter County*, n.p.

7. According to Claude Woods, the director of the Healdton Oil Museum, the Wirt State Bank finally closed in 1934 because it had been robbed many times.

8. Franks, Kenny A., *Ragtown: A History of the Greater Healdton-Hewitt Oil Field*, 85.

9. Ibid.

10. Interview with Claude Woods, Healdton, Oklahoma, August 21, 2000.

11. Ardmore Junior Chamber of Commerce, *The History of Carter County*, n.p.

12. Ibid.

13. Kenny A. Franks, *Ragtown: A History of the Greater Healdton-Hewitt Oil Field*, 79–82.

14. *The Ardmore Statesman*, January 22, 1915.

15. Ibid.; Gilbert L. Robinson, "History of the Healdton Oil Field" (Thesis, The University of Oklahoma, 1937), 63. In the confusion caused by the fire, Roberts managed to escape authorities and was never apprehended.

16. Gilbert L. Robinson, "History of the Healdton Oil Field," 62.

17. Ibid., 60; Kenny A. Franks, *Ragtown: A History of the Greater Healdton-Hewitt Oil Field*, 99.

18. Gilbert L. Robinson, "History of the Healdton Oil Field," 62.

19. Bill Burchart, "The Oil Rush Wild West," *True West*, December 1966.

BUCK GARRETT

1. William Krohn, "Some Thrilling Experiences in Lives of Buck Garrett and Bud Ballew," *The Daily Oklahoman* (Oklahoma City), February 20, 1921. Always a strong supporter of the Garrett regime, the state capital's *Daily Oklahoman* would often praise Buck Garrett, Bud Ballew, and their accomplishments. Reporter Bill Krohn was a personal friend of both men.

2. Patty Virginia Norton and Layton R. Sutton, comps. and eds., *Indian Territory and Carter County, Oklahoma, Pioneers, Including Pickens County, Chickasaw Nation, Vol. 1, 1840–1926* (Dallas: Taylor Publishing Co., 1983), 190; Dan L Thrapp, *Encyclopedia of Frontier Biography, Vol. II, G–O* (Lincoln: Bison Books, University of Nebraska Press, 1988), 540.

3. Ibid. It has been stated on numerous occasions that Buck Garrett was the nephew or other relative of noted Southwest lawman and killer of Billy the Kid, Patrick Floyd Garrett. This is untrue. There is no known familial relationship between the two men.

4. Patty Virginia Norton, and Layton R. Sutton, comps. and eds.; William Krohn, "Some Thrilling Experiences in Lives of Buck Garrett and Bud Ballew"; *The Daily Oklahoman* (Oklahoma City), February 20, 1921.

5. William Krohn, "Some Thrilling Experiences in Lives of Buck Garrett and Bud Ballew," *The Daily Oklahoman* (Oklahoma City), February 20, 1921.

6. Howard K. Berry, ed. by Richard E. Jones, *He Made It Safe to Murder, The Life of Moman Pruiett* (Oklahoma City: Oklahoma Heritage Association, 2001), 45–108.

7. Patty Virginia Norton and Layton R. Sutton, comps. and eds., *Indian Territory and Carter County, Oklahoma, Pioneers,* p.190; William Krohn, "Some Thrilling Experiences in Lives of Buck Garrett and Bud Ballew," *The Daily Oklahoman* (Oklahoma City), February 20, 1921.

8. *Fort Worth Gazette,* November 26, 1891.

9. Helena Huntington Smith, *The War on Powder River,* 185–264; Robert K. DeArment, *Alias Frank Canton,* 120–144; William Krohn, "Some Thrilling Experiences in Lives of Buck Garrett and Bud Ballew," *The Daily Oklahoman,* February 20, 1921. Krohn, who no doubt got his information from Buck Garrett, portrayed the Johnson County War and Garrett's role in it in a much more heroic, but surprisingly realistic, manner.

10. Helena Huntington Smith, *The War on Powder River,* 264.

11. Patty Virginia Norton and Layton R. Sutton, comps. and eds., *Indian Territory and Carter County, Oklahoma, Pioneers,* 190; William Krohn, "Some Thrilling Experiences in Lives of Buck Garrett and Bud Ballew," *The Daily Oklahoman* (Oklahoma City), February 20, 1921. Ida Garrett, or "Ma" as she came to be called by everyone, was a woman almost as tough as her husband. In her article "Buck Garrett, Man and Legend" (*True West,* Vol. 17, No. 3, February, 1970, p.25), Louise Riotte, an Ardmore newspaper reporter and historian who was able to interview people who had known Mrs. Garrett personally, called her "a woman plain almost to the point of homeliness." Going further, Riotte declared Ida Garrett to be "a large, heavy woman. She had an extensive vocabulary of 'cuss' words and used them frequently, yet those who knew her best have always declared her to be the most generous and kindly of women."

12. *Daily Ardmoreite,* November 5, 1894.

13. Ibid., May 27, 1900.

14. I.e., ibid., October 9, 1900, the arrest of John Duke for a serious assault at Durwood; March 1, 1901, the rearrest of E. D. Martin at Wynnewood following Martin's escape from the Ardmore jail.

15. Lou Carpenter-Bowers-Emmerson-Reynolds, but known to every lawman in Texas, Oklahoma, and Kansas as Lou Bowers, was a well-known female miscreant in the tradition of Belle Starr and Flora Quick. Born in Mississippi in 1878, Bowers moved as a child to the Indian Territory with her family. Orphaned at a young age, Bowers followed her brother, who formed his own band of outlaws. Eventually captured by a posse of U.S. deputy marshals near Emmerson, Oklahoma, at which time her brother John was seriously wounded, Bowers was charged with horse theft but acquitted. Later she threw in her lot with one William Hill, an alleged member of the Starr gang. Hill and Bowers rode together until both were eventually run to

ground by lawmen. Hill received a sentence of ten years for horse theft. Once again Bowers managed an acquittal. At length the outlaw groupie hooked up with Scarface Jim Watson. After Watson's death in 1901 Bowers drifted about the Southwest. In May 1912 the incorrigible female found herself in Sheriff Buck Garrett's Ardmore jail for her connection to the misdeeds of her current paramour. The eventual fate of Lou Bowers is unknown. *Daily Ardmoreite*, May 2, 1912.

16. William Krohn, "Some Thrilling Experiences in Lives of Buck Garrett and Bud Ballew," *The Daily Oklahoman*, February 20, 1921.

17. Ibid.; *Daily Ardmoreite*, July 5, 7, 1901; Elmer LeRoy Baker, *Gunman's Territory* (San Antonio, Texas: The Naylor Company, 1969), 148–149.

18. *Daily Ardmoreite*, July 15, August 15, September 1, 1901.

19. Ibid., October 21, 1901, May 2, 1912; William Krohn, "Some Thrilling Experiences in Lives of Buck Garrett and Bud Ballew," *The Daily Oklahoman*, February 20, 1921.

20. *Daily Ardmoreite*, September 18, October 21, 1901.

21. Ibid., October 21, 1901, May 2, 1912; Elmer LeRoy Baker, *Gunman's Territory*, 154–155. In a somewhat odd relationship U.S. Deputy Marshal and later Ardmore, Oklahoma, Police Chief Bob Hutchins was a friend of "Scarface" Jim Watson. Watson apparently even rode in a number of Hutchins's posses in pursuit of other ne'er-do-wells. According to biographer Elmer LeRoy Baker, Hutchins "always thought of Scar Faced Jim Watson as a man who hated a thief worse than the devil hates holy water. Jim did not believe there was any harm done in selling whiskey." Baker quoted Hutchins as saying of Bowers, "Lou Bowers was so cold-blooded, hard-boiled and bull-headed, she had to kick the bucket to go to her eternal reward to get warm!" Elmer LeRoy Baker, *Gunman's Territory*, 148–155.

22. *Daily Ardmoreite*, February 2, 1902.

23. Ibid., February 3, 1902.

24. Ibid., February 5, 1902.

25. In his court testimony Garrett's companion, Hal Castleberry, would admit that they "had been drinking a little bitters."

26. *Daily Ardmoreite*, June 8, 1902.

27. Ibid.

28. Ibid., February 16, 1905; Patty Virginia Norton, and Layton R. Sutton, comps. and eds. Indian Territory and Carter County, Oklahoma, pioneers Norton and Sutton state that Garrett joined the Ardmore police force in 1905. By February

1905, however, he had already declared himself a candidate for chief of police suggesting he had already been a member of the force at least a few months before declaring his candidacy.

29. *Daily Ardmoreite*, February 16, 1905.

30. Ibid., April 5, 1905.

31. Ibid., March 6, 28, 1906.

32. Upon reaching the station first thing in the morning and learning of the shooting, Hubatka sent Officer Light to place Garrett under arrest. Shortly, Light appeared back at the station house by himself. According to Light: "I was coming to the office with Garrett when he saw two deputy sheriffs approaching and thought they had a warrant for his arrest. He did not want to be arrested, did not know what to do, so he walked away. He said he would come here later and make a statement of the affair in full." Hubatka then sent his man back out a second time to make the arrest. *Daily Ardmoreite*, March 6, 1906.

33. George Garrison was a pioneer Oklahoma lawman and personal friend of Buck Garrett. Born in Upsur County, Texas, Garrison served as a peace officer in Texas and Arkansas before moving to Oklahoma Territory in 1897. Elected Oklahoma County sheriff in 1904, he would serve two terms in that office. On June 5, 1908, Garrison and two deputies attempted the arrest of Alf Hunter, a wanted murderer. In the resulting gun battle Sheriff Garrison received a mortal bullet wound. Hunter was eventually captured, convicted, and legally hanged. Ron Owens, *Oklahoma Heroes* (Paducah, Kentucky: Turner Publishing Company, 2000), 97–98.

34. *Daily Ardmoreite*, March 28, 1906.

35. Ibid., January 19, 21, 1908.

36. Howard K. Berry, ed. by Richard E. Jones, *He Made It Safe to Murder, The Life of Moman Pruiett*, pp. 234–236. It has been suggested that the shooting of Jim Peters was not an accident and that Buck Garrett actually hit the man he was aiming at following some unknown disagreement with Peters, the case being contrived and camouflaged by that master tactician of the courtroom Moman Pruiett. Howard K. Berry, in his book *He Made It Safe to Murder, The Life of Moman Pruiett*, utilizing his personal acquaintance and hours of interviews with Pruiett, hints at such when he writes (235): "A little difference arose in the parlor. Buck and another patron, named James Peters, started to settle. The Chickasaw marshal tried the case, and after hasty deliberation, found his adversary of (*sic*) contempt and assessed the maximum for punishment. Afraid of a successful appeal, he entered hasty execution—a pair of lead slugs through the bowels. Jim Peters died; Buck was held on a charge of murder."

He also quotes Pruiett as making a somewhat odd comment about Garrett. "Buck's a privileged character. He's got a technique to his killin' that makes it artistic. People don't mind gettin' killed by Buck Garrett."(236)

If this is not a fabrication on the part of Berry, perhaps there is more to this rumor than has previously been realized. Who better than Moman Pruiett to know the inside secrets of a case he defended? Perhaps the truth will never be known.

37. Shortly after being cleared of the Peters trouble, in March 1908, Buck Garrett and his father-in-law Jim Chancellor would face, in the Carter County court, the far less serious charge of "forcibly detaining possession of real estate." The outcome of the case it not of record.

38. *The Daily Oklahoman*, February 20, 1921.

39. "A Glimpse into the Past," www.brightok.net/~bridges/glimpse.html.

40. Over his long career Gains would set a record for the number of illegal whiskey stills he would eventually find and destroy. Bill Ward would twice run, unsuccessfully, for sheriff of Carter County. He would later serve as police chief of Wilson. Mac McGalliard, *Reporter's Notebook* (Ardmore, Oklahoma: Sprekelmeyer Printing Company, 1973), 106–107; Born about 1868 in Savannah, Georgia, William Frank Bishop moved with his wife, Allie, from McKinney, Texas, to Ardmore, ca. 1895. Serving as a deputy and jailer throughout Buck Garret's entire tenure as sheriff, Bishop retired from law enforcement to run a restaurant and domino parlor in Ardmore until 1940. He died in Ardmore at the age of seventy-five in 1943, survived by eight children and numerous grandchildren. Patty Virginia Norton and Layton R. Sutton, 62–63.

VICTIM #2—ARCH CAMPBELL

1. William Richard "Dick" Highnight was born in Texas ca. 1873. By 1901 he and his wife, Ruth, were living in Oklahoma Territory. The couple would eventually have at least four children: Ella born about 1901; Walter ca. 1903; Julia ca. 1906; and Carter ca. 1911. Stationed at Ardmore in his capacity as a deputy U.S. marshal, Highnight would later fill the office of Ardmore chief of police and be a close personal associate and business partner of well-known law officer and gunman Dow Braziel. Federal Census of the United States, 1920, State of Oklahoma, County of Carter, Ardmore City, Sup. Dist. No. 3, Enum. Dist. No. 39, Sheet No. 3, House #21, Dwelling #57, Family #62, enumerated January 5, 1920 by census enumerator Mrs. Mary A. Ledbetter.

2. Herz had been a former chief deputy U.S. marshal under U.S. Marshal Hammer out of the Ardmore federal court in the early 1900s.

3. *Statesman Ardmore Directory, 1916, Ardmore Statesman*, Ardmore, Oklahoma, 10–11. This particular edition of the *Ardmore Directory*, located in the Ardmore Public Library, has some unique hand written notations contained in it. On one of the inside front pages is written, "Private Property of Bob Hutchins—Chief of Police—Do not take me off." On the last page of the volume someone, possibly Chief Hutchins himself wrote, "This book belongs to Bob Hutchins. And it is Private Property. Don't take out office (*sic*)."

4. Ardmore Junior Chamber of Commerce, *The History of Carter County* (Fort Worth, Texas: University Supply and Equipment Company, 1957), n.p.

5. *Ardmore Statesman*, January 29, 1916.

6. *Daily Ardmoreite*, January 26, 1916. *Ardmore Statesman*, January 29, 1916.

7. *Daily Ardmoreite*, January 26, 1916.

8. *Daily Ardmoreite*, January 3, 1916.

9. Ibid., March 15, 1916; *Ardmore Statesman*, February 26, 1916; Gilbert L. Robinson, "History of the Healdton Oil Field" (Thesis, University of Oklahoma, 1937), 63–64.

10. *Daily Ardmoreite*, May 22, 1916, *Ardmore Statesman*, May 25, June 29, 1916.

11. Ibid. All quotes from the *Daily Ardmoreite* and *Statesman* news coverage.

12. *Daily Ardmoreite*, May 22, 1916; *Ardmore Statesman*, May 25, June 29, 1916.

13. *Ardmore Statesman*, May 25, 1916.

14. Ibid.

15. Ibid.

16. Ibid.

17. *Daily Ardmoreite*, May 22, 1916.

EX-DEPUTY BALLEW

1. There were rumors that it had actually been Bryant who had been involved in the bootlegging activities on Bud's Lone Grove ranch. *Statesman's Ardmore Directory, 1916. Ardmore Statesman*, Ardmore, Oklahoma, 283.

2. *Ardmore Statesman*, May 11, 1922; *The Daily Oklahoman*, May 6, 1922.

3. Mac McGalliard, *Reporter's Notebook, Number 6*, scrapbooks in the collections of the Greater Southwest Historical Museum, Ardmore, Oklahoma, clipped from *Daily Ardmoreite*, January 27, 1980, n.p.

4. *Daily Ardmoreite,* June 25, 1916; *Ardmore Statesman,* June 29, 1916.

5. Ibid.

6. *Ardmore Statesman,* July 27, 1916.

7. Ibid.

8. *Daily Ardmoreite,* September 3, 1916.

9. In February 1916 Jones had been arrested on liquor charges but managed to gain his release. Gilbert L. Robinson, "History of the Healdton Oil Field" (Thesis, University of Oklahoma, 1937), 63.

10. Gilbert L. Robinson, "History of The Healdton Oil Field," 66; Kenny A. Franks, *Ragtown: A History of the Greater Healdton-Hewitt Oil Field* (Oklahoma City: Oklahoma Heritage Association, Western Heritage Books, Inc., 1986), 99.

11. *Ardmore Statesman,* October 12, 1916.

12. Ibid. In all, the October 1916 term of the District Court faced a total of five murder indictments and fourteen cases of assault to kill mixed in with the various liquor law violations and other charges, a testament to the violent atmosphere of Carter County at the time.

13. *Ardmore Statesman,* October 19, 1916. The *Statesman* reproduced the damning grand jury report in full.

14. Ibid.

15. Ibid.

16. Ibid., November 9, 1916.

17. *Daily Ardmoreite,* November 6, 1916; Kenny A. Franks, *Ragtown: A History of the Greater Healdton Oil Field,* 80.

18. *Ardmore Statesman,* January 4, 1917.

19. *Daily Ardmoreite,* May 2, 1917.

20. *Ardmore Statesman,* July 19, 1917; Harvey-Douglas Funeral Records, 1898–1995, 8.

21. *Ardmore Statesman,* July 19, 1917.

22. Ibid. McLish Avenue was notorious for its speeding violators, and Earley had been making numerous arrests of speeding motorists at this time. But, as the *Statesman* put it, "stopping Bud Ballew when he is in a hurry is a serious undertaking only embarked in by those who feel compelled by duty, or are reckless as to consequences."

23. Ibid.

VICTIM #3—STEVE TALKINGTON

1. Pershing had led the troops, which pursued Mexican revolutionary Pancho Villa into Mexico in March 1916.

2. Mac McGalliard, *Reporter's Notebook*, Sprekelmeyer Printing Company, Ardmore, Oklahoma, 1973, 106–107. Will Ward served throughout Buck Garrett's regime as a deputy sheriff stationed in Wilson. At least twice into the 1920s, he ran unsuccessfully for sheriff of Carter County. He later served as chief of the Wilson Police Department.

3. *Daily Ardmoreite*, January 26, 1905.

4. Ibid., September 13, 1905.

5. Letter to the author from Richard E. Jones, Oklahoma City, Oklahoma, May 10, 2002. Besides being an expert on the life of lawyer Moman Pruiett and editor of the book *He Made It Safe to Murder*, Mr. Jones has also done extensive research on Bud Ballew and Carter County.

6. *Ardmore Statesman*, October 4, 1917.

7. The *Daily Ardmoreite* stated that "Lewis has a bad record behind him for killing and other sorts of trouble."

8. *Daily Ardmoreite*, June 8, 1915.

9. Ibid.

10. *Statesman's Ardmore Directory, 1916*, Ardmore Statesman, Ardmore, Oklahoma, 291. In the Wirt section of the *1916 Directory*, Talkington's name is misspelled "Tarktington."

11. *Daily Ardmoreite*, February 29, 1916.

12. Ibid., October 11, 1916; *Ardmore Statesman*, October 12, 1916.

13. *Daily Ardmoreite*, October 11, 1916.

14. *Ardmore Statesman*, August 30, 1917. *R.L. Polk & Co.'s Ardmore City Directory, 1918* (Sioux City, Iowa, St. Paul, Minnesota, Detroit, Michigan: R.L. Polk & Co.), 222.

15. *Daily Ardmoreite*, August 27, September 28, 1917; *Ardmore Statesman*, October 4, 1917.

16. Letter to the author from Richard E. Jones, Oklahoma City, Oklahoma, May 10, 2002.

17. *Ardmore Statesman*, August 9, 1917; *Daily Ardmoreite*, September 28, 1917. At this point the *Statesman* was also misspelling Talkington's surname as "Tarkington."

18. *Ardmore Statesman*, October 4, 1917.

19. *Daily Ardmoreite*, August 27, 1917.

20. Ibid., September 28, 1917, taken from Bud Ballew's court testimony at his subsequent trial for the death of Steve Talkington.

21. It would later be alleged by certain witnesses that Talkington feared that the pistol he apparently carried in his pocket was malfunctioning and might not operate properly if he attempted to use it.

22. *Daily Ardmoreite*, August 30, 1917, taken from the testimony of Dr. Walter Hardy at Ballew's preliminary hearing. Hardy testified that either of these two wounds would have proved fatal.

23. *Daily Ardmoreite*, August 27, 30, September 28, 1917; *Ardmore Statesman*, October 4, 1917. Quotes taken from the various testimony reported in the local newspapers.

24. *Daily Ardmoreite*, August 30, 1917; Fred Croson testimony at Ballew's preliminary hearing.

25. *Daily Ardmoreite*, August 27, 1917; *Ardmore Statesman* October 4, 1917.

26. *Daily Ardmoreite*, August 27, 1917. The *Ardmoreite* erred in printing Judge T. W. Champion's initials as "J. B." J.B. was his brother, who was an Ardmore attorney.

27. Ibid., August 30, 1917.

28. Ibid.

29. Ibid., September 28, 1917.

30. Ibid.; *Ardmore Statesman*, October 4, 1917.

31. *Daily Ardmoreite*, September 28, 1917.

32. Ibid.

33. Ibid.; *Ardmore Statesman*, October 4, 1917.

34. Letter to the author from Richard E. Jones, Oklahoma City, Oklahoma, May 10, 2002.

35. *Ardmore Statesman*, October 4, 1917.

36. Kenny A. Franks, *Ragtown: A History of the Greater Healdton-Hewitt Oil Field* (Oklahoma City: Oklahoma Heritage Association, Western Heritage Books, Inc., 1986), 102–103, 133.

37. *Ardmore Statesman*, August 30, 1917.

38. *R.L. Polk & Co.'s Ardmore City Directory, 1918*, p. 222. The fate of Gus Talkington is unknown.

VICTIM #4—RUFUS P. HIGHNOTE

1. *Daily Ardmoreite*, December 31, 1917; Robinson, Gilbert L., *History of the Healdton Oil Field* (Thesis, University of Oklahoma, 1937), 66–67.

2. *Daily Ardmoreite*, January 23, 1918.

3. I.W.W. was the acronym for the militant trade union Industrial Workers of the World, also known as "wobblies," notorious at the time for their alleged involvement in riot and murder in order to achieve their aims. Referring to a "blind tiger" or illegal booze emporium. *Ardmore Statesman*, February 28, 1918.

4. *Daily Ardmoreite*, March 18, 1918.

5. Ibid., March 22, 1918. Previously the twenty-eight-year-old Costello had been arrested and jailed for vagrancy. The *Ardmoreite* said that Costello was "subject to the draft. He says he is registered at Tulsa."

6. Ibid., April 1, 1918.

7. Ibid., April 7, 1918.

8. His name was usually given as "R. P. Highnote" in the local press. Occasionally this would be varied with "R. E. Highnote" or "Hynote." The Ardmore City Directory of 1918 gives his first name as Rufus. *R.L. Polk & Co.'s Ardmore City Directory, 1918* (Sioux City, Iowa, St. Paul, Minnesota, Detroit, Michigan: R.L. Polk & Co.), 126.

9. *Daily Ardmoreite*, April 7, 8, 1918. At the time of his death, the *Ardmoreite* refers to him as "about 60 years of age."

10. Ibid., April 8, 10, 1918; *Ardmore Statesman*, April 11, 1918.

11. *Daily Ardmoreite*, April 10, 1918; *Ardmore Statesman*, April 11, 1918.

12. *Daily Ardmoreite*, April 8, 1918.

13. Ibid., April 7, 1918.

14. Sam Henderson, "The Oklahoma Moonshine War," *Oldtimers Wild West* (December, 1979): 38.

15. *Statesman's Ardmore Directory, 1916*, Ardmore Statesman, Ardmore, Oklahoma, 115.

16. *Daily Ardmoreite*, May 2, 1917.

17. *R.L. Polk & Co.'s Ardmore Directory, 1918*, 126. The directory lists Rufus "E." Highnote as president of his company. His residence is still given as 105 D. Street S.W. in Ardmore.

18. *Daily Ardmoreite*, April 8, 1918.

19. Ibid. From Buck Garrett's later court testimony at Bud Ballew's preliminary trial for the death of Highnote.

20. *Daily Ardmoreite*, April 8, 1918.

21. Ibid.

22. Kenny A. Franks, *Ragtown: A History of the Greater Healdton-Hewitt Oil Field* (Oklahoma City; Oklahoma Heritage Association, Western Heritage Books, 1986), 100.

23. *Daily Ardmoreite*, April 8, 1918.

24. Ibid., April 10, 1918; *Ardmore Statesman*, April 11, 1918.

25. *Daily Ardmoreite*, April 8, 1918.

26. *Daily Ardmoreite*, April 10, 1918, reporting Blackburn's testimony at Bud Ballew's preliminary hearing on April 9.

27. Ibid., Testimony of Dr. S. M. Alexander.

28. Ibid., Testimony of A. G. Chapman.

29. Ibid., Testimony of Cecile Sherell.

30. Ibid., Testimony of Arthur Johnson.

31. Ibid., April 8, 1918.

32. Ibid., April 10, 1918. Testimony of J. M. Chandler.

33. Ibid., Testimony of Bud Ballew.

34. Ibid., April 7, 8, 10, 1918; *Ardmore Statesman*, April 11, 1918.

35. *Daily Ardmoreite*, April 8, 10, 1918.

36. Ibid., April 10, 1918.

37. Ibid.

38. Ibid.; *Ardmore Statesman*, April 11, 1918.

39. *Daily Ardmoreite*, April 10, 1918.

WHISKEY AND MURDER

1. *Daily Ardmoreite*, June 3, 1918.

2. *R.L. Polk & Co.'s Ardmore City Directory, 1918* (Sioux City, Iowa, St. Paul, Minnesota, Detroit, Michigan: R.L. Polk & Co.), 108. Raymond E. Garrett is listed as living with his father and mother at 221 N. Washington Street in the 1918 directory. At the time of the publication of the 1918 directory Raymond was not yet married to his soon-to-be-wife Sallie.

3. *Ardmore Statesman*, August 29, 1918.

4. Ibid.

5. Ibid. *The Statesman* went on to report that, according to Dr. Hardy and the Garrett family "the only shot he (Garrett) received was 'in the arm,' and was delivered by Doctor Walter Hardy to control the malady from which he was suffering. And that the only women with him on the trip were his wife and his son's wife."

6. *Daily Ardmoreite*, August 29, 1918. "Choc," or Choctaw beer, was a synthetic drink that originated in the Choctaw Nation and had been brewed for many years. Ingredients included barley, hops, tobacco, fish berries, and a small amount of alcohol, which happened to be just over the legal limit allowed during Prohibition.

7. Interview with Sharon Graham, Ardmore, Oklahoma, August 16, 2000.

8. *Daily Ardmoreite*, August 31, 1918.

9. Ibid. Tom Slaughter was one of the rare breeds of outlaws emerging in the second decade of the twentieth century who bridged the gap between the horseback outlaws of the Old West era and the more modern automobile and tommy-gun criminals of the gangster time period.

10. Ibid., September 10, 1918.

11. *Ardmore Statesman*, October 17, 1918.

12. Ibid., October 10, 1918.

13. Ibid.; *Daily Ardmoreite*, May 8, 1922. Buster Ballew's death notice in the *Statesman* appears alongside the newspaper's solicitation for entries in its Spanish Flu writing contest.

14. *Daily Ardmoreite*, November 19, 30, 1918.

15. Ibid., November 30, 1918.

16. Ibid., November 26, 1918.

17. Ibid., December 12, 1918.

18. Ibid.

19. Ibid., January 9, 1919.

20. Bessie Estella McCullough (nee Tanner) was the daughter of Jessie James Tanner and Tallitha Floyd Tanner (nee Elliner or Ellenor). Bessie Tanner was born on December 20, 1889. She married Henry Thomas McCullough on October 7, 1906. Bessie's mother, Tallitha Elliner, was one of six children born to L. J. and Louisa Elliner. Tallitha was born on February 6, 1862. She married Jesse J. Tanner on January 14, 1883. According to various family findings, it would seem that Tallitha was somehow related to Bryant Ballew, Bud Ballew's father. Family chart compiled by Velma Lee (McCullough) Flowers, supplied by Norman Flowers, Ardmore, Oklahoma.

21. Interview with Norman Flowers, (third cousin of Bud Ballew) Ardmore, Oklahoma, August 23, 2000.

VICTIM #5—DOW BRAZIEL

1. *A. Owen Jennings' Ardmore City Directory for 1904-1905*, A. Owen Jennings, Springfield, Missouri, 43; *Statesman's Ardmore Directory, 1916*, Ardmore Statesman, Ardmore, Oklahoma, 40; *Daily Ardmoreite*, February 5, 1915. By 1915 two of Braziel's sisters lived in Durant, Oklahoma. One married a Lee White while the other, Lula, married a Greer. Another sister, Lillian, moved to New Mexico and wed an Austin. The remaining two Braziel girls remained in Ardmore. One married Dave Holley while the other was wed to the disreputable Caddo Street rough Ben Franklin; *A. Owen Jennings' Ardmore City Directory for 1904-1905*, 43.

2. *Statesman's Ardmore Directory*, 1916, 40; *R.L. Polk & Co.'s Ardmore City Directory, 1918* (Sioux City, Iowa, St. Paul, Minnesota, Detroit Michigan: R.L. Polk & Co., Publishers), 58; *Daily Ardmoreite*, May 31, 1907.

3. Ibid., March 2, 22, 1908.

4. *Daily Ardmoreite*, May 5, June 4, 1908; The outcome of these charges is not of record. *Daily Ardmoreite*, June 10, 1908; One of the ads for the Keep-U-Neat Pressing Club, "Dow Braziel, Prop." contains the blurb WE CALL FOR AND DELIVER

ALL WORK. Perhaps some reading between the lines could translate this into the pick-up of orders and delivery of liquor. A second ad proclaims WANTED! 1,000 SPRING SUITS TO CLEAN AND PRESS. A message understood only by those in the need to know? Certainly it could be termed most unusual for a laundry business to be called a "club"; *Daily Ardmoreite*, November 3, 1908; *Wichita Daily Times*, November 3, 1908. Quotes taken from the reporting in the *Daily Ardmoreite*; *Daily Ardmoreite*, November 3, 1908.

5. *Daily Ardmoreite*, November 3, 1908.

6. Ibid.

7. Prison Records, State of Oklahoma, Oklahoma Department of Corrections, # 680, John Braziel. Braziel is listed as twenty-nine years of age, standing five feet, eleven and three-quarter inches and weighing 170 pounds. He stated that he had six years of schooling and left home at age seventeen. Asked if he smoked, chewed tobacco or drank Braziel answered, "yes" to all three. He is also listed as being able to read and write. His religion is declared as "none." Although he is listed as a married man with one child, for some reason Braziel did not give his wife's name in the "name and address of parents and family or correspondents" section, giving only his father, Robert H., and mother, N. J. Braziel, residing at Ardmore.

8. *Daily Ardmoreite*, May 10, 1911.

9. Ibid., December 18, 1911.

10. Ibid., *The Ardmoreite* declared that Booker had a petition:
    Signed with 125 signatures of the best business and professional men in the city asking the commissioner to appoint him as chief of police.
    Mr. Booker . . . was an officer for fifteen years in this district and in that time there was never a charge preferred against him of any sort. He did his duty fearlessly and impartially and when a "bad man" started to create a disturbance "Dave" usually convinced him that his play would not go through. If the commissioner of police appoints D. E. Booker chief of police he may be rest assured of this fact, that he will have appointed a man who will do his duty without fear or favor of any one.

11. Ibid., January 11, 1912. The city commissioners deadlocked at two apiece, Commissioners George P. Selvidge and Ikard voting for, and Commissioners W. R. Burnitt and Thomas C. Bridgman voting against, Braziel. It was necessary for mayor D. H. Dawson to break the deadlock, and he cast his vote for Dow Braziel.
    Thomas Bridgman operated the Bridgman Undertaking Parlor and later became a prominent insurance agent in Ardmore. George Selvidge served a term as mayor of Ardmore, 1931 to 1933. Selvidge Park, located at the end of D Street N.W. in Ardmore is named in honor of him for donating the land to

the city. Ardmore Junior Chamber of Commerce, *The History of Carter County* (Fort Worth, Texas: University Supply and Equipment Company, 1957), n.p.; *Statesman's Ardmore Directory, 1916*. 41; *R. L. Polk & Co.'s Ardmore City Directory, 1918*, 59; *Daily Ardmoreite*, January 11, 1912, February 5, 1911. Wilson was jailed and tried in Marietta court for his assault on Franklin.

12. *Daily Ardmoreite*, January 11, 1912.

13. *Daily Ardmoreite*, March 11, 1912.

14. Ibid., May 13, 1912. Apparently a bystander, one Sherman Joines, was able to point out to Braziel in which room the fight was taking place by the powder smoke drifting out of the window.

15. Various issues of the Ardmore newspaper label Braziel an "Enforcement Officer." The January 31, 1915 *Daily Ardmoreite* calls him "Dow Braziel, a special enforcement officer commissioned as such by the United States interior department."

16. Ron Owens, *Oklahoma Heroes* (Paducah, Kentucky: Turner Publishing Company, 2000), 55; *Ardmore Statesman*, September 26, 1914. *The Statesman* terms Braziel "a deputy U.S. marshal, enforcement officer . . ."

17. The culprits in the conspiracy against Hignight were a trio of underworld characters named Bert Elliot, George Riggs and O. C. Youngblood. Apparently a bounty of $500 had been placed on Hignight's head. According to *the Statesman*: "in case one of the alleged conspirators fell down in doing the job, one of the others was to go ahead with the work to 'bump Dick off,' and the third was to act as treasurer and collect the money." Eventually Hignight got wind of the plot against him, and all three men were arrested and bought up on charges in federal court. *Ardmore Statesman*, September 26, 1914.

18. *Ardmore Statesman*, September 26, 1914.

19. Ibid. Chapman was released under a bail bond of $5,000 pending trial in the district court. As usual in such cases he was eventually exonerated on the grounds of having conducted the shooting of Dorris in his function as a law officer performing his regular, appointed duties.

20. Most witnesses failed to hear the remark. Bob Key, however, stated at Braziel's later preliminary hearing that Dow Braziel asked them "if they had their guns." According to Key, Greenwood answered he "did not have one, nor did he think he needed one for any purpose whatever." *Daily Ardmoreite*, September 29, 1914.

21. *Daily Ardmoreite*, September 14, 29, 1914, January 28, 29, 1915; *Ardmore Statesman* September 26, 1914; *Wichita Daily Times*, May 7, 1922.

22. *Ardmore Statesman*, September 26, 1914.

23. *Daily Ardmoreite*, September 29, 1914.

24. Ibid., November 2, 1914.

25. Ibid., January 31, 1915. *The Ardmoreite* of January 29 would state, "a great deal of acrimony was developed . . . by opposing counsel . . ." The jury were withdrawn a number of times "while attorneys argued the admissibility of certain testimony."

26. Ibid., January 28, 31, 1915.

27. The accusations of a Dow Braziel protection racket would extend into 1922, three years after his death. The issue would arise during the ouster proceedings against the then Ardmore Chief of Police Dick Hignight. It would be testified to that Braziel and Hignight were paid "$5 for each barrel of beer and $2.50 for each case of whiskey." It must be taken into consideration that the accuser on this occasion was none other than Gus Key "self-confessed king of the local bootleggers" and brother of Bob Key, the man who had been walking with Tom Greenwood when he was shot by Dow Braziel. The Keys, of course, had little use for either Braziel or his partner, Dick Hignight. *Daily Ardmoreite*, February 20, 1922; *Ardmore Statesman*, February 23, 1922; according to the *Daily Ardmoreite* of January 31, 1915:

    In the concluding argument, Attorney Pruitt (*sic*) began speaking a little before midnight, but it was well past the midnight hour when he concluded what was perhaps the most eloquent appeal ever addressed to a jury in any courtroom in Oklahoma. Mr. Pruitt's fame as a lawyer had preceded him, and the courtroom was filled to its capacity by those who desired to hear him speak. The large crowd was very attentive throughout, and were rewarded for their patience; *Daily Ardmoreite*, January 28, 29, 31, 1915; *Ardmore Statesman*, January 30, 1915.

28. *Daily Ardmoreite*, November 14, 1915.

29. Ibid., November 15, 1915.

30. *Statesman's Ardmore Directory, 1916,* Ardmore Statesman, Ardmore Oklahoma, 40.

31. Louise Riotte, "Marshal Braziel and Bud Ballew," *Frontier Times* (Vol. 54, No 6, October-November, 1980): 39. Mrs. Riotte, an Ardmore newspaper reporter and historian, had occasion to interview many witnesses of the Bud Ballew/Dow Braziel era in the 1960s and '70s. Unfortunately she fails to date this incident or identify the witness who related it to her.

32. *Daily Ardmoreite,* September 3, 1916; It would seem that by September 1916 Alexander's father was deceased. His mother, Mrs. W. J. Alexander, three brothers, Marshall, Adam, and Charles, and sister, Mrs. R. E. Grisham, all lived in Ardmore. Of his two remaining sisters, Mrs. E. L. Little resided at Greenville, South Carolina, while Mrs. Charles Laws made her home at Gainesville, Georgia.

33. *Daily Ardmoreite,* September 29, 1912.

34. Interestingly, Les Segler's brother-in-law was a Love from Ardmore—the husband of Segler's sister, Bonnie. There is no record as to whether this particular Love was related to George and Mose Love. *Ardmore Statesman*, December 11, 1919.

35. *Daily Ardmoreite*, September 3, 1916; *Ardmore Statesman*, September 7, 1916.

36. *Daily Ardmoreite*, September 3, 1916; *Ardmore Statesman*, September 7, 1916.

37. The local newspapers would state on a number of occasions that Ballew and Braziel had some sort of old feud brewing; however, the cause of this "feud" is never explained in detail—perhaps because they were also in the dark on the matter.

38. In her writings on early Ardmore characters, historian Louise Riotte, an obvious Dow Braziel supporter, would claim that Bud Ballew acquired a certain jealously toward Braziel for Braziel's good looks and flashy dress, i.e.:

    The Braziels were a well-to-do, educated family. They were all fine looking people, very straight, very tall and always stylishly and expensively dressed.

    . . . Dow was like the rest of the family, handsome, meticulously dressed, wearing expensive clothes and handmade boots. And, according to those who knew him, he always "looked like a million dollars."

    Bud Ballew, on the other hand, was rather small of stature, stockily built, a little on the heavy side, and had a mop of unruly red hair, his clothes were clean and he was always neatly shaven, but somehow he looked slightly rumpled and unpressed no matter how he was dressed.

    No matter how accurate these descriptions may have been, this can almost certainly be ruled out as a major factor in the enmity between the two men. Neither Ballew nor Braziel was the type to quibble over such insignificant details. Louise Riotte, "Marshall Braziel and Bud Ballew," *Frontier Times* (Vol.54, No.6, October-November, 1980): 38; There have also been those who claim Ballew was jealous of Braziel's position as a federal officer. Again, this is highly unlikely. The prestige and reputation Bud Ballew had acquired during his career in Carter County as a deputy sheriff probably far outstripped Braziel's situation as a federal prohibition agent, the feds being fairly unpopular during the era of Prohibition.

39. *Daily Ardmoreite*, November 2, 1916.

40. Ibid, November 5, 1916.

41. Ibid., November 28, 1916. The case was a rather notorious one. During the robbery of the Santa Fe train No. 405 near Bliss, Oklahoma, on October 18, 1916, the robbers shot and killed U.S. Mail Clerk Percy Norman. United States Special Officer Butler had been trailing the gang ever since the Apache, Arizona, robbery in August. Taking a swing through Ardmore, Butler recruited Dow Braziel and the pair, along with Purcell Chief of Police Franks, cornered the bandits in a house in Purcell. According to the newspaper report:

Special Officer Dow Braziel of this city, who was at Purcell last night, was chosen by the officers to lead the way in making the arrests. As the alleged bandits were seated at the supper table he noiselessly opened the door, and with a big gun in his hand ordered everyone to "hands up." One of the supposed bandits was a trifle slow in complying, and it was only when he was told that so much as the batting of an eyelash meant his death that he complied with the demands of Braziel.

The five train robbers were Joe L. Mays, W. F. Wells, John Borgen, John Courtney, and a woman named Lula Cobb. The newspaper speculated that Braziel would be sharing in a hefty reward for the important collar.

42. *Daily Ardmoreite,* May 29, 1917.

43. Ibid, August 11, 1918. For a number of months, Joe Duane had been a suspicious character in and around Ardmore. In early 1918 he had been jailed in Ardmore by Deputy U.S. Marshal Dick Hignight on suspicion of being a German spy. He was again jailed by Les Segler, at that time acting as registrar of German aliens, when he failed to come in and register before the time for registration had expired. According to evidence Duane and Bailey, a local farmer, argued over the sale of a harness. The fact that Bailey's wife divorced him and later married Duane in June 1918 was also said to have played a part in the incident.

44. Federal Census of the U.S., 1920, State of Oklahoma, County of Carter, Township of Morgan, City of Ardmore, 1ˢᵗ Ward, Super. Dist. No. 3, Enum. Dist. No. 39, enumerated on January 5, 1920, House No. 21, Family No.62; *R.L. Polk & Co's Ardmore City Directory, 1918* (Sioux City, Iowa, St. Paul, Minnesota, Detroit, Michigan: R.L. Polk & Co.), 126.

45. *Statesman's Ardmore Directory, 1916,* 115.

46. *R.L. Polk & Co.'s Ardmore City Directory, 1918,* 58, 126.

47. Ibid., p. 58. John Braziel is listed as living at 116 C Street N.W. and his occupation is listed as "auto livery."

48. Louise Riotte, "Marshall Braziel and Bud Ballew": 36-37.

49. Many later-day sources spell the name "Sigler." Most contemporary sources, however, used the Segler spelling.

50. *Ardmore Statesman,* December 11, 1919.

51. The census of 1910 listed Segler's age as twenty-six. Federal Census of the U.S., 1910, State of Oklahoma, County of Carter, Morgan Township, Dwelling #60, Family #60; Federal Census of the U.S., 1910. Also living with the family at this time was a "hired man" named Lenard Clark. Living on the farm next to the Les Segler family was his father Joseph M. Segler, aged fifty-four years, along with Les's brother, Joe Jr., and two sisters, Daisey and "Bonney" (sic).

52. *Ardmore Statesman,* December 11, 1919; *Statesman's Ardmore Directory, 1916,* 12.

53. *Daily Ardmoreite,* August 11, 1918.

54. *Daily Ardmoreite,* May 14, 1918. The "Reservation" was a group of four large buildings, which had originally been built on the outskirts of the city, but by 1918, had been incorporated into the Ardmore city limits. The Reservation featured every vice imaginable from booze to gambling and drugs to prostitution. At its height in 1918 it gave Caddo Street a run for its money as the vice capitol of Ardmore. Numerous brawls and several killings took place within its domain.

55. Ibid.

56. *Ardmore Statesman,* November 6, 1919.

57. Ibid., January 30, 1919. The individual is not identified in the news reports.

58. Ibid., November 6, 1919.

59. Ibid., January 30, 1919.

60. Ibid., January 30, November 6, 1919; *Daily Ardmoreite,* January 31, 1919; McGalliard, Mac, Reporters, Notebook #8, scrapbooks contained in archives of the Greater Southwest Historical Museum, Ardmore, Oklahoma, clipping from *Daily Ardmoreite,* October 5, 1980; Ron Owens, *Oklahoma Heroes* (Paducah, Oklahoma: Turner Publishing Company, 2000) 55–56; Louise Riotte, "Marshal Braziel and Bud Ballew": 36–37.

61. *Daily Ardmoreite,* January 31, 1919; *Ardmore Statesman,* January 30, 1919.

62. *Daily Ardmoreite,* January 31, 1919.

63. Louise Riotte, "Marshal Braziel and Bud Ballew": 36–38. Mrs. Riotte fails to identify her witness.

64. Richard E. Jones to author, May 10, 2002.

65. *Daily Ardmoreite,* January 31, 1919.

66. Richard E. Jones to author, May 10, 2002. Mr. Jones is the chief proponent of the Garrett/Ballew protection racket in early Carter County.

VICTIM #6—RUSTY MILLS

1. *Daily Ardmoreite,* February 1, 1919.

2. Ibid.

3. Louise Riotte, "Marshall Braziel and Bud Ballew," *Frontier Times* (November, 1980, Vol. 54, No.6): 39.

4. Prison Records, State of Oklahoma, Oklahoma Department of Corrections, No. 680, John Braziel.

5. *Daily Ardmoreite*, March 1, 1919. Due to lack of prosecution, the case against Ballew for the shooting death of Highnote died on the docket and was dismissed by County Attorney Russell Brown.

6. John Washington Gauntt was born in Henderson County, Texas, on November 11, 1870. He moved with his family to Thackerville, Indian Territory, in about 1878. John Gauntt, twenty-nine, married twenty-five-year-old Hattie Ballew in 1899. Gauntt conducted various businesses out of Lone Grove including hauling of equipment by freight line into the oil fields, truck gardening, and a donkey stud service as well as involvement in the formation of the Chickasaw Telephone Company. The couple had seven children, Herman Burnett, Dugar Edgar, Ethel Geneva, Marilyn Obed, Jessie Lee, Jonny B., and Royce Edward. Also a part of the family were Gauntt's four children by a previous marriage to Dora Cowger. John Gauntt died in Lone Grove on December 24, 1958. Hattie Gauntt (nee Ballew) followed her husband in death on February 8, 1964. Both are buried in Lone Grove cemetery near the grave of Bud Ballew and family. Patty Virginia Norton and Layton R. Sutton comp. and eds., *Indian Territory and Carter County, Oklahoma, Pioneers Including Pickens County, Chickasaw Nation, Vol. 1, 1840-1926* (Dallas, Texas: Taylor Publishing Company, 1983) 193.

7. *Daily Ardmoreite*, March 12, 1919.

8. Ibid., April 9, 1919.

9. Ibid., April 10, 1919.

10. Ibid., April 15, 21, 1919; *Ardmore Statesman*, April 17, 1919.

11. It later came to light that both the automobile and Mills's diamond ring were stolen property. *Daily Ardmoreite*, April 18, 1919.

12. Ibid.

13. *Daily Ardmoreite*, April 15, 1919; Prison Records, State of Oklahoma, Oklahoma Department of Corrections, No. 5722 and No. 7592, Arthur Mills. Mills's March 30, 1915, incarceration in the Oklahoma State Penitentiary at McAlister, Oklahoma, lists him as nineteen years old. His second induction of March 4, 1917, lists his age as twenty-one.

14. Prison Records, State of Oklahoma, Oklahoma Department of Corrections, No. 5722, Arthur Mills. Mills told prison officials that his occupation was that of a "teamster"; however, he had not been gainfully employed for the past six months before his arrest. At his trial he pled guilty and was not represented by counsel. He stated that he could read and write, had eight years of schooling, and had left home at his present age of nineteen apparently not long before his troubles with the law. He told officials he had no religion and that he smoked, drank, and chewed tobacco. In answer to the question "cause of downfall?" he replied "hard luck." Mills listed both of his parents as living in Los Angeles, California, and listed two sisters but was not married. In the "parents and family or correspondents" section he listed his father as T. G. Mills of Los Angeles, California.

15. Ibid.

16. Prison Records, State of Oklahoma, Oklahoma Department of Corrections, No. 7592, Arthur Mills. Once again Mills failed to obtain legal representation at his trial and pled guilty to the charge. This time he stated that he had only lived in Oklahoma for the last six years leaving the possibility that he was originally from California where his parents were known to have been living at the time. On this occasion he listed "women" as the cause of his "downfall." He apparently had no connection with any family members at this time as he is listed as having "no correspondents."

17. Ibid. At the bottom of Mills prison record is the following notation:
    Wanted; notify U.S. Marshal, of Muskogee Eastern District of Oklahoma, Thirty-Days before expiration of sentence.
    Also notify Chief Inspector P.O. [Post Office] Dept., Washington, D.C. before expiration.
    Wanted by B.A. Enloe Jr. U.S. Marshal West Dist. of Okla. See letter in jacket. Whether these notifications were carried out is not known.

18. *Daily Ardmoreite*, April 15, 1919.

19. Ibid., April 21, 1919. At Buck Garrett and Bud Ballew's later preliminary hearing for the death of Arthur Mills, J. A. Thomas, no relation to Charlie but a secret service operative of the Oklahoma City Police Department, stated that he "had known Arthur Mills for nine years, since the young man was 15 years old, and had first met Charlie Thomas five or six months ago, when both were arrested in the northwest part of Oklahoma City for stealing some coils and tools from an automobile."

20. Ibid., April 15, 21, 1919; *Ardmore Statesman*, April 17, 1919.

21. William Krohn, "Some Thrilling Experiences in the Lives of Buck Garrett and Bud Ballew" *Daily Oklahoman* (February 20, 1921). Employing information gleaned from Buck Garrett, Krohn wrote:

> The method of following one another employed by Buck and Bud during the hold-up is still in use by the two men [Garrett and Ballew]. They do it for two reasons, one of which is for the sake of safety, in the event one of them gets into a hazardous position and the other is so they might observe the actions of suspicious characters whom they pass. Not only do these officers employ such methods when using automobiles, but also when walking on the streets, or riding on horseback. Garrett explains that if he should be the preceding man when Bud and he are walking the street, and passed a suspicious character, that that person will act in a manner which will prove his guilt after Buck has passed him. The guilty action will be observed by Ballew.

22. *Ardmore Statesman*, April 17, 1919.

23. Ibid.

24. Ibid.; *Daily Ardmoreite*, April 15, 21, 1919; William Krohn, "Some Thrilling Experiences in the Lives of Buck Garrett and Bud Ballew," *Daily Oklahoman* (February 20, 1921). This gunfight would be cited by Buck Garrett in the years to come as the day Bud Ballew saved his life. William Krohn, Oklahoma City newspaperman and friend of both Garrett and Ballew would later write:

> It appears that the magnetic influence which makes such a great feeling of friendship spring up between some men when they get acquainted with each other, occurred in the case of Buck and Bud. Their bonds of friendship were greatly strengthened by an incident which occurred after the men had formed this great acquaintance. Buck owes his life to Bud.

Krohn is no doubt referring to the Mills/Thomas gunfight.

25. *Ardmore Statesman*, April 17, 1919.

26. If Charlie Thomas did stand trial (and it is hard to believe he did not have some sort of court repercussions following the robbery and gun battle), he was not sentenced to any term in the Oklahoma State Penitentiary as no Charlie Thomas can be found in that institution's records. E-mail, Richard E. Greene, Manager, Offender Records Unit, Oklahoma Department of Correction, to author, April 26, 2001.

27. *Daily Ardmoreite*, April 18, 1919.

28. *Ardmore Statesman*, April 17, 1919.

29. *Daily Ardmoreite*, April 21, 1919.

VICTIM #7—JOHNNIE PIERCE

1. The area is still known as "Black Town" to this day. Interview with Libby Long, Ardmore, Oklahoma, August 17, 2000.

2. *Daily Ardmoreite*, August 27, 1919.

3. Ibid.

4. Ibid., August 29, 31, 1919.

5. Ibid., August 31, 1919.

6. Ibid.

7. *Ardmore Statesman*, May 11, 1922. In a review of the life of Bud Ballew the *Statesman* reported in regard to the Pierce affair:
   . . . both he [Ballew] and Fred (*sic*) Williams shot at the fleeing Negro James Perie (*sic*), whom they had under arrest, who jumped from the train at the Santa Fe depot and ran, both officers shooting at, and killing him.

8. *Daily Ardmoreite*, August 31, 1919.

9. Walter Munford Harrison, *Me And My Big Mouth* (Oklahoma City: Britton Print Company, 1954), 108.

10. Ibid.

11. *Daily Ardmoreite*, August 31, 1919.

12. Ibid., October 12, 1919.

13. Ibid.

14. Ibid., October 31, November 1, 1919.

15. Ibid., November 5, 1919; *Ardmore Statesman*, November 6, 1919.

16. *Daily Ardmoreite*, November 5, 1919.

17. *Ardmore Statesman*, November 6, 1919.

18. *Daily Ardmoreite*, November 16, 1919.

19. Ibid.

20. *Ardmore Statesman*, December 11, 1919.

21. *R.L. Polk & Co's Ardmore City Directory, 1920* (Sioux City, Iowa, St. Paul, Minnesota, Detroit, Michigan: R.L. Polk & Co.), 71. The 1920 Ardmore city directory lists James M. Chancellor, chief of police, and wife, Mary, living at 203 G. Street

N.E. Also living at the Chancellor residence was a daughter, Fannie, who worked as a telephone operator for S.W. Bell Telephone Co. and a son, Thomas E., laborer, with his wife, Gertrude.

22. *Ardmore Statesman*, December 11, 1919. It is not known if Bonnie Love was a widow in her own right or if she divided her time between her own home and her brother Les's.

23. At Braziel's later trial for the murder of Les Segler, Mrs. Jinnie Gillham testified that she was standing near Segler when she heard someone yell, "Look out, woman! I'm going to shoot!" At that point Bob Braziel ran up and shot a surprised Segler.

    Another witness, G. A. Larkin, testified that Braziel said to the woman, "Lady, you had better get out of the way for there's going to be shooting here." Larkin continued that Braziel then calmly approached Segler and asked him, "Well, do you know me?" Before Segler could reply, Larkin stated, Braziel remarked to him, "If you have your gun with you, you had better get to it, for I'm going to kill you." According to Larkin, Braziel then fired the three shots before Segler made any move for a pistol.

    According to J. W. Riggs, he witnessed Segler and Braziel walking together down the sidewalk. After they had walked past him Riggs heard three shots and saw Segler fall, Braziel walking rapidly off down the street.

    Another alleged witness claimed to have seen Segler reach to a pocket as if going for a weapon before Braziel opened fire.

    Another witness proved to be one T. Alexander. At Bob Braziel's preliminary hearing on December 9, Alexander made a sworn statement: "I was shaking hands with Sigler (*sic*) when Bob Braziel stepped out of a stairway about 10 feet from us. Braziel walked up to Sigler and pocked his gun up against Sigler's head and shot him. Sigler fell to the ground and Bob shot him twice again. I know Sigler never saw him. He did not reach for his gun nor make any sign of reaching for it." *Daily Ardmoreite*. December 7, 10, 1919, September 19, 1920.

24. *Ardmore Statesman*, December 11, 1919; *Daily Ardmoreite*, December 7, 10, 1919, September 19, 1920; Ron Owens, *Oklahoma Heroes* (Paducah, Kentucky: Turner Publishing Company, 2000), 180.

25. *Daily Ardmoreite*, December 7, 1919.

26. Ibid., December 10, 1919.

27. Ibid., December 11, 1919.

28. Ibid., December 22, 1919.

29. Braziel claimed to be carrying the same revolver that had been carried by his brother Dow Braziel the day that he had been killed by Bud Ballew in Ardmore back on the morning of January 30, 1919.

30. *Daily Ardmoreite,* September 19, 1920.

31. Ibid.

THE JAKE HAMON AFFAIR

1. A native born son of Indian Territory Moses Edgar "Babe" Pruitt first came into the world on October 31, 1889. Moving to Carter County at a young age, he took up farming until 1911. At this time the twenty-two-year-old Pruitt went to work as a deputy sheriff for Buck Garrett. Pruitt would be one of Garrett's longest serving deputies, continuing to work as a deputy throughout Garrett's entire tenure as Carter County sheriff. When Garrett left the sheriff's office in 1922, Pruitt resigned his deputy sheriff commission and went to work as a constable in Berwyn (present-day Gene Autry). Pruitt would be shot by a black man named Semi Roberts while attempting a raid on a African-American dice game near Berywn. He would die from his wound one day after being shot, October 12, 1930, at the age of forty years. Ron Owens, *Oklahoma Heroes* (Paducah, Kentucky: Turner Publishing Company, 2000), 164.

2. James A. Simms was born May 20, ca. 1864, in Lawrence County, Tennessee. The U.S. census of 1920 enumerates the police sergeant as living on 1st Avenue in Ardmore with this fifty-six year old wife "Mamie" J. (name difficult to decipher on schedule) and two sons, Larry M., aged twenty-four and James L. Jr., nineteen years old. Simms himself is listed as fifty-four years old giving him a possible birth year of 1865. Both sons are reported to have been born in Tennessee suggesting that the Simms family did not move to Oklahoma until sometime after ca. 1900. Larry Simms's occupation is listed as "Washer at Laundry." James Jr. worked as a grocery store clerk. Federal Census of the United States, 1920, 1st Ward, City of Ardmore, Ardmore Township, County of Carter, State of Oklahoma, Sup. Distr. No. 3, Enum. Dist. No. 39, Sheet No. 3, Dwelling #63, Family #73, enumerated January 1920; Ron Owens, *Oklahoma Heroes,* 181.

3. *Daily Ardmoreite,* May 20, 1920; Ron Owens, *Oklahoma Heroes,* 181.

4. Ron Owens, *Oklahoma Heroes,* 164.Following his brother's death at the hands of Semi Roberts on October 11, 1930, a furious Claude Pruitt stormed into the Ardmore Hospital armed with a revolver and searching for the room of Roberts, who had been wounded by Babe. Finally finding the bed-ridden man, Pruitt opened fire at him. Struck with another bullet, Roberts frantically dived out a window and sprinted off across an adjacent field.

    Running outside, Pruitt jumped into a vehicle driven by his father. The two Pruitts sped off in pursuit of the fleeing Roberts. About one half mile from the hospital, Roberts ran out of the bush in an attempt to cross the road. Seeing him, the elder Pruitt put his foot down on the gas pedal and struck the already wounded man with the vehicle. As Roberts lay in the road Claude Pruitt exited the car with a revolver in each hand. Walking up to the prostrate form of Roberts, Pruitt fired both guns into the man's body. Shot five times, Roberts was pronounced dead at the scene.

Arrested by Ardmore Police Chief Jess Dunn and Detective Con Kiersey, Pruitt was charged with the murder of Semi Roberts.

5. *Daily Ardmoreite*, May 24, 1920. The three gave their names as S. T. Smith, F. H. Baker, and Edgar O'Mera with residences at Forth Worth, Dallas, and Wichita Falls, Texas, although Garrett felt they were fabricating information.

6. *Ardmore Statesman*, November 18, 1920.

7. Ibid.

8. The 1920 census of Carter County shows Buck Garrett living on North Washington Street with his wife, Ida; twenty-one-year-old-son, Raymond E.; and Raymond's sixteen-year-old wife, Sallie-Joe. At this time Raymond's occupation is listed as "mechanic, construction Co." Also living in the household were six boarders: Harry O. Delaney, a thirty-one-year-old driller in the oil fields; Ernest C. White, twenty-six years old, working as an "oil salesman"; Dick A. Eckel, thirty-three, brick layer; John A. Cunningham, twenty-six, pharmacist; Lee E. Williford, thirty-seven, a French-speaking hotel chef; and James E. Carter, thirty-three years old, one of Garrett's own deputy sheriffs. Federal Census of the United States, 1920, State of Oklahoma, County of Carter, Morgan Township, City of Ardmore, 1st Ward, Sup. Dist. No.3, Enum. Dist. No. 39, Sheet No.3, Dwelling # 170, family # 209, enumerated January 5, 1920, Mrs. Mary A. Ledbetter, Enumerator. The 1920 Carter County census shows a forty-two-year-old David M. Ballew living on D. Street in Wilson with his wife, Fanny M., thirty-six, and son, Dorris L., sixteen years old. Living in the house next door were Fanny's parents, Dr. William M. Harper, now eighty-one years old, and his seventy-nine-year-old wife, Anna S. Federal Census of the United States, 1920, State of Oklahoma, County of Carter, City of Wilson, 3rd Ward, Sup. Dist. No. 3, Enum, Dist. No. 55, Sheet No. 16, Dwelling #'s 230 and 231, family #'s 240 and 241, enumerated February 16, 1920, William U. Henderson, Enumerator.

9. *Daily Ardmoreite*, November 29, 1920.

10. Ibid., November 26, 29, 1920.

11. Ibid., November 29, 1920.

12. Ibid., November 26, 29, 1920.

13. Ibid., November 28, 1916. Other partners in the venture were Charles C. Wilson, another wealthy Chicago businessman; H.A. Coomer, railroad operations expert; P. C. Dings, president of the Guaranty State Bank; and C. L. Anderson, founder of the First National Bank of Ardmore.

14. Letter from Richard Jones, Oklahoma City, Oklahoma, to author January 5, 2003.

15. James H. Mathers as told to Marshall Houts, *From Gun to Gavel* (New York: William Morrow & Company, 1954), 98-99.

16. Elmer LeRoy Baker, *Gunman's Territory* (San Antonio, Texas: The Naylor Company, 1969), 301.

17. For some reason James Mathers misrepresents his time of service as Carter County attorney in his book *From Gun to Gavel*. In the book he claims a service of fourteen years straight as county attorney resigning in 1921 in order to defend Clara Smith for the shooting of Jake Hamon. In actuality Mathers served two separate stretches of four years and a little over a year respectively with a space of nine years in between. First elected in 1907, he held the office until 1911. Following Mathers' shooting of Bill Ballew in 1911, Andy Hardy, brother of Dr. Walter Hardy, served until 1918. In 1918 Russell Brown took over as county attorney. Between 1912 and 1920 Mathers conducted a successful private practice in Ardmore. In November 1920 he defeated Russell Brown at the polls to commence his second occupancy in the office. Disqualified by special agreement to act as county attorney in the Clara Smith trial due to his being hired by Smith as her defense council, Mathers picked up his county duties following the trial. After serving only fifteen months of this term, Mathers would resign in late February 1922 only six days after the ouster of Sheriff Buck Garrett.

18. James H. Mathers as told to Marshall Houts, *From Gun to Gavel*, 98. Mathers calls Jake Hamon "Frank Thaxton."

19. Ibid., 99-100; Elmer LeRoy Baker, *Gunman's Territory*, 307; *Daily Ardmoreite*, November 26, 1920.

20. James H. Mathers, as told to Marshall Houts, *From Gun To Gavel*, 98.

21. *Daily Ardmoreite*, November 22, 1920; *Ardmore Statesman*, November 25, 1920.

22. *Daily Ardmoreite*, November 22, 1920.

23. Ibid.; *Ardmore Statesman*, November 25, 1920.

24. James H. Mathers, as told to Marshall Houts, *From Gun to Gavel*, 100–103. Mathers stated that he and his wife were close friends of Hamon and Smith. In his book he reports that Smith came to their house immediately after the shooting distraught and claiming to have shot Hamon. While Hamon recovered in the hos-

pital following the removal of the bullet, Mathers claimed that the wounded man confided in him that he had been shot by Smith in a scuffle over the gun following their having argued about Hamon's proposed move to Washington. Mathers further claimed that Hamon told him he "didn't want any fuss made over the incident" and to have Smith sent to Mexico pending his recovery. Elmer LeRoy Baker, *Gunman's Territory*, 311–312.

25. *Daily Ardmoreite*, November 26, 1920.

26. *Daily Ardmoreite*, November 23, 24, 25, 1920; *Ardmore Statesman*, November 25, 1920. *Daily Ardmoreite*, November 26, 1920; *Ardmore Statesman*, November 25, 1920.

27. *Daily Ardmoreite*, November 28, 29, December 23, 26, 1920; *Ardmore Statesman*, December 9, 23, 1920; Elmer LeRoy Baker, *Gunman's Territory*, 314–317.

28. *Daily Ardmoreite*, December 23, 1920; *Ardmore Statesman*, December 30, 1920.

29. *Daily Ardmoreite*, December 26, 1920; *Ardmore Statesman*, December 30, 1920.

30. The *Ardmore Statesman* of December 30, 1920 reported:
    James A. Mathers, who will qualify as county attorney next Monday, will be disqualified to act as prosecutor because of his having been retained as attorney for the defendant, and, Judge Champion will name a special county attorney to prosecute the case. Russell B. Brown, present county attorney, will probably be named, and paid special fees for his service, as provided by the statutes of the state.
    Howard K. Berry, *He Made It Safe to Murder* (Oklahoma City: Oklahoma Heritage Association, 2001), 530. Despite his understandable dislike of Clara Smith following the death of Jake Hamon, Pruiett would seem to have been another of those captivated by the woman's obvious charms. Referring to his first meeting with her sometime before Hamon's death [532], Pruiett described her as:
    . . . twenty-three or twenty-four years old; radiant, stalwart, voluptuous. The V at her throat was a trifle low and the hem of her skirt a trifle high . . . for a young woman to wear. . . . Pale, tan, freckles across the bridge of her nose and high on the smooth cheeks detracted nothing from her natural charm. They added a natural accompaniment to the picture of health which her superbly developed figure suggested.

31. *Daily Ardmoreite*, December 26, 1920; *Ardmore Statesman*, December 30, 1920.

32. *Ardmore Statesman*, January 20, 1921.

33. Ibid., February 3, 1921.

34. John P. Gilday and Mark H. Salt, editors, *Oklahoma History South of the Canadian* (Chicago: The S.J. Clarke Publishing Co., 1925), 449.

35. The prospect of the possible existence of motion-picture footage of Bud Ballew, Buck Garrett, and all the other personalities of the Ardmore of the day proved greatly intriguing. In speaking with a representative of Liberty Home Video located in Tulsa, Oklahoma, one of the largest depositories of old Pathe movie reels, however, it was learned that most of the news reels from the period of the Clara Smith trial no longer exist. They, at least, do not have any film of the Smith trial. Telephone interview with representative of Liberty Home Video, Tulsa, Oklahoma, February 2003.

36. *Ardmore Statesman*, January 20, March 3, 1921.

37. McGalliard, Mac, *Reporters Notebook Number Three*, scrapbooks located in the archives of the Greater Southwest Historical Museum, Ardmore, Oklahoma, clipping from the *Daily Ardmoreite*, August 10, 1973.

38. *Daily Oklahoman*, (Oklahoma City), May 6, 1922.

39. *Daily Ardmoreite*, March 10, 11, 14, 15, 16, 17, 18, 1921; *Daily Oklahoman*, March 10, 11, 14, 15, 16, 17, 18, 1921.

40. Hamon's personal bodyguard, Bob Hutchins, told his biographer that, for all intents and purposes, he believed political enemies of Hamon had baited Clara Smith to shoot the oilman using her jealously at the fact that Hamon planned to drop her in order to move into a position of political power in Washington, D.C., with his wife. Elmer LeRoy Baker, *Gunman's Territory*, 304–310.

41. James Mathers, as told to Marshall Houts, *From Gun to Gavel*, 105–109. In his memoirs Mathers related Clara Smith's story of the Hamon shooting as she herself related it on the witness stand as a witness in her own defense. According to Mathers:

She told how Frank [Jake Hamon] entered the room, not drunk, but it was obvious he had received his share of liquor and champagne at the party [a banquet Hamon had attended that evening]. He was a bit unsteady on his feet and talked louder than normal.

As he came toward her, she rose to meet him, and he took her in his arms and began to kiss her. He insisted that they go to bed, but she knew his train was leaving in a little over an hour and he must be on it. [Apparently Hamon and two companions were planning a trip to either Texas or Montana, depending on the source, to check on Hamon's business interests.] But Frank sat down on the bed and tugged at her. The pistol was in the drawer of the bureau near the bed and she reached out her hand and took it—foolishly just to tease him, to make him realize he must stop his playing and get to the train. He pulled her down toward him and made an effort to knock the gun aside. But it fired.

42. *Daily Ardmoreite*, March 18, 1921; Elmer LeRoy Baker, *Gunman's Territory*, 321; James Mathers as told to Marshall Houts, *From Gun to Gavel*, 109.

43. *Daily Oklahoman*, May 6, 1922.

44. *Daily Ardmoreite*, August 23, 1921.

45. *Ardmore Statesman*, May 11, 1922.

BUD "BALLEW-IZES" ARDMORE

1. Mac McGalliard, *Reporter's Notebook #6*, scrapbooks located in the archives of the Greater Southwest Historical Museum, photo. Besides Scott Ballew and Chief of Police Jim Chancellor other officers identified in the photo include policemen Bill Ratliff, J. B. McCullar, Floyd Randolph, Barney Ross, Jim Lathrop, Dick Rayburn, John T. Spears, Dick Naler, and Pat Rogers.

2. *Daily Ardmoreite*, March 24, 1921.

3. Apparently the name of the aircraft.

4. Interestingly the man responsible for the first bombing of an American city by a foreign power was a pioneer aviator and native of Ardmore, Oklahoma, named Patrick Murphy. Hiring himself and his aeroplane out to the forces of rebel Governor Fausto Topete in his rebellion against the forces of Mexican President Emilio Portes Gill in 1929, Murphy participated in the attempt to dislodge government troops from Naco, Sonora. Employing homemade bombs rigged up in suitcases, Murphy over flew the government trenches in an attempt to bomb them into submission. Some of Murphy's suitcase bombs flew over the international line damaging property in neighboring Naco, Arizona. Following the battle Murphy was jailed in Nogales, Arizona, but quickly gained his release and returned to Ardmore. The ultimate fate of the first man to bomb a U.S. city, over twenty years before Pearl Harbor, Irishman and Ardmore native Patrick Murphy is unknown. Douglas V. Meed, *Bloody Border* (Tucson, Arizona: Westernlore Press, 1992), 219–228.

5. *Daily Ardmoreite*, July 6, 7, 1921.

6. *Ardmore Statesman*, September 29, 1921.

7. Ibid. Although the *Statesman* refers to the Ballew incident they do not identify him by name calling him "a county official." There is no doubt, however, that the "county official" referred to is Bud Ballew.

8. *Daily Ardmoreite*, November 9, 1921, January 3, 1922. None of the assailants of Mrs. Casey are identified.

9. Ibid., January 3, 1922.

10. Ibid., November 9, 1921.

11. This statement of Brown would seem to indicate that he had attempted to acquire state involvement in the affairs of Carter County earlier during his term as county attorney.

12. *Daily Ardmoreite*, November 9, 1921.

13. For most of 1921 James Mathers had been afflicted with a crippling case of rheumatism preventing him from taking an active part in many of the major cases for that year. Assistant County Attorney Hodge handled these in most cases. I.e.: *Daily Ardmoreite*, March 24, 1921, the Newt Ashcroft prosecution.

14. *Daily Ardmoreite*, November 9, 1921. All aspects of the meeting garnered from the article headed, "Mass Meeting of Citizens Cry Out Against Lax Law Enforcement Appoint a Committee to Ask the Governor to Investigate and Then to Prosecute. Mention of Ku Klux Klan Greeted With Prolonged Applause."

15. James Mathers as told to Marshall Houts, *From Gun to Gavel* (New York: William Morrow & Company, 1954), 235–236.

16. Ibid., 235.

17. Mac McGalliard, *Reporters Notebook #3*, scrapbooks contained in the archives of the Greater Southwest Historical Museum, Ardmore, Oklahoma, clipping from *Daily Ardmoreite*, August 10, 1978.

18. *Daily Ardmoreite*, November 9, 1921.

19. Kenny A Franks, *Ragtown: A History of the Greater Healdton—Hewitt Oil Field* (Oklahoma City: Oklahoma Heritage Association, Western Heritage Books, Inc., 1986), 104–105.

20. Ibid., 104.

21. *Daily Ardmoreite*, December 4, 1921.

22. Ibid.

GUN BATTLE AT WILSON

1. At Sims's death in 1921 the *Daily Ardmoreite* reported that he was forty-two years old. *Daily Ardmoreite*, December 16, 1921.

2. Ibid.; Ron Owens, *Oklahoma Heroes* (Paducah, Kentucky: Turner Publishing Company, 2000), 248.

3. *Daily Ardmoreite*, March 21, 1915, December 16, 1921. An ad for Sims's livery and sale business appears in the *Ardmoreite* of March 21, 1915. Under his photo is the script:
C. G. Sims
I have 15 head of
HORSES AND MARES
FOR SALE,
Or will trade for city property or
Farm Land
Phone 35
222 A St., N.E., Ardmore, Okla.

4. *Daily Ardmoreite*, December 16, 1921.

5. Ibid.

6. *Ardmore Statesman*, December 1, 1921.

7. Ibid., December 22, 1921, *Daily Ardmoreite*, December 16, 1921.

8. *Daily Ardmoreite*, December 16, 1921.

9. Jeff Smith later testified to the presence of a number of feather pillows and the mention of tar at the meeting place suggesting a possible tar and feathering was contemplated. *Daily Ardmoreite*, December 23, 1921, *Ardmore Statesman*, December 22, 1921.

10. Although Walter Carroll later testified that this man was Ardmore automobile dealer Ray Beede, it is more likely, from evidence, that the man was C. G. Sims.

11. *Daily Ardmoreite*, December 16, 1921. Joe Carroll was survived by a wife and four children.

12. The many facts concerning the Wilson gun battle can be gleaned from the following: *Daily Ardmoreite*, December 16, 22, 23, 1921; *Ardmore Statesman*, December 22, 29, 1921; Ron Owens, *Oklahoma Heroes*, 248-249; Kenny A. Franks, *Ragtown: A History of the Greater Healdton-Hewitt Oil Field* (Oklahoma City: Oklahoma Heritage Association, 1986), 105–107. John Smith left a wife and three children.

13. *Daily Ardmoreite*, December 16, 1921; *Ardmore Statesman*, December 22, 1921.

14. *Ardmore Statesman*, December 22, 1921.

15. *Daily Ardmoreite*, December 16, 1921.

16. Ibid., December 30, 1921.

17. *Daily Oklahoman*, December 22, 1921.

18. *Daily Ardmoreite*, December 16, 1921.

19. Ibid., December 18, 1921; *Ardmore Statesman*, December 22, 1921.

20. Ibid.

21. *Daily Ardmoreite*, December 19, 1921; *Ardmore Statesman*, December 22, 1921.

22. *Daily Ardmoreite*, December 21, 1921; *Ardmore Statesman*, December 22, 1921.

23. *Daily Ardmoreite*, December 20, 1921.

24. Ibid., December 19, 1921.

25. Ibid.; *Ardmore Statesman*, December 22, 1921.

26. *Daily Ardmoreite*, December 20, 1921, *Ardmore Statesman*, December 22, 1921.

27. *Daily Ardmoreite*, December 20, 1921, *Ardmore Statesman*, December 22, 1921.

28. *Daily Ardmoreite*, December 20, 1921.

29. Ibid.; *Ardmore Statesman*, December 22, 1921.

30. Ibid.

31. Ibid.

32. Ibid.; *Daily Ardmoreite*, December 21, 1921.

33. *Daily Ardmoreite*, December 21, 1921.

34. Ibid.

35. Ibid.

36. Ibid., December 22, 1921.

37. Ibid.; *Ardmore Statesman*, December 29, 1921.

38. *Daily Ardmoreite*, December 21, 1921; December 22, 1921; *Ardmore Statesman*, December 29, 1921.

39. *Ardmore Statesman*, December 29, 1921.

40. *Daily Ardmoreite*, December 27, 1921.

41. Ibid., December 23, 1921; *Ardmore Statesman*, December 29, 1921.

42. *Daily Ardmoreite*, December 27, 1921; *Ardmore Statesman*, December 29, 1921; *Daily Oklahoman*, December 28, 29, 1921.

43. The cases had been set for January 16, 1922. At this time, however, Prince Freeling was involved in an important hearing in the United States Supreme Court known as the "Red River Line Case," thus resulting in the first postponement. *Ardmore Statesman*, January 5, 1922; *Daily Ardmoreite*, January 2, 1922.

44. *Ardmore Statesman*, January 5, 1922.

45. Ibid., *Daily Ardmoreite*, December 30, 1921. In part, Carroll's statement read:

First—That I fully realize that I have been for sometime past a very undesirable citizen and have not lived within the law.

Second—That, notwithstanding any former statement I may have made, I cannot identify any person or persons who were in anyway connected with the above mentioned shooting affair at Wilson in which my brother Joe Carroll was killed.

Third—That I make the foregoing statement of my own free will and accord and that I am sincerely sorry for the way I have lived in the past and for any untrue statements which I have made in regard to the above mentioned shooting affray and that it is my sincere desire to lead a good and useful life, strictly within the bounds of the law, at all times in the future. I truly hope and pray that the good people of Carter County will extend me the helping hand at all time [*sic*] in the future in order that I may succeed in staying on the right path and make of myself a good and true citizen. I want to further state that I hold no malice or ill feeling toward any person whether or not they were in any respect connected with the unfortunate affair in which my brother Joe Carroll lost his life. Three of my brothers have lost their lives because of whiskey and it is my sincere wish that the illicit booze traffic be done away with forever.

46. *Daily Ardmoreite*, December 30, 1921. In part, Carroll's revised second statement read:

I, Walter Carroll, upon my oath do state, that I have just read the purported statement, published in the *Wilson Gazette* . . . and that the statement as published is not true and was not made by me.

As many as five automobiles loaded with men have been following me; one time nine automobiles loaded with men followed me. I am now afraid and have constantly been afraid that they would kill me.

Wren met me on yesterday in Wilson and told me that if I would sign a statement stating that I would go to work and be a man and not violate the law and that I would come home and go to work; and make a living for my family and do what was right, that he would do all in his power with the help of the citizens of Carter County, to see that my rights and my life was thoroughly protected, as long as I stayed within the law, which I promised to do. The only reason I made any statement at all was because I was then and now am afraid that I would be killed.

47. *Daily Ardmoreite*, December 30, 1921.

48. Ibid., *Ardmore Statesman*, January 5, 1922. *The Statesman* called Sims's letter "a peach."

OUSTER

1. The son of Dr. and Mrs. J. F. Young, Deputy Young was no stranger to controversy in his life. In addition to his fractious career as a Garrett deputy, Young, in his early life experienced another incident that became somewhat of a cause celebre in Carter County. Harrell McCullough relates the story in the biography of his grandfather, *Selden Lindsey, U.S. Deputy Marshal.*

In the early 1900 both Earl Young and Shelby "Sheb" Lindsey, Selden Lindsey's nephew, were foremen for the large Westheimer ranching concern. By all accounts Sheb Lindsey's wife, Roxie, was a stunning beauty, and Earl Young fell in love with her. Apparently his affections were not spurned by Roxie Lindsey. In fact she seems to have returned her affections in kind.

On Thanksgiving Day 1909, Lindsey and his wife were alone at the ranch headquarters southeast of Mill Creek. Suddenly a shot rang out, and Roxie Lindsey fell dead, a bullet hole above her left breast. Although it was officially ruled a suicide, many were of the opinion that, having become aware of the affair between Young and Roxie, Sheb had dealt his wife a fatal bullet.

At the funeral of Roxie Lindsey, Earl Young collapsed as he approached Roxie's open casket. Later when Sheb Lindsey's mother asked Young if a strange ring on Roxie's finger belonged to him, Young nodded in the affirmative. When asked if he wanted the ring back, Young reportedly replied, "No, leave it where it is." Therefore Roxie Lindsey was buried with the ring of Earl Young still on her finger.

Harrell McCullough, *Selden Lindsey, U.S. Deputy Marshal* (Oklahoma City: Paragon Publishing, 1990) 285–287.

2. Harrell McCullough, *Selden Lindsey, U.S. Deputy Marshal*, 284–285.

3. *Daily Ardmoreite*, January 2, 1922; *Ardmore Statesman*, January 5, 1922.

4. By 1922 Dick Hignight's brother, Joe Hignight, was serving as a sergeant under him on the Ardmore police force. *Polk's Ardmore City Directory, 1922* (Sioux City, Iowa, St. Paul, Minnesota, Detroit, Michigan: R.L. Polk & Co., Publishers), 149; Born ca. 1872, J. H. Langston was fifty years old in early 1922. When the city of Healdton was incorporated in 1918, Langston became defacto mayor, his real title being chairman of the board of city trustees. Langston was married, and the father of a number of children by 1922. *Daily Ardmoreite*, January 4, 1922; N. A. "Lem" Bates was born ca. 1872 and was about fifty years old in 1922. In 1918, with the

incorporation of the city of Healdton, Bates was elected as Healdton's first city marshal. Later resigning the office, Bates was only a few months into his second term as marshal by the time of the ouster charges in early 1922.

5. *Daily Ardmoreite*, January 4, 1922. It would seem from future developments that James Mathers saw the writing on the wall and realized his future was determined.

6. Ibid., January 2, 1922.

7. Ibid., January 3, 1922.

8. Ibid., January 4, 1922; *Ardmore Statesman*, January 5, 1922.

9. *Daily Ardmoreite*, January 5, 1922; *Ardmore Statesman*, January 5, 1922.

10. *Daily Ardmoreite*, January 5, 1922; *Ardmore Statesman*, January 5, 1922.; *Daily Ardmoreite*, January 25, 1922.

11. *Daily Ardmoreite*, January 5, 1922.

12. Ibid.

13. Ibid., January 3, 9, 1922.

14. Ibid., January 5, 1922.

15. Ibid. A statement that Hignight and Garrett were at loggerheads had appeared earlier in the *Daily Oklahoman* of Oklahoma City.

16. *Daily Ardmoreite*, January 3, 5, 6, 9, 1922.

17. *Daily Ardmoreite*, January 3, 5, 6, 9, 1922.

18. Ibid., January 11, 1922.

19. Ibid., January 9, 1922.

20. Ibid., January 11, 1922.

21. *Ardmore Statesman*, January 19, 1922.

22. Ibid.; *Daily Ardmoreite*, January 19, 1922.

23. Ibid.

24. *Daily Ardmoreite*, January 19, 1922.

25. Ibid.

26. Ibid., January 25, 1922.

27. *Ardmore Statesman*, February 9, 1922. Freeling accepted a fee of $15,000 to prosecute the cases in Washington and felt he would no longer be able to attend to his

duties as attorney general of Oklahoma. One of his assistants, George F. Short, a thirty-two-year-old native of Kentucky, received appointment as the new attorney general of the state.

28. *Ardmore Statesman*, February 9, 1922; *Daily Ardmoreite*, February 8, 1922.

29. *Daily Ardmoreite*, February 8, 1922; *Ardmore Statesman*, February 9, 1922.

30. *Ardmore Statesman*, February 9, 1922.

31. Ibid. The witness was identified in the press as a "Mr. Cornell."

32. *Ardmore Statesman*, February 9, 1922; *Daily Ardmoreite*, February 8, 1922.

33. *Ardmore Statesman*, February 9, 1922; *Daily Ardmoreite*, February 8, 1922.

34. *Daily Ardmoreite*, February 9, 1922

35. *Daily Ardmoreite*, January 25, 1922. In the fifth count of the charges against Buck Garrett, that of prisoners serving terms in the county jail being released before their terms had expired, the following examples were provided by Attorney Fulton:

   W. B. Wright, sentenced to jail for 30 days and pay a fine of $50 for violation of the prohibitory laws.

   F. J. Rutledge, sentenced to jail Nov. 24, 1921, for 30 days and pay a fine and costs of $77 for violation of prohibitory laws.

   J. C. Thompson, ordered to jail Nov. 2, 1921, to serve 30 days and pay fine and costs of $73.

   J. C. Beck, ordered to jail Nov. 3, 1921, for 30 days and to pay fine and costs of $75.

   Jim Staples, committed to jail Jan. 1, 1922, for 30 days and to pay fine and costs of $93.35; *Daily Ardmoreite*, February 9, 1922; *Ardmore Statesman*, February 9, 1922.

36. *Ardmore Statesman*, February 9, 1922.

37. Ibid.; *Daily Ardmoreite*, February 9, 1922.

38. *Daily Ardmoreite*, February 9, 1922.

39. Ibid., February 10, 1922.

40. Ibid.

41. Ibid., February 13, 1922.

42. Ibid.

43. Ibid., February 14, 1922.

44. Ibid., February 15, 1922. Earl Young also had a chance at this time to explain his conduct during the Jordan Rooms affair at which time he had been accused of opposing the city police force with an armed presence. Young declared that he himself had been conducting a raid on the Jordan on the night in question. He denied the accusations of opposing the Ardmore police. His gun was drawn at the time of the Ardmore officers' arrival, he said, because he had been having trouble with an inmate of the establishment.

45. Ibid.

46. Ibid., February 16, 1922.

47. Ibid.

48. Ibid.; *Ardmore Statesman*, February 23, 1922.

49. Ibid.

50. The count on aiding certain persons in their cases before the courts, specifically the Fords, et al., in the Casey case, had been dropped by the state during the course of the trial.

51. *Daily Ardmoreite*, February 17, 1922; *Ardmore Statesman*, February 23, 1922. Buck Garrett was only the second sheriff in Carter County history, being elected in 1911 and having held the position continuously until his ouster in 1922.

52. *Daily Ardmoreite*, February 20, 21, 1922; *Ardmore Statesman*, February 23, 1922.

53. *Daily Ardmoreite*, February 17, 1922.

54. Ibid.

55. Ibid.

56. Ibid.

SHOOT-OUT AT THE COURTHOUSE

1. *Ardmore Statesman*, February 23, 1922.

2. Ibid.

3. Ibid.

4. Ibid.

5. Ibid.

6. *Daily Ardmoreite*, February 21, 1922.

7. Ibid.

8. *Ardmore Statesman*, February 23, 1922.

9. Ewing London swore the initial two shots were fired inside the office. Others on the scene felt they came from outside. It was never determined who fired these shots or where their point of origin had been.

10. The two best sources for the courthouse battle are: *Ardmore Statesman*, February 23, 1922; *Daily Ardmoreite*, February 20, 21, 1922. Quotes are taken directly from the *Statesman* coverage of the fight. In its excitement to publish something the day of the battle, the *Ardmoreite* of February 20 made a mistake in its sub-headline of the sparse report declaring "Ballew, Richardson (*sic*) and Cowles Shot In Gun Battle Today." Of course, there was no "Richardson" involved in the affray, the paper no doubt meaning Whitson.

11. *Ardmore Statesman*, February 23, 1922.

12. *Daily Ardmoreite*, February 21, 1922.

13. Ibid., February 22, 1922.

14. Ibid., February 20, 1922.

15. Ibid., February 21, 1922.

16. Ibid.

17. Ibid., February 22, 1922.

18. *Ardmore Statesman*, February 23, 1922.

19. Ibid., February 23, April 27, 1922; *Daily Ardmoreite*, April 25, 1922.

20. *Ardmore Statesman*, February 23, 1922.

21. Ibid.

22. *Daily Ardmoreite*, February 23, 1922.

23. *Ardmore Statesman*, February 23, 1922.

24. *Daily Ardmoreite*, February 23, 1922.

25. *Ardmore Statesman*, March 9, 1922.

26. Ibid.

27. Ibid.

28. *Wichita* (Texas) *Daily Times*, May 6, 1922.

29. *Daily Ardmoreite*, March 6, 1922.

30. *Wichita Daily Times*, May 6, 1922; *Daily Ardmoreite*, May 7, 1922; *Polk's Ardmore City Directory, 1922* (Sioux City, Iowa, St. Paul, Minnesota, Detroit, Michigan: R.L. Polk & Co., Publisher), 128. The directory lists: Garrett, Buck (Ida M.), Pres. Southwestern Anti Car Thief Assn., 221 N. Washn.

31. Walter Munford Harrison, , *Me and My Big Mouth* (Oklahoma City: Britton Print Co., 1954), 108–109. In his book Harrison claims, "After the amazing Jack Walton was elected Governor he brought Buck Garrett and Bud Ballew to Oklahoma City as the head of his strong-arm squad." This is impossible for, at the time of Walton's election in January 1923, Bud Ballew had already been dead for over eight months. Harrison goes on to relate a story concerning an encounter he had with Ballew during the Walton era in which he said Ballew "scares the wits out of me." If the episode happened at all it would have to have occurred before Walton became governor, sometime in the period between February 1922, when the Farmer-Labor Reconstruction League picked Walton as its candidate, and early May 1922, the time of Bud Ballew's death, a very short window indeed.

Jack Walton is remembered as one of the most corrupt, or misunderstood, governors in the history of the state of Oklahoma. Elected by the biggest majority in state history, he ended up serving the shortest governorship in Oklahoma history, being impeached on November 19, 1923, following various indiscretions.

32. *Ardmore Statesman*, April 27, 1922.

33. Ibid.; *Daily Ardmoreite*, April 25, 1922.

34. *Ardmore Statesman*, April 27, 1922.

VICTIM—BUD BALLEW

1. *Daily Ardmoreite*, May 7, 1922; *Wichita (Texas) Daily Times*, May 6, 1922. The *Wichita Daily Times* even headed one of their many articles dealing with Ballew's death: "Bud Ballew Dies As He Had Wished To End His Career."

2. Lone Grove section map supplied courtesy of Ann Ballew Carlton. According to Ann Carlton, Ballew owned section 18-T-45-R-1E containing 282.43 acres; section 27-T45R-1W containing 10 acres; and section 26-T45 R1W containing 40 acres. Sections 26 and 27 are located along highway 70 in present-day Lone Grove, one section containing the old Ballew house, which is still standing. In fact, the house was still in use up to a few years ago; *Daily Ardmoreite*, May 5, 1922.

3. *Ardmore Statesman*, May 11, 1922.

4. *Daily Ardmoreite*, March 6, 1919.

5. Ibid.

6. *Wichita Daily Times*, April 9, 1909.

7. Ancestor Charts, compiled by Malcolm R. Dixon, grandson of Joseph and Martha Ballew, San Antonio, Texas, May 19, 1990, November 10, 1991; Family Group Charts, compiled by Douthitt M. McKay and Doris Rische, Corpus Christi, Texas, March 9, 1978, courtesy Malcolm R. Dixon; Cemetery records of J. U. Ballew family, compiled by Douthitt M. McKay, courtesy Malcolm R. Dixon; Family Sheet of Harvey Ballew family, courtesy Ann Ballew Carlton, Natchez, Mississippi. Joe and Martha Ann Ballew raised their large family of ten children in or near Wichita Falls, Texas, where they cultivated a small farm. Both are buried in Wichita Falls' Riverside Cemetery.

8. *Wichita Daily Times*, May 5, 1922.

9. Ibid.; May 5, 6, 1922; *Daily Ardmoreite*, May 7; *Ardmore Statesman*, May 11, 1922.

10. *Wichita Daily Times*, May 7, 1922; *Ardmore Statesman*, May 11, 1922.

11. *Wichita Daily Times*, May 2, 1922.

12. Ibid., May 3, 1922.

13. Ibid., May 5, 1922.

14. Ibid., May 4, 1922.

15. Ibid., May 5, 1922.

16. Ibid.

17. Ibid., May 6, 1922; E. M. Dickey, "Nevada Dick," letter to *True West* magazine, Truly Western, *True West*, Vol. 18, No.1 (September-October, 1970): 4; *Wichita Daily Times*, May 5, 6, 1922.

18. Ibid., May 6, 7, 1922; *Daily Ardmoreite*, May 7, 1922.

19. *Wichita Daily Times*, May 6, 1922.

20. Ibid.

21. Ibid., May 5, 1922.

22. Like Bud Ballew, Tom Hickman may also have been in Wichita Falls at the time to act as a judge during the rodeo. According to renowned Texas Ranger historian Walter Prescott Webb, Hickman "is widely known as a judge of stock shows and rodeos. He has judged rodeos all over the West, and in Chicago, New York and London." Walter Prescott Webb, *The Texas Rangers, A Century of Frontier Defense* (Austin: University of Texas Press, 1991 reprint), 550.

23. *Wichita Daily Times*, May 7, 1922.

24. Dickey says "the first night in town"; however, since he also says this was the night before the Ballew/McCormick encounter, which took place on Friday afternoon, Thursday evening is a more likely time frame.

25. E. M. Dickey, "Nevada Dick," letter to the *True West* magazine. All quotes are taken from Dickey's remembrances of the story told to him by Foghorn Clancy who died in Florida in 1957.

26. The best sources concerning the shooting are the contemporary newspaper reports of the incident: *Wichita Daily Times*, May 5, 6, 1922; *Daily Ardmoreite*, May 5, 7, 1922; *Ardmore Statesman*, May 11, 1922; *Daily Oklahoman*, (Oklahoma City), May 6, 1922. All quotes are taken from *Wichita Daily Times* coverage of the killing. Other sources dealing with Ballew's death include: Ron Owens, *Oklahoma Heroes* (Paducah, Kentucky: Turner Publishing Company, 2000), 44; E. M. Dickey, "Nevada Dick," letter to *True West* magazine; Louise Riotte, "Marshal Braziel and Bud Ballew," *Frontier Times*, Vol. 54, No. 6 (October-November, 1980): 40.

27. *Daily Ardmoreite*, May 5, 1922; *Wichita Daily Times*, May 5, 1922. The case of Ballew's guns and his method of handling them are a major enigma if the press reports are to be believed. It seems quite obvious that the Colt six-shooter found on Ballew after his death had been marked with six notches, apparently indicating six men killed. Gun notching has long been considered something out of Hollywood fantasy that was rarely indulged in by real-life western gunmen. Yet, it seems Bud Ballew did it, as two newspapers, one each based in Ardmore and Wichita Falls reported such to be a fact the day following his death. Oklahoma City's *Daily Oklahoman* of May 6, 1922, went one step further by claiming that Ballew had named his revolver "Betsy" and printed:
    Notches on Bud's Betsy
    Dusty (*sic*) Mills, killed by Ballew to save Garrett.
    _____ Highnote, killed after shooting Ballew twice in the abdomen.
    Steve Talkington, killed in a raid at Wirt.
    Arch Campbell, killed in Ardmore barbershop.
    Pete Bynum, killed in oil field resort.
    (In addition to the above Ballew is said to have shot a Negro, name unknown, and another white man.)
    The Negro, no doubt, would be Johnnie Pierce, shot in 1919. Who the "other white man" could be is a mystery unless there wasn't one. If that were the case, and Ballew followed the legendary procedure of "not counting Negroes," that would make the notches on his "Betsy," six, absolutely correct.
    If we are to believe another contemporary newspaper, Ballew's style of shooting flew in the face of every self-respecting Old West shootist. He was claimed to have been a "gun fanner," a method of shooting a revolver, which saw the

shooter fire his weapon by slapping the hammer back with the palm of the hand rather than simply pulling the trigger. This style of shooting was said to have been disdained by any real western gunman worth his salt and, again, more a Hollywood affectation than an actual practice. Yet the *Wichita Daily Times*, in an article datelined Ardmore, Okla., May 6 (1922), reported:

While Bud usually wore two guns strapped to him, he was a one-gun man. He never became accustomed to what he termed the new fangled automatic revolvers, but depended on a single action .45 pistol. He "fanned" the trigger (*sic*) as he drew and discharged each shot.

28. *Wichita Daily Times*, May 6, 1922.

29. Ibid., May 5, 1922.

30. Ibid.

31. Ibid., May 5, 6, 1922. Those who signed McCormack's bond were J. W. McCormick himself, A. H. Carrigan, W. W. Gardner, J. R. Monroe, J. M. Bland, John C. Kay, W. S. Curlee, S. M. Gose, Scott Bowers, P. J. Lee, Pat H. Simmons, Tom F. Hunter, N. O. Monroe, J. M. Alexander, Lester Jones, and G. N. Monroe.

32. *Wichita Daily Times*, May 5, 6, 1922.

33. Ibid., May 6, 1922; *Ardmore Statesman* May 11, 1922.

34. *Wichita Daily Times*, May 5, 6, 1922; *Ardmore Statesman* May 11, 1922.

35. *Wichita Daily Times*, May 6, 1922.

36. Ibid.

AFTERMATH

1. Mrs. Allie Gardner, interview conducted by Vella Howard, Ringling, Oklahoma, August 20, 2000. Born in ca. 1910 Mrs. Gardner was ninety-years-old at the time she related the story to Mrs. Howard.

2. Butch Bridges, Carter County historian, interview conducted by Lauretta Ritchie-McInnes, Ardmore, Oklahoma, August 18, 2000.

3. *Daily Ardmoreite*, May 7, 1922; *Wichita Daily Times*, May 6, 1922.

4. Ibid.

5. Ibid.

6. *Daily Oklahoman*, (Oklahoma City), May 5, 1922.

7. *Daily Ardmoreite*, May 5, 1922. Despite ruling against Garrett, Oldfield did decide that the defendant would not have to shoulder the entire cost of the trial, only his part of it. It was estimated that the cost of the proceedings would total over $2,000.

8. *Wichita Daily Times*, May 6, 1922.

9. Ibid.

10. *Daily Ardmoreite*, May 7, 1922

11. Ibid.

12. Ibid.; *Wichita Daily Times*, May 6, 7, 1922.

13. *Wichita Daily Times*, May 6, 1922.

14. Ibid. One example of this is the letter sent by the pastor of a local Wichita Falls church, J. H. Groseclose, which appeared in the May 6, 1922 issue of the *Wichita Daily Times*:

> Editor of the Times:
>
> Our new chief of police is on the job. In the few days he has been in office he has been bringing in the violators of the law by the scores. The time is here for the good people to get behind him. He is going to run into something that even some good people would rather he had not discovered. He will soon develop opposition. No officer ever did his duty without creating opposition. He will arrest some boy or girl or some man or woman whose prominence will cause a ripple. It is never popular to arrest "respectable" people. It is always popular to arrest Negroes and low whites. He is going after crime. He is not counting the cost. Let's get behind and back him up!
>
> With this in mind I am going to devote a considerable part of my sermon Sunday night to a commendation of the police department of our city. The men of the force have been invited to come to the service. They have accepted the invitation. As many as can be spared will be present. If you believe in what Commissioner Fitts and Chief McCormick and his men are doing, come out to the Floral Heights Church Sunday night at 7:45 and help us back them up in this "clean up" program they have inaugurated under the new management.
>
> J. H. Groseclose

15. *Ardmore Statesman*, May 11, 1922.

16. *Wichita Daily Times*, May 8, 1922.

17. Harvey Douglas Funeral Records, Ballew, Bud, 05/05/22. Ref. B.8.

18. *Daily Ardmoreite*, May 7, 1922; *Ardmore Statesman*, May 11, 1922.

19. *Ardmore Statesman*, May 11, 1922.

20. *Wichita Daily Times*, May 7, 1922.

21. The *Daily Ardmoreite* of Monday, May 8, 1922 recorded, "Not since 1908 has Ardmore and vicinity been visited with such rains"; *Wichita Daily Times*, May 8, 1922.

22. Bud Ballew Memorial Record, courtesy Ann Ballew Carlton; *Daily Ardmoreite*, May 8, 1922; *Ardmore Statesman*, May 11, 1922; *Wichita Daily Times*, May 9, 1922.

23. Bud Ballew Memorial Record, courtesy Ann Ballew Carlton.

24. Ibid. Other floral offerings were received from John Harrell, Mr. J. E. McCarty, Paul and James Sullivan, Mr. C. H. Williams, Mr. and Mrs. J. A. Lathrop, Frank Ketch, Mrs. E. L. Wheeler, Miss Hilda Lawrence, Mr. and Mrs. Coakley, Mrs. Geo. W. Wyatt and sister, Dr. Sullivan, Frank Carter, Dr. and Mrs. S. A. Hefflin, Mr. and Mrs. Jack Grimes, Mrs. Jack Hoban, Mr. and Mrs. G. B. Brown, Mr. and Mrs. Barringer and Jeanette, Mr. C. W. Petty, Mr. W. N. Whitford, Mr. W. R. McClusky, Mr. Morris Sass, Mr. and Mrs. E. R. Bulter, Laura and Nell Nolan, John Baker, Freddie and Henry Wheeler, and Robert R. Scivally.

25. *Wichita Daily Times*, May 15, 1922.

26. Ibid.

27. Ibid., June 27, 1922

28. Ibid., July 3, 1922.

29. Richard E. Jones, Oklahoma City, Oklahoma, letter to author, May 10, 2002.

30. Norman Flowers, interview from Ardmore, Oklahoma with author, September 9, 2000.

31. Sally Gray, telephone interview from Ardmore, Oklahoma with author, September 9, 2000.

32. *Daily Oklahoman*, May 6, 1922.

AFTERWORD: FUTURE LIVES, FUTURE TIMES

1. Louise Riotte, "Buck Garrett: Man and Legend," *True West*, Vol. 17, No. 3 (February, 1970): 25; Dan L. Thrapp, *Encyclopedia of Frontier Biography, Vol. II, G-O* (Lincoln: University of Nebraska Press, 1991), 540.

2. Kenny A. Franks, *Ragtown: A History of the Greater Healdton-Hewitt Oil Field* (Oklahoma City: Oklahoma Heritage Association, Western Heritage Books, Inc., 1994), 108; *A Glimpse into the Past*, www.brightok.net/~bridges/glimpse.html

3. Ibid. Whether Jim Cruce was related to former Ardmore native and governor of Oklahoma Lee Cruce is not of record.

4. Kenny A. Franks, *Ragtown: A History of the Greater Healdton- Hewitt Oil Field*, 108.

5. Louise Riotte, "Buck Garrett: Man and Legend," 44–45; Dan L. Thrapp, *Encyclopedia of Frontier Biography, Vol. II, G-O*, 540–541.

6. Ibid; B. A. Botkin, Ed., *Folk-Say: A Regional Miscellany* (Norman, Oklahoma: The Oklahoma Folklore Society, 1929), 147.

7. Ibid.

8. Vella Howard, telephone interview with author, from Ringling, Oklahoma, September 7, 2000.

9. Ibid.

10. Ibid.; Ron Owens, *Oklahoma Heroes* (Paducah, Kentucky: Turner Publishing Company, 2000), 124.

11. *A Glimpse Into the Past*, www.brightok.net/~bridges/glimpse.html.

12. Ron Owens, *Oklahoma Heroes*, 146–147.

13. Ibid., 211–212.

14. Ibid., 208.

15. Ibid., 175–176.

16. Ardmore Junior Chamber of Commerce, *The History of Carter County* (Fort Worth, Texas: University Supply and Equipment Company, 1957), n.p.

17. Elizabeth A. Long, *Songs Unsung* (Lakeville, Minnesota: Galde Press, Inc., 1997), 72.

18. Ibid., 73.

19. Ballew Family Bible, courtesy Ann Ballew Carlton. Rev. Willie Webb of Wilson, Oklahoma, wed the couple. Witnesses were Mrs. Myrtle McGuire of Wilson, Mrs. Cora Arnold of Lone Grove; Mrs. Willie Coffey of Lone Grove; Bill Harris of Wilson; Irene Tidmore of Wilson; and Thelma Young of Wilson.

20. Ann Lum Ballew (wife of Bud Ballew's grandson Dorris Eugene Ballew), telephone interview with author from Natchez, Mississippi, September 17, 2000. Eugene and Ann Ballew visited with Fannie shortly before her death.

21. Family Chart, courtesy Ann Ballew Carlton. Also in the Lone Grove cemetery at this time was Bud's stepmother, Martha Ballew, wife of Bryant, who died in 1945.

22. Howard K. Linger, "Dorris Ballew, President Mississippi Quarter Horse Association, Dies Suddenly," *Mississippi Valley Stockman-Farmer*, Vol. 16, No. 8 (May, 1962): 4, 17.

23. Ann Carlton Ballew and Ann Lum Ballew, telephone interview with author from Natchez, Mississippi, September 17, 2000; Ballew Family Chart, courtesy Ann Ballew Carlton; Ballew Family Bible, courtesy Ann Ballew Carlton. Mildred Wright was born July 16, 1907, in Sedan, Kansas.

24. Ann Lum Ballew, telephone interview with author from Natchez, Mississippi, September 17, 2000; "A Tribute to Dorris Ballew," *The Southern Horseman*, Vol. II, No. V (May 1963). This issue featured a full cover portrait of Dorris Ballew.

25. "A Tribute to Dorris Ballew," *The Southern Horseman*, Vol. II, No. V (May 1963); Ann Lum Ballew, Natchez, Mississippi, letter to author, September 17, 2000.

26. "A Tribute to Dorris Ballew," *The Southern Horseman*, Vol. II, No. V (May 1963); Ann Lum Ballew, Natchez, Mississippi, letter to author, September 17, 2000.

27. Howard K. Linger, "Dorris Ballew, President Mississippi Quarter Horse Association, Dies Suddenly," *Mississippi Valley Stockman-Farmer*, Vol. 16, No. 8 (May, 1962): 4, 17.

28. Ibid.

29. "A Tribute to Dorris Ballew" 10–11.

30. Ballew Family Chart, courtesy Ann Ballew Carlton.

31. Ibid.

32. Ibid.

33. All born in Natchez, Mississippi, Ann Wright Ballew was born March 27, 1953. She would wed Charles Carlton and have two children, Margaret Paige Carlton, February 5, 1979, and John Ballew Carlton, January 12, 1981. Susan Gayle Ballew, born April 14, 1954, wed Jamie Cummins. They have three children, Susan Ashley Cummins, August 3, 1977; Amy Elizabeth Cummins, September 9, 1981; and Jamie Tyler Cummins, November 7, 1985. Louise Hamilton Ballew, born August 19, 1957, is the mother of three children, Paul Freeman, January 30, 1983; Preston Gene Freeman, October 5, 1987; and Leigh Hamilton Freeman, October 11, 1993. Eugene and Ann's youngest daughter, Jeannie Lum Ballew, was born March 28, 1959. She is the mother of Kendric Ann Hinson, June 18, 1981; Megan Lauren Hinson, April 26, 1985; William Taylor Hinson, September 4, 1988; and Gena Britton Hinson, November 17, 1989. At this writing all reside in the Natchez area. Family Chart, courtesy Ann Ballew Carlton.

34. "A Tribute to Dorris Ballew," 10.

35. Family Chart, courtesy Ann Ballew Carlton; Ann Lum Ballew, telephone interview with author from Natchez, Mississippi, September 17, 2000.

36. *Natchez Democrat*, February 5, 2000.

──Bibliography──────────────────────────────────

BOOKS

A. Owen Jennings' Ardmore City Directory for 1904-1905. A. Owen Jennings, Springfield, Missouri.

Ardmore Junior Chamber of Commerce. *The History of Carter County*. Fort Worth, Texas: University Supply and Equipment Company, 1957.

Baker, Elmer LeRoy. *Gunman's Territory*. San Antonio, Texas: The Naylor Company, 1969.

Berry, Howard K., ed. by Richard E. Jones. *He Made It Safe to Murder: The Life of Moman Pruiett*. Oklahoma City: Oklahoma Heritage Association, 2001.

Botkin, B.A., ed. *Folk-Say: A Regional Miscellany*. Norman, Oklahoma: The Oklahoma Folklore Society, University of Oklahoma Press, 1929.

Chronicle of the 20th Century. Mount Kisco, New York: Chronicle Publications Inc., 1987.

DeArment, Robert, K. *Alias Frank Canton*. Norman: University of Oklahoma Press, 1996.

────. *George Scarborough: The Life and Death of a Lawman on the Closing Frontier*. Norman: University of Oklahoma Press, 1992.

Dobie, J. Frank. *Texas and Southwestern Lore*. Austin, Texas: Texas Folk-Lore Society, 1927.

Franks, Kenny A. *Ragtown: A History of the Greater Healdton-Hewitt Oil Field*. Oklahoma City: Oklahoma Heritage Association, Western Heritage Books, Inc., 1986.

243

Harris, Larry A. *Pancho Villa: Strong Man of the Revolution*. Silver City, New Mexico: High-Lonesome Books, Reprint, 1989.

Harrison, Walter Munford. *Me and My Big Mouth*. Oklahoma City, Oklahoma: Britton Print Company, 1954.

Johnson, Roy M., John P. Gilday and Mark H. Salt, eds. *Oklahoma History, South of the Canadian, Historical and Biographical*. Chicago: S. J. Clarke Publishing Co., 1925.

Kinard, Mary Turner. *Chickasaw Nation Groom Index, 1895-1907*. n.p., n.d.

Long, Elizabeth, A. *Songs Unsung*. Lakeville, Minnesota: Galde Press, Inc., 1997.

Mathers, James H., as told to Marshall Houts. *From Gun to Gavel: The Courtroom Recollections of James Mathers of Oklahoma*. New York: William Morrow and Company, 1954.

McCullough, Harrell. *Selden Lindsey: U.S. Deputy Marshal*. Oklahoma City, Oklahoma: Paragon Publishing, 1990.

McGalliard, Mac. *Reporter's Notebook*. Ardmore, Oklahoma: Sprekelmeyer Printing Company, 1973.

———. *Reporter's Notebook, No. 1-15*, scrapbooks in the collections of the Greater Southwest Historical Museum, Ardmore, Oklahoma.

Meed, Douglas V. *Bloody Border*. Tucson, Arizona: Westernlore Press, 1992.

Metz, Leon. *John Wesley Hardin: Dark Angel of Texas*. El Paso, Texas: Mangan Books, 1996.

Norton, Patty Virginia and Layton R. Sutton, comps. and eds. *Indian Territory and Carter County, Oklahoma, Pioneers Including Pickens County, Chickasaw Nation, Vol. 1, 1840–1926*. Dallas: Taylor Publishing Company, 1983.

Noyes, Stanley. *Comanches in the New West, 1895–1908*. Austin: University of Texas Press, 1999.

Owens, Ron. *Oklahoma Heroes*. Paducah, Kentucky: Turner Publishing Company, 2000.

Polk's Ardmore City Directory, 1922. Sioux City, Iowa, St. Paul, Minnesota, Detroit, Michigan: R.L. Polk & Co., Publishers.

R.L. Polk & Co.'s Ardmore City Directory, 1918. Sioux City, Iowa, St. Paul, Minnesota, Detroit, Michigan: R.L. Polk & Co., Publishers.

R.L. Polk & Co.'s Ardmore City Directory, 1920. Sioux City, Iowa, St. Paul, Minnesota, Detroit, Michigan: R.L. Polk & Co., Publishers.

Shirley, Glenn. *Guardian of the Law: The Life and Times of William Matthew Tilghman.* Austin, Texas: Eakin Press, 1988.

Smith, Helena Huntington. *The War on Powder River.* New York: McGraw-Hill Book Company 1966.

Statesman's Ardmore Directory, 1916. Ardmore, Oklahoma: Ardmore Statesman.

Sterling, William Warren. *Trials and Trails of a Texas Ranger.* Self published, 1959.

Thrapp, Dan L. *Encyclopedia of Frontier Biography,* three volumes. Lincoln: University of Nebraska Press, 1988.

Watson, Larry S., ed. *Smith's First Directory of Oklahoma Territory for the Year Commencing August 1, 1890.* Guthrie, Oklahoma Territory: James W. Smith, Publisher, reprint, Histree, 1989.

Williams, Neville. *Chronology of the Modern World.* New York: David McKay Company, Inc., 1967.

ARTICLES

Burchart, Bill. "The Oil Rush Wild West." *True West,* December 1966.

Dickey, E.M. (Nevada Dick). Letter to the editor, "The End of Bud Ballew." "Truly Western," *True West* 18, no. 1, September–October, 1970.

Franks, Kenny A. and Clyda R. Franks. "Last of the Wild West: Oklahoma's Oil Boomtowns." *Oklahoma: Magazine of the Oklahoma Heritage Association* 7, no. 1, Spring–Summer, 2002.

Hall, Christina. "Family Tradition." *The Natchez Democrat,* February 5, 2000.

"Hardy and Straughn Exhibits Re-open." Greater Southwest Historical Museum, GSHM Report, Vol. 1 Issue 1, Summer 2000.

Henderson, Sam. "The Many Careers of Sheriff Buck Garrett." *The West* 9, no. 2, July, 1968.

———. "The Oklahoma Moonshine War." *Oldtimers Wild West,* December, 1979.

Krohn, William. "Some Thrilling Experiences in the Lives of Buck Garrett and Bud Ballew." *The Daily Oklahoman,* February 20, 1921.

Linger, Howard K. "Dorris Ballew, President Mississippi Quarter Horse Association, Dies Suddenly." *Mississippi Valley Stockman-Farmer* 16, no. 8, May, 1962.

McInnes, Elmer D. "Bud Ballew: The Legend of Carter County." *Quarterly of the National Association for Outlaw and Lawman History*, Inc., Vol. XXVI, No. 1, January–March 2002.

Riner, Stephen W. "Ardmore's Noted Killer." http://bsriner0.tripod.com/ballew.html.

Riotte, Louise. "Buck Garrett, Man and Legend." *True West* 17, no. 3, February, 1970.

———. Marshal Braziel and Bud Ballew." *Frontier Times* 54, no. 6, October–November, 1980.

———. "Shoot Out At the California Cafe." *Western Frontier*, July, 1983.

"A Tribute to Dorris Ballew." *The Southern Horseman*, Vol. II, No. V, May 1962.

UNPUBLISHED SOURCES

Frame, Paul N. "A History of Ardmore, Oklahoma." Masters Thesis, University of Oklahoma, 1949.

Robinson, Gilbert L. "History of the Healdton Oil Field." Thesis, University of Oklahoma, 1937.

NEWSPAPERS

Ardmore Statesman, selected issues 1906–1923.

Daily Ardmoreite (Ardmore), selected issues 1895-1923, 1980.

Daily Oklahoman (Oklahoma City), selected issues, 1915–1922.

Dallas Morning News, selected issues, 1885–1891.

Fort Worth Gazette, selected issues, 1893–1895.

Natchez Democrat, February 5, 2000.

Tulsa World, 1912.

Wichita Daily Times (Wichita Falls, Texas), 1900-1913, 1922-1923.

PUBLIC RECORDS

Ballow, Meredith. Estate Records. Ashe County, North Carolina, 1847, 1899.

Braziel, John. Prison Records. State of Oklahoma, Oklahoma Department of Corrections, Inmate #680.

BIBLIOGRAPHY

Federal Census of the United States. Ashe County, North Carolina, 1800, 1810, 1830, 1840, 1850.

Federal Census of the United States. Burke County, North Carolina, 1810, 1820, 1830.

Federal Census of the United States. Carter County, Oklahoma, 1910, 1920.

Federal Census of the United States. Eastland County, Texas, 1880.

Federal Census of the United States. Fannin County, Texas, 1860, 1880, 1900, 1910.

Federal Census of the United States. Indian Territory, Chickasaw Nation, Soundex, 1900.

Federal Census of the United States. Jones County, Texas, 1880.

Federal Census of the United States. Pontotoc County, Oklahoma, Soundex, 1910.

Federal Census of the United States. Russell County, Kentucky, 1840, 1850.

Federal Census of the United States. Wichita County, Texas, 1900.

Fooshee, John. Prison Records. State of Oklahoma, Oklahoma Department of Corrections, Inmate # 682.

Fooshee, "Jonah." Prison Records. State of Oklahoma, Oklahoma Department of Corrections, Inmate # 681.

Harvey-Douglas Funeral Records, 1898–1995. n.p., n.d.

Marriage Record Book E. Indian Territory, Southern District.

Marriage Bonds. Russell County, Kentucky, Book 1.

Mills, Arthur. Prison Records. State of Oklahoma, Oklahoma Department of Corrections, Inmate #s 5722 and 7592.

FAMILY RECORDS

Ancestor Chart. Courtesy Malcolm R. Dixon. San Antonio, Texas, compiled May 19, 1990.

Ancestor Chart. Courtesy Malcolm R. Dixon. San Antonio, Texas, compiled by Douthitt McKay, San Antonio, Texas, March 9, 1978.

Ballew, Bud, Family Chart. Courtesy Ann Ballew Carlton. Natchez, Mississippi.

Ballew, Bud, Memorial Record. Courtesy Ann Ballew Carlton.

BIBLIOGRAPHY

Ballew Family Bible. Courtesy Ann Ballew Carlton.

Ballew, J. U., Family Cemetery Records. Courtesy Malcolm R. Dixon, complied by Douthitt M. McKay.

Ballow, Baker, Family Group Chart. Prepared by Nancy A. Manning. Fairview, North Carolina, June 18, 2001.

Ballow, Leonard. Family Group Chart. Prepared by Nancy Manning, June 18, 2001.

Ballow, Meredith. Family Group Chart. Prepared by Nancy Manning, June 12, 2001.

Family Chart. Courtesy Ann Ballew Carlton.

Family Chart. Courtesy Norman Flowers, Ardmore, Oklahoma. Compiled by Velma Lee (McCullough) Flowers.

Lone Grove Section map. Courtesy of Ann Ballew Carlton.

Manning, Nancy. "The Ancestry of Bud Ballew and Bill Ballew." Genealogical Report, June, 2001.

INTERVIEWS

Bridges, Butch. Ardmore, Oklahoma, August 17, 18, 2000.

Carlton, Ann Ballew and Ann Lum Ballew. Telephone interview. Natchez, Mississippi, September 10 and 17, 2000.

Dixon, Malcolm R. Telephone interview. San Antonio, Texas, August 16, 2001.

Flowers, Norman. Ardmore, Oklahoma, August 23, 2000.

Franks, Joyce. Telephone interview. Ardmore, Oklahoma, September 8, 2000.

Gardner, Allie. Telephone interview with Vella Howard. August 20, 2000.

Graham, Sharon. Ardmore, Oklahoma, August 16, 2000.

Gray, Sallie. Telephone interview. Ardmore, Oklahoma, September 9, 2000.

Howard, Don and Vella. Howard Ranch, near Ringling, Oklahoma, August 20, 2000.

Howard, Vella. Telephone interview. Howard Ranch, near Ringling, Oklahoma, September 7, 2000.

Liberty Home Video representative. Telephone interview. Tulsa, Oklahoma, February, 2003.

BIBLIOGRAPHY

Long, Libby. Ardmore, Oklahoma, August 17, 2000.

Maxwell, Steve, Carter County Deputy Sheriff. Ardmore, Oklahoma, August 21, 2000.

Walser, Diane. Wichita Falls, Texas, August 22, 2000.

Woods, Claude. Healdton, Oklahoma, August 21, 2000.

CORRESPONDENCE

Ballew, Ann Lum. Natchez, Mississippi. Letter to author. September 17, 2000.

Greene, Richard E. Oklahoma Department of Corrections, E-mail to author. April 26, 2001.

Jones, Richard E. Oklahoma City, Oklahoma. Letters to author. May 10, September 24, 2002; January 5, 2003.

WEB SITES

A Glimpse Into the Past, www.brightok.net/~bridges/glimpse.html.

Police Guide, www.policeguide.com/bud-ballew-killed.htm.

About the Authors

Elmer McInnes is the author of *Gamblers and Gunmen along the Northern Pacific,* as well as numerous published journal articles. A highly sought-after public speaker, Elmer has long been considered an expert on the Old West's most famous, infamous, and fascinating characters. His research and writing have covered the gamut of characters from the business partner of Wyatt Earp to outlaw Con Murphy. He is a member of numerous associations, including the National Association for Outlaw and Lawman History, Western Outlaw Lawman History Association, Oklahombres, and the Oklahoma Outlaws Lawmen History Association. He is a former member of the James Gang Historical Organization, Friends of the Youngers, Friends of the James Farm, Outlaw Trail History Centre, and the English Westerners Society. Elmer is also a registered researcher with the Oklahoma Historical Society and the Nebraska Historical Society. He lives with his wife, Lauretta Ritchie-McInnes, research assistant on this title, in Yorkton, Saskatchewan.